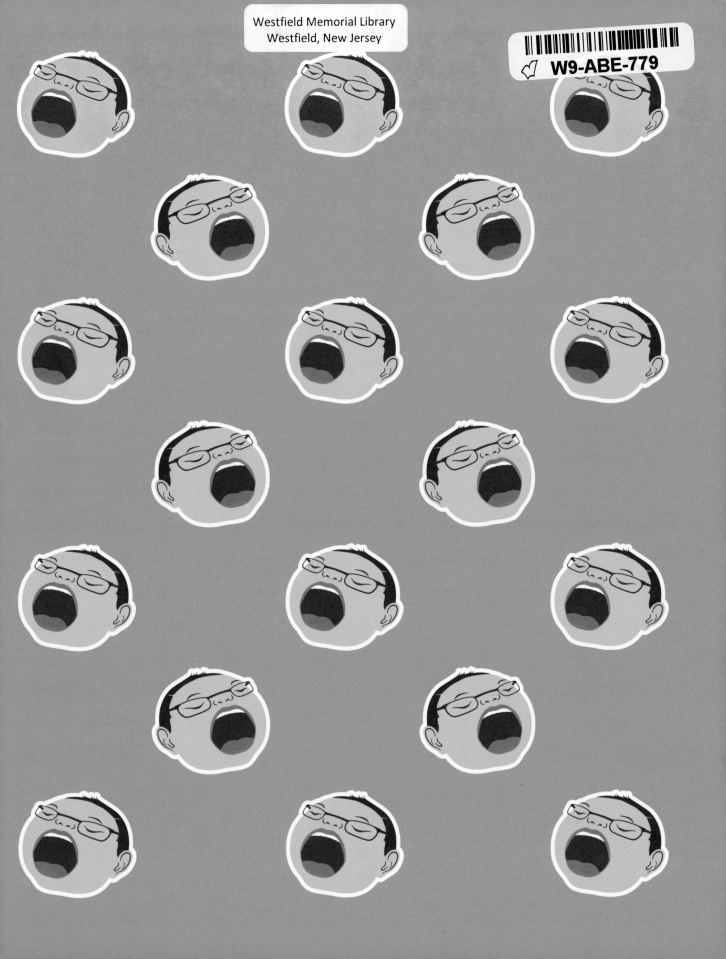

ASIAN-AMERICAN

PROUDLY INAUTHENTIC RECIPES FROM THE PHILIPPINES TO BROOKLYN

DALE TALDE

with JJ GOODE

New York Boston

Grand Central Life & Style
Hachette Book Group
1290 Avenue of the Americas
New York, NY 10104

www.GrandCentralLifeandStyle.com

Printed in the United States of America

Q-MA

First Edition: September 2015
10 9 8 7 6 5 4 3 2 1

Grand Central Life & Style is an imprint of Grand Central Publishing.
The Grand Central Life & Style name and logo are trademarks
of Hachette Book Group, Inc.

The Hachette Speakers Bureau provides a wide range of authors
for speaking events. To find out more, go to
www.HachetteSpeakersBureau.com or call (866) 376-6591.

The publisher is not responsible for websites (or their content)
that are not owned by the publisher.

Library of Congress Cataloging-in-Publication Data

Talde, Dale, 1978–
Asian-American : a cookbook / Dale Talde with JJ Goode. —First Edition.
    pages cm
Includes index.
  ISBN 978-1-4555-8526-7 (hardback)—ISBN 978-1-4555-8525-0 (ebook)   1. Asian
american cooking.   I. Goode, J. J.   II. Title.
  TX715.2.A74T35 2015
  641.759'073—dc23   641.595
                                                        2015021783

To my family—my father, Salvador; my mother, Eva;
my brother, Ian; and my sister, Aileen

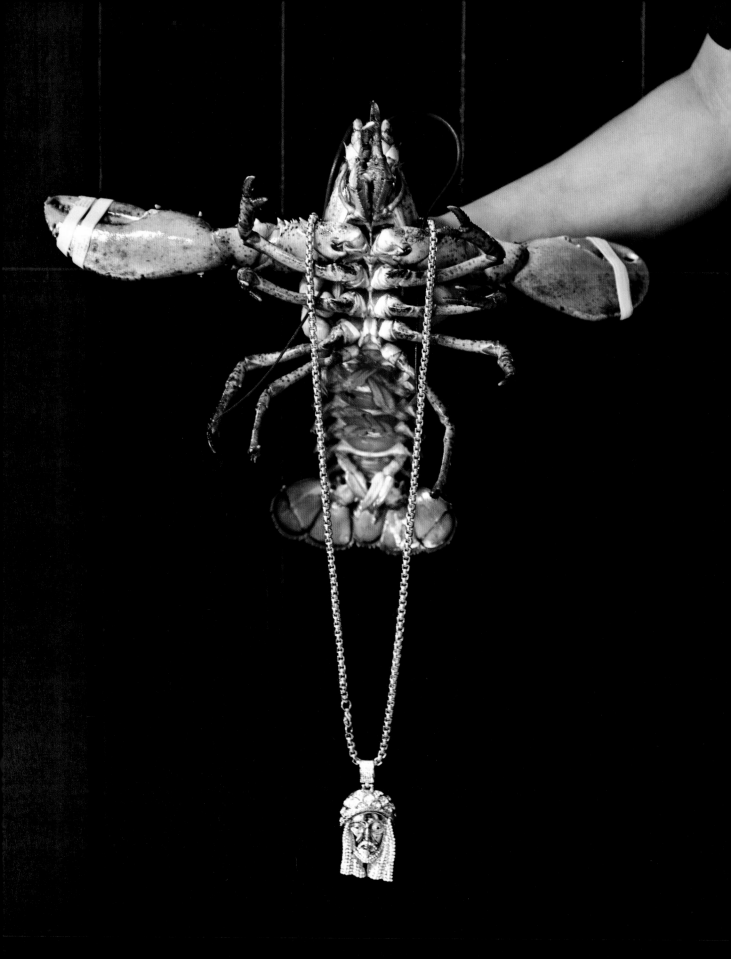

Contents

Where ★★★★★ I'm From

There's a pig's head in the oven again. I'm just a kid, no more than six years old, but I'm not surprised when I peer over my aunt's shoulder as she opens the oven and I see the pig's sleepy eyes staring back at me. At my aunt's house, there was often a pig's head in the oven. I'm not talking about on special occasions. I'm talking about on some random Thursday—even when she had no reason to think we were coming over. The pig's head was the Filipino equivalent of cheese and crackers. It was just-in-case-there's-company food.

My mom preferred fish heads to pig. She was always hitting the supermarket to ask the fish guy whether he had any lying around that he'd be willing to part with at no charge. He typically did, because none of his other customers wanted them. Way before nose-to-tail cooking was a chef's badge of honor, Filipino moms were eating off-cuts for the thrift of it.

After my mom's 16-hour shift at the Chicago hospital where she worked as a nurse, she got to come home to cook dinner—lucky her—for my dad, my brother and sister, and my bratty ass. She cooked Filipino food almost exclusively—or at least an immigrant's approximation. It was called Fil-Am food (short for Filipino-American) and was as Filipino as you could get without having access to half of the proper ingredients. When we made fried rice, we made do without the Filipino sausage called *longaniza* and used Spam instead. At some point, Mom got fed up with the lack of Asian vegetables around town and started trafficking, sneaking seeds back into the U.S. in her purse when she returned from trips to the Motherland and planting them in the garden. That way, we could have bitter melon and water spinach. Mom was thrilled that she could get canned sardines, though. It might have been her favorite ingredient. She would cook soffrito, the Spanish and Italian flavor base made from slowly sizzled vegetables, the Filipino way—tomato, garlic, and onions cooked down until the onions were almost burnt but in a good way—and dump in cans of sardines in tomato sauce. She'd mash it all up and use the result as a sort of sauce for rice or eggs.

Heads were just one of the many things that ended up on our table, which seemed to be always filled with food. It became a joke among the Filipino families we rolled with: Whenever anyone came to our place, whenever we visited Filipino friends, even if we'd just gotten back from dinner, someone's mom, aunt, or cousin would ask, "So, who's hungry?" Just in case we were, a table of food was usually waiting. More often than not, the spread was pork-heavy. Sausage, chops, stew, head. Sometimes the pork was served with more pork—Filipinos are fucked-up like that—such as crunchy pork rinds for sprinkling or Mang Tomas, a sort of gravy made with sugar, vinegar, bread crumbs, and pork liver.

Sometimes Mom would make *dinuguan*, a nasty-looking, deep-brown slop from the region of the Philippines my parents come from. The first few times she made it for us, she tried to get us kids to eat it by calling the stew by its nickname: chocolate meat. That was a well-worn trick used by Filipino parents to make *dinuguan* seem like something a kid might want to eat. A couple of disappointing bites and we were on to her. There was no chocolate in there. The color came from cooked blood. And this stuff was organ-ed out—there was liver, heart, and lung, not to mention ear and snout. Even though we eventually came to like the stuff, we developed a rule of thumb for *dinuguan*: Only eat it if you know

the person who made it. Otherwise, you're taking your life in your hands.

And there was always rice. *Always.* Even when Mom occasionally gave in and made non-Filipino food for dinner. One time she made spaghetti for dinner and my dad absolutely killed his bowl, which I swear was like one of those family-style portions you'd get at Olive Garden. Then he asks Mom, "Where's the rice?" That's commitment right there. He ended up launching right into meal number two: a bowl of rice and canned sardines with chile-spiked vinegar on the side. There was always something on the side, no matter what we ate: tiny fried dried fish, shrimp paste mixed with vinegar, or bowls of fresh bird chiles as long as my thumbnail, which we'd eat whenever we craved pain.

For years, this all seemed normal to me—pig heads in the oven, fish heads in the pot, rice in bowls, and a shrimp-paste smell in the air.

Normal to my friends, too. When there are only a few Asian kids at

"I grew up infatuated with burgers and pizza and fried chicken and tacos because they had the thrill of the forbidden."

school, they band together. There was an undeniable comfort in our sameness, and that was part of what brought and kept us close. None of them looked at me funny when they came over and saw the rice cooker on the counter. They all had one, too. When I visited my friend Robert, who's Korean, his house always smelled like kimchi. I didn't exactly know what kimchi was, but I did know that his house stunk just like mine did. I also had a couple of Indian friends. The experience at their houses was slightly different—I stared the first time I saw grown-ups using their hands to shovel food into their mouths—but they ate rice with every meal and bit into tiny chiles, just like we did.

My white friends were the ones with the strangest eating habits. One guy, Sean, scored ten dollars from his mom every night for dinner at The Works, the dope gyro shop in our neighborhood. I was shocked: "You get to eat that every day?" I'd ask, extremely jealous. "Your mom cooks?" he'd ask, looking at me as if I'd just told him that she could fly.

I rarely, if ever, got to eat crap at

home. Which I think is why I had so much love for fast food. My mom thought it was going to kill Dad, who had high cholesterol, and was afraid it'd take me, my brother, and my sister out with him. Practically anything that came in patty form, had melted cheese, or didn't include rice was banned. No matter that roasted pig's head isn't exactly low-fat, low-cal. Dad didn't care about cholesterol, but he cared about Mom, so for a long time he kept his lunch trips under wraps. One day, though, he decided to let me in on his secret.

My dad fixed industrial boilers so big that he had to go inside them to do repairs. The work was no joke, so when lunchtime came, he and his work buddies treated themselves right. He'd hit up places frequented by union guys and other laborers. The first place he took me to was a tiny burger joint near Evanston. We walked in to a chorus of "What's up, Sal?" and Dad (real name Salvador) introduced me to the crowd. The place served buns piled with as many thin burger patties as you wanted. The minimum anyone got was a double. Most guys ordered four with cheese, fries, and the largest Coke on offer. I still remember exactly what those burgers taste like.

Another time Dad asked if I wanted tacos. Of course I did. So he took me to a narrow grocery store in Wicker Park that reeked of cumin and cilantro. I followed him past the *Jesus Cristo* candles for sale, past shelves of herbs and cornhusks and long, pale sticks of cinnamon. All the way in the back, invisible to anyone passing by or just stopping in to grab a soda, there was a counter with 12 stools and a line of 20 people waiting for one to open up. Dad got the same reception here, except in Spanish: "*Hola*, Sal. *Cómo estás?*" I ordered what Dad ordered, because I knew he knew what was good.

I grew up infatuated with burgers and pizza and fried chicken and tacos because they had the thrill of the forbidden. Because they felt special. Because Dad loved them. Oh, and because they were bangin'. I reveled in the processed-food bliss of sugary white bread, the way American cheese melted like no other cheese can, the way a natural-casing hot dog snapped when you bit into it. Still do.

When I was a teenager, I found these pleasures even in chain fast food. I know it's bad for me. I know what it represents. Still, to this day, I'll crush a Double Quarter Pounder with Cheese. I'll hit up Popeyes for legs, thighs, and biscuits. I'll even do Pizza Hut for those thick pan pizzas hot from the oven, crispy on the outside and soft in the middle, like some expertly made focaccia.

My Filipino friends and I lived two lives. There was the Filipino one: the cotillions, where Filipino families celebrated a girl's 18th birthday and my boys and I awkwardly hollered at her friends decked out in fly dresses. The PBA (Philippine Basketball Association), where you weren't allowed to play unless you were a grade-A Filipino. Seriously. When my boy showed up with two 6-foot-5 "cousins," the rest of us asked to see their birth certificates. We never saw those cousins again. Ain't no real Filipinos that tall.

Yet even though I was rolling with all Filipino kids, after those basketball games and dances we never said, "Let's get some *sinigang* for dinner." Never. We wanted burgers. We wanted Buffalo wings. We wanted shrimp toast and lo mein. Anything but Filipino food. In part, it was straight-up rebellion: Our moms made us eat fish heads and chocolate meat. Now that it was up to us, we chose our second life: the American one.

It's not that we didn't want to be Filipino. We just badly wanted to be American, or at least to find a way to fit in. In my family and many Filipino families, the U.S. looms large, whether you live here or not. America saved us during World War II. Ten hours after the Japanese attacked Pearl Harbor, they hit the Philippines. Like many of her neighbors, my grandma fled her house and hid in the wooded hills to escape the Japanese occupation. In the Philippines, there are statues of General MacArthur and highways named for him.

Of course, when I was in high school I didn't know shit about MacArthur. But I did know about De La Soul. American culture was my thing, specifically the world of hip-hop, of rappers and B-boys. I definitely wasn't the first Asian kid who looked to hip-hop and black culture for role models. When you're 14 years old and no one

> "Our moms made us eat fish heads and chocolate meat. Now that it was up to us, we chose our second life: the American one."

main features were machine guns and malls. When we arrived at the airport in Iloilo Province, where my mom's family comes from, I saw that, instead of the relatively polite TSA agents who had ferried us through security at O'Hare, there were military-looking guys with AKs at the ready. On the streets, I saw the same thing. Everyone seemed to have very obvious private security, as if intimidation was the best way not to get your ass kidnapped. Maybe I should've been worried that the guy who took me and my cousins to the mall only brought three pistols. We spent most of our time in the Philippines at that mall, playing video games in the AC and eating Quarter Pounders at McDonald's.

Some people decide they want to cook for a living on their first trip to Paris or Spain. Me, I was in a grocery store. I was a broke-ass high schooler working the checkout line at Butera, a small family-run chain. I liked my job. I liked memorizing and entering the numbers that corresponded to each fruit and vegetable. I liked being surprised by what people bought.

Because this was Chicago, the customers came in various colors. Mexican families handed me bags of fresh green chiles and what looked like green tomatoes covered in papery husks. Tomatillos, I soon learned. Indian families bought coriander, cardamom, and huge tubs of cottage cheese, which I'd later learn they'd press to make paneer. Why, I wondered, did they never buy meat? Polish families certainly did, leaving with pounds of sausage and bacon as well as a shitload of potatoes and sacks of sauerkraut. After a while, I

on TV, in magazines, or in any position of authority looks like you, you search for someone else to identify with. I chose other outsiders who celebrated their outsider status. First it was A Tribe Called Quest and De La, and my friends and I sported Starter jerseys, baggy shorts, and Jordans. Then it was Wu-Tang, and we rocked bubble goose vests and fitted caps, butterscotch Tims and enormous jeans with one leg rolled up. By high school, we were going to house parties that bumped booty-shaking music so loud it drowned out the cha-cha music blaring at those cotillions.

I embraced my American identity, though my Filipino life kept intruding. When my grandfather in the Philippines got sick, my parents took us on the endless flight "home." Whenever Mom said "home," I knew right away that she didn't mean our place in Chicago. She meant the Philippines, where she grew up but where I had spent only a few years when I was a toddler. We got off the plane and my impression was that this place was weird, hot, and loud. I decided that the country's

started piecing together different food cultures from the contents of transparent bags. Classic combinations took shape in my head—tomatillo, chiles, and garlic always seemed to go together; so did cumin, coriander, and cardamom. Butera was my first culinary class, Ethnic American Food 101.

⟨✦⟩

When I graduated from high school, all I really knew was that I didn't want a desk job and I liked food. So I enrolled at the Culinary Institute of America, with the full support of my parents. I took culinary school about as seriously as an 18-year-old can. Early on, I remember hearing a speech from the dean, a pudgy German guy. He told my class that we were going to learn how to cook many different things in the course of our time there, but that one of the greatest things we'd ever cook was a simple roast chicken. This sentiment seems profound to me now. Back then, I was rolling my eyes: My parents are paying for the best cooking school in the world and this guy's talking up roast chicken? I also found myself missing rice. The first time I had steak *au poivre*, all I could think of was how badly it needed a bowl of those warm, steamy grains alongside.

While I was a mediocre student from kindergarten through high school, I did better in culinary school. I finally got to learn by watching and doing, which I was good at, rather than by reading and writing, which I was not good at. Sure, if I could go back, I'd probably choose to focus more and not show up to class hungover or stoned—if you ask me, culinary schools should have an NBA-style age restriction to prevent dumbasses like me from going before they're mature enough. Still, the tech-

niques I learned stuck. I swear that even though I haven't made a classic fish quenelle in the 15 years since my first big culinary school exam, I could still knock one out right now, tarragon beurre blanc and all—no problem. More important than that, though, culinary school taught me that I was actually good at something.

When I started working in kitchens, I was always the one Asian guy among Mexicans. There was Flaco, Gordo, Feo, and me, Chino. My first gig, by the way, was at an Outback Steakhouse, where my $60K education qualified me to make grilled shrimp pastas on the sauté station. When I took jobs in "serious" kitchens, I was the one Asian among Mexicans and a few well-off white boys. Like me, the white boys weren't there to feed their families; we aspired to make velouté and veal stock in fancy kitchen after fancy kitchen until one day we would be the guys who got to tell people to make the velouté and veal stock.

After our shifts, my cook friends and I would pound beers and fantasize about being named one of the ten best new chefs by *Food & Wine* magazine. I even had my photo spread planned out: All nine other winners would be in the typical group shot. Flip the page and you'd find my photo—styled by Hype Williams, the man behind what seemed like every hip-hop music video of the 1990s. I'd be rocking a chinchilla-fur chef's coat, a gorgeous woman under each arm, and a gold chain blazing, "F&W 1999."

My friends were kind. They never broke it to me that that wasn't going to happen. I was a mediocre cook. And a lazy one, too. Before my shifts at Vong, the Chicago outpost of Jean-Georges Vongerichten's trailblazing Southeast Asian–influenced restaurant, I'd get

> "I swear, molecular gastronomy was like weed in high school—all my friends were doing it, so I did too."

stoned outside. I kept my job solely because I showed up and didn't give a fuck what I was getting paid. I kept this up for a while, living out "my college years," which I'd missed out on in the almost military environment of culinary school.

My conversion from slacker to hard worker was spurred on by a come-to-Jesus moment: I needed money. I had bills to pay. I had moved out of my parents' place to live on my own, so at 23 years old I started a job running the kitchen at a French-Vietnamese café, where I had no idea what I was doing. I did, however, get myself a ride (an Acura CL Type S), and like a good Asian kid, I tricked it out with some fat rims—even though I could barely afford my monthly car payments. It never quite became a rice burner, those completely pimped-out cars with giant mufflers, spoilers, and rims. But I did manage to spend about 50 Gs that I didn't have. Then I quit my job after a huge fight with the owner.

In debt, I took two jobs—an a.m. and a p.m. gig. From 8 a.m. to 2:30 p.m., I worked at a three-star spot that

was unfortunately called Kevin. After a half-hour break, I went to my second gig at the three-star Naha, where I worked until close. I did this for a year and a half, taking only the occasional day off. Time seemed to both crawl and fly.

During that year and a half, my perception of cooking started to change. Early on, I'd aspired to open a tasting-menu-only restaurant that served Expressionist-art-looking plates of food that reflected my mood. This was the late 1990s, early 2000s, after all, when everyone was sweating Arzak and El Bulli. I swear, molecular gastronomy was like weed in high school— all my friends were doing it, so I did, too. I added soy lecithin to sauces and frothed them up. I smoked salmon tableside under a dome. I dreamed up dishes with 16 components. Instead of just letting people taste my food, I'd first hit them with a prologue filled with descriptions of all the complicated techniques I employed to make it. And as if the pretention wasn't bad enough, the food itself was really, really bad, too.

My outlook began to shift while working under Carrie Nahabedian at Naha. When I first started, she served this pan-seared fillet of striped bass with mashed potatoes and tomatoes cooked slowly in olive oil. At the time I remember thinking, "Seriously, Chef, can't we do better than this?" It seemed too simple. In retrospect, it was perfect. Beautifully seared fish, incredibly sweet tomatoes, top-notch olive oil, a sneaky bit of preserved lemon. The dish was exactly what it promised to be, but tasted so much better than I ever thought it could.

And I attribute some of my transformation to the fact that with two jobs I had no mental space for creativity or food-is-art bullshit and no time to fuck around. I got my shit together. It helped to work beside a lot of Mexican guys, who busted their asses all day every day. They didn't complain when they had to work lunch and dinner. Cooking wasn't a life's ambition. They did a good job, shared a few jokes, then went home to their families. So I came in, prepped my station, and made what the boss wanted me to make. I was learning a trade, like my dad had when he learned to fix boilers. Like my mom had when she learned to take blood pressure and read sonograms. I knew I wasn't particularly bright. But I could do well if I worked hard, and I got better as a cook. By the time I took my next job at a good restaurant, I was ready to fulfill my destiny—to become Mr. Asia.

The typecasting actually began at Naha. The chef came up to me, handed me a box of squash blossoms, and asked, "Do you know how to make tempura?" I'm not sure if she meant it this way, but I took her question as, You're Asian, you must know how to do it. And hey, I wasn't offended. So what if tempura is Japanese and I'm Filipino? I didn't know how to cook Filipino food either, so I wasn't about to jump on my high horse. Truth was, I was trained to make *béchamel*, *brandade*, and *blanquette de* fucking *veau*. I didn't know any more about making tempura than I did about making falafel. Still, if I had to be Mr. Asia, I figured I might as well use it to my advantage. So I shouted my best "Yes, Chef!" I went back to my station, and I flipped over the cornstarch box. There, I saw a recipe for tempura. Fifteen minutes later I handed the chef some banging tempura squash blossoms. My reputation was born.

At my next job, I became the dumpling expert. So what if I'd never made dumplings in my life? The chef asked me to make him some, I said "Yes, Chef," and when I went home that night I googled how to make dumplings. I came in the next day and made some. I'm not saying they were the best dumplings, but the chef was thrilled. I credit my small Asian hands. That's why we Asians have crazy dexterity. That's why we're so good at badminton and Ping-Pong. That's why we can school your ass on an abacus. (At least, that's one reason; we also invented that shit.) Everyone else in the kitchen had these clumsy sausage fingers. When they tried to form the little folds that distinguish good-looking dumplings, they could only make four of them. I was rocking eight-fold dumplings and looking like the man.

After a while, I figured that since I liked Asian food and everyone kept asking me to make it, I might as well really learn how. I decided to do that in New York, forever a restaurant mecca and as good a place as any to double down on my new dumpling direction.

"I was ready to fulfill my destiny—to become Mr. Asia."

I got a job at Morimoto, the Iron Chef's flagship Manhattan restaurant, where I learned how to make sushi rice, and that the chef had the temper of a yakuza boss.

Fortunately for me, Asian food was about to blow up. Or more accurately, blow up even more. I was in high school when Nobu Matsuhisa opened his eponymous restaurant in New York City. That dude was brilliant: He had people happily dropping triple digits on miso-glazed black cod and other re-issued Asian standards. I was also lucky to learn from another pioneer of Asian flavors, Jean-Georges Vongerichten. Yet even at the peak of Nobu's reign, no one could've anticipated the success of Danny Bowien, a skinny Korean dude rocking tiny shorts, patent leather shoes, and long blond hair, who has people lining up for his take on Sichuan-style double-cooked pork. No one thought a white guy from Vermont named Andy Ricker would win awards for re-creating the food of Northern Thailand.

At this point, I'd been cooking professionally for almost a decade and had achieved more than I ever thought I could. After my stint at Morimoto, I scored a sous chef position at Buddakan, the New York location of Philly restaurateur Stephen Starr's baller modern Chinese spot. I was happy, but restless. Like a kid with a matchbook, I had only one idea: I had to do something stupid. I had to start a fire. One day on the way to work, I passed by the location of the open-call audition for *Top Chef*'s fourth season. I was a fan of the show and an even bigger fan of competition. As a kid, I was always finding a reason to talk shit. As

a man, competing didn't mean skipping rocks and playing basketball. It meant flaunting my knife and wok skills. I mentioned the audition to my cooks and they suggested I try out: "TV people love assholes," one said. "And you're a real asshole." He was right on both counts. The casting agents had just finished packing up for the day when I walked into the audition spot. "Shit, I'm late, huh?" I said, ready to bounce and not look back. "We have time for one more," one agent said.

Being on *Top Chef* turned out to be one of the oddest and greatest experiences I've had as a cook. It's like being in jail minus the shanks and the communal showers. You arrive—in chef's whites, not orange jumpsuits—and immediately you size everyone up. Instead of "What are you in for?" you're asked "Where did you cook?" If you can say that you've cooked with Thomas Keller, Eric Ripert, or another well-respected big-name chef, that's like saying you're in for a triple homicide. People are scared of you. If you say you're a caterer, God help you. That's like ending up in Riker's Island for snatching an old lady's purse. You're fucked.

Everyone developed a rep. He takes shortcuts, she's a slob, he's a shitty cook, she's the one to beat. Mine was as the punk Asian kid, which, to be fair, I was. And I found myself playing into it, just like I did in kitchens. Chefs assumed I could make dumplings, so I made them. My fellow contestants thought I was a punk, so I got in people's faces and punched walls. Some of that attitude I borrowed from hip-hop: the alpha-male, I'm-the-best-here swagger. If you act and talk like you're the shit, people might just start thinking you're the shit. Some of it came from the stress of knowing that every single day you were on the show you could basically be promoted or fired. Some of it, though, came from legitimate anger issues, which I ultimately went to therapy to fix.

I learned a lot about myself on that show. I learned that I hate losing. I also learned that I had it out for people who I thought had it easy—apparently I thought that I didn't. My parents worked hard all my life to provide for me and my siblings. We weren't ever dirt poor, but we struggled. Seemingly small stuff had big stakes, so when I did something dumb, my dad's belt came out. Not just that; I'd have to go get the belt myself. When Dad asked me to close the windows—that way the white neighbors wouldn't judge Filipino-style parenting from my shrieks—I knew I was going to get it bad. I'm not an advocate of violence, but I do know that I grew up with a healthy respect for my father. And fear, too.

On the show, I reserved most of my rage for the few people there who acted like they had it easy, like they grew up with the notion that everyone wins in life, whether you worked hard or not. These were people who, I could tell just by looking at them, had never been straight punched in the face on the basketball court. Once in a while, it's good for you to get hit, to have to cover your face, tears flowing and one hand up, like "Alright, alright, chill, chill." I know I need a beatdown sometimes.

First impressions, of course, were just a starting point. Reputations were built on competition wins and the degree of those victories. Win with a dish everyone knew was dope, or dominate a particularly tough challenge, and your culinary stock rose. My greatest moment: I won a knife-skills challenge laid down by guest judge Daniel Boulud.

Knife skills are the ultimate in kitchen cred. Daniel Boulud is one of the chefs most respected by other chefs. Winning that was like hearing Big L tell you that you're a dope freestyler, or Jay Z telling you your girl is fly. I should've just quit the show right there. Because when I did get kicked off the show, I lost big. I like to blame a perfect storm of bad luck. But I can't front. What did me in were my miso-butterscotch scallops. As Anthony Bourdain put it, they were jaw-droppingly bad. But hey, you don't hit home runs without striking out. Whiffing on TV, though? Not a good look.

All in all, the show was great for me as a chef and as a person. I met great people. I confronted my anger issues. Even more important, people suddenly knew who I was, including a guy named Dave Massoni. One night, I took my girl at the time to 'Inoteca, an Italian spot on the Lower East Side. We showed up at 9:30 p.m., the place was poppin', and got quoted a two-hour wait. Typical New York. We figure we'd wait, for a while at least, and took a stroll around the hood. We dipped into a sex toy shop, just for kicks, and started acting stupid. Next thing you know, I've got some vibrating ring on my finger and I'm pretending to fight my girl with a giant swordlike, uh, thing. That's when I heard someone call my name and looked up, frozen mid-battle. Dave, a Teddy bear–looking dude wearing a Polo shirt with a popped collar, who was then 'Inoteca's general manager, had recognized me from *Top Chef*. "We have a table waiting for you," he said. "When you're done here."

Despite our weird start, Dave and I became friends. A year or so later, Dave opened a restaurant in Park Slope called Thistle Hill Tavern with a friend of his, a veteran bartender, slightly terrifying and tattooed from ankle to wrist, named

> "I learned a lot about myself on that show. I learned that I hate losing. I also learned that I had it out for people who I thought had it easy—apparently I thought that I didn't."

John Bush. I came to Brooklyn to check it out and to pick their brains. I had just been on *Top Chef*: *All Stars*, a spin-off of *Top Chef* that pitted the best (or in my case, the most notorious) former contestants against one another. I doubted I'd ever be on TV again.

I wanted to open my own place one day and figured I had better stir-fry while the wok was hot. Before I made the trip to Park Slope from the Lower East Side, I had been to Brooklyn approximately three times and had all the typical prejudices of a longtime Manhattanite. Brooklyn, I thought, was either scary or suburban, with more strollers than potential customers. Then one day, at Dave's insistence, I spent rush hour standing outside the F-train stop at Ninth Avenue and my mind got less narrow with every person who spilled out of the station. Not only were there plenty of potential customers, but at the time there weren't nearly enough restaurants to feed them all. Add to that the fact that space was cheap compared to rents in Manhattan and that the three of us got along like brothers, and you know what came next.

When we finally found a space,

I had to figure out what the hell I'd serve there. If I'd had to decide just a few years earlier, I might have come up with some soy lecithin–spiked, tasting-menu-only, smoke-and-mirrors bullshit. But my experience on *Top Chef* cemented who I was as a chef. I started to have more fun cooking. I realized that food is just food. Don't get me wrong, I spend almost every waking minute—probably most of my non-waking ones, too—thinking about cooking it and eating it. But it's not such a serious thing. So instead of forcing high-tech gizmos and high-end ingredients into my cooking, I began to embrace the food I liked, whether I'd discovered it on fine china in a dining room or in a bag at the drive-thru.

On the show, some contestants complained that all I did was cook Asian food, as if Asia were a country, not a vast continent, and as if cooking with soy sauce, ginger, and chiles were cheating. And as if anyone would whine about an Italian chef who cooked Italian food. I stopped worrying about what I *should* cook. Now I channeled a different kind of hip-hop swagger, not that I'm-the-shit bluster but an attitude that was, as the Brand Nubian song goes, "Love me or leave me alone." My food too spicy for you? Too fishy? Too salty? OK, then go somewhere else. In a way, I got lucky. Diners used to want food to be a pat on the back, not an uppercut to the chin. By the time I opened my first restaurant, they were ready to be transported or challenged. People wanted food that took them somewhere new, somewhere unexpected.

And I realized that "Asian," "modern Asian," or "Asian fusion" doesn't describe my food. I prefer Asian-American.

The New Asian-American Cuisine

My first restaurant, Talde, doesn't have Buddha ice sculptures, tatami mats, Chinese lanterns, or other typical Asian restaurant trappings. That's because it's not an Asian restaurant. I'm Filipino, sure, but really I'm an American chef who just happens to be Filipino. Instead, Talde looks like a classic American tavern, bar up front, dark wood booths in back, with just a few dragon statues and samurai-warrior wood carvings hinting that we don't serve straight-up Buffalo wings and burgers. The food here is my version of Asian-American cuisine, which is about as American as it is Asian.

My food is decidedly different from my mom's Asian-American home cooking (Filipino dishes made with American ingredients) and different from old-school Asian-American restaurant grub (classic Asian dishes re-jiggered to appeal to the American palate). It celebrates the culinary spirit of both, of Asian immigrants (and really, all immigrants) who re-create the flavors of home with what's available at the local supermarket and who hawk General Tso's chicken and spicy tuna rolls to provide for their families.

Yet while mine is also an immigrant's cuisine, I'm not the same kind of immigrant as my parents are. While "home" for my mom means the Philippines, for me it means Brooklyn. When I was younger, it meant Chicago. My palate was defined as much by my mom's food as it was by American food. And to me, American food not only means meat loaf and hot dogs, but also *shawarma* and roti, tacos and yakitori.

When I opened Talde, I didn't realize I was part of a culinary movement. But it's true: I make food for members of Generation Steamed Bun. These are the masses who were raised on take-out pad thai and egg rolls, who will travel two hours for real-deal Sichuan, and who would just as soon eat some dope pho as they would dine at Alinea. These are some Momofuku-loving, pork bun–eating motherfuckers. My food, though, is different from my peers' food. Some of the chefs making waves right now cook food meant to transport you—to Northern Thailand or Sichuan Province, to Vietnam or Tokyo. My food is meant to remind you that you're home, in that strange and awesome country where we live. My greatest influence comes from the diners, gyro shops, Polish delis, taquerias, burger joints, Chinese spots, and other food meccas that make up my American landscape.

For instance, chicken wings, the American bar staple, are my jam, but so is the classic Sichuan dish of kung pao chicken. So why not toss them in kung pao sauce? And since every good chicken wing needs a dairy dip, I serve them with buttermilk Ranch, the only thing on earth that could top blue cheese dressing.

To me, buttered toast is tied with ramen for the best breakfast food. Why not come up with a way to unite the two? That's how the Talde brunch bowl was born: ramen noodles in broth infused with the flavor of buttered toast, plus bacon and a poached egg for good measure. There's "phot roast" (pot roast stewed with ingredients you'd find in Vietnamese pho). There's fish basted with Chinese fermented black bean–infused brown butter. There's bacon, egg, and cheese— the holy trinity of the New York City bodega sandwich—made into fried rice. The book's overarching premise is, Why not?

I even occasionally pay direct homage to the fast food I loved as a kid. Let's all agree that there's no one in his right mind who doesn't love (secretly or not) McDonald's chicken nuggets with the three essential dipping sauces: honey mustard, sweet chile, and BBQ. I'm the president of their fan club, so at my restaurant Pork Slope I serve my version—all-white-meat chicken marinated in yogurt and hot sauce and fried in a rice-flour batter, with mostly homemade sauces on the side—which elevates the dish without sacrificing its easy-to-love, proudly unsophisticated qualities.

That's the kind of food you'll find in this cookbook: exciting, straight-

forward, ridiculously tasty food. To have the most fun with this book, there are a few things to keep in mind.

1. Invite a bunch of friends over. You know how every restaurant serves "small plates" now, like that's a new thing? Well, we *been* doing that. From Tokyo to Taipei, from Cebu to Chiang Mai, Asians have been eating meals composed of many different dishes that everyone shares. Each dish balances the others. At Talde, food is served in this spirit, too. At home, making seven dishes for dinner for two isn't realistic. But just know, the more people you invite over, the more dishes you'll make and the better the food will taste.

2. Flip to the Sauces chapter. I made this a sauce-heavy book on purpose. Bless you if you're down to deep-fry chicken, roast whole fish, or make dumplings. In case you're not, pick a sauce that sounds good—tomato jam, green sambal, pepperoni marinara— and pour it on a sautéed chicken breast, a grilled piece of steak, or a steamed lobster. If you want to make

kung pao sauce but not Kung Pao Chicken Wings (page 30), go ahead. If you want to make Korean Fried Chicken with Kimchi Yogurt (page 104), make the kimchi yogurt and grab spicy legs and thighs from Popeyes. Not just because it's a whole lot easier—but also because, let's be honest, Popeyes is damn good.

3. Do yourself a favor and flip the script. I'm not the food police. Recipes mean different things to different people. If you're new to cooking, stick to the script the first time you cook, say, Fish with Black-Bean Brown Butter (page 135). But if you're a good cook and want to mess around and apply the butter to shrimp, scallops, or lobster, do your thing. If you mess up, don't worry: It's just food.

Get Lazy

I'm not afraid to admit it: I'm a lazy cook. Nowadays, menus everywhere announce house-made ricotta, pickles, pasta, and even plates. I know I should be on some "We make our own *bao* buns and so should you" kick. But I can't front. We buy ours from a bakery. And so should you.

Look, I'm not trying to be the Asian Sandra Lee. I'm definitely not trying to hate on books that teach you how to make bread or noodles or salami. It's fun to make bread at home, even when you know some bakery can make it better. I'm just saying you shouldn't feel bad about being a little lazy.

When I do make something at my restaurants, the reason is typically economics (I make XO sauce because I had to do something with all the ham scraps I had) or because I was having trouble buying a good version in sufficient quantity (when I could finally get cheap enough cases of Barrio Fiesta brand *ginisang bagoong*, I stopped making my own shrimp-paste soffrito). Part of the reason I like Asian cooking in the first place is its affection for the dump-and-stir method of cooking. When a Chinese cook makes a stir-fry, he doesn't start by brewing his own oyster sauce. He combines a few bottled liquids in the right way and boom, dope dish.

At home, the reality is that the more tasks you plan to take on, the less likely you are to actually find the time to perform any of them. At least, that's how I feel during my downtime, when I don't have a small army of cooks to do the hard work for me. Here's the secret, though: If you live in a city, you do have your own troops.

You could call it urban foraging. City dwellers everywhere do it to some degree. You buy bread from the dope bakery down the block. You get the butcher to butterfly a leg of lamb for you. I like to take the "Let someone else do it" philosophy even further. Especially when that someone does it better or more efficiently than you do. You could steam your own lobster or find a fishmonger to do it for you. You could make your own rice noodles, or you could buy them from the lady on Canal Street who charges 80 cents a pound. Some might call it taking the easy way out. I call it delegating.

You'll figure out what shortcuts make sense for you. If you roll like my mom and always have rice left over from dinner the night before, good for you. You'll be able to whip up fried rice in 15 minutes. If not, then you're stuck cooking rice, waiting a day or two, then frying it. But if you buy the rice at Panda Delight for $1.50, that's one less task and one less pot to clean.

So choose your battles. Your cooking will be more successful and you'll have more fun. The recipes in this book are filled with shortcuts. Using Hellman's or Duke's for my XO Tartar Sauce (page 193) or Garlic-Vinegar Mayo (page 193) is a no-brainer. Buying cooked rice from your local Japanese spot for Crispy Sushi Rice with Yuzu Guacamole and Ham (page 26) is not just an option but a recommendation. You could wash, trim, cut, and blanch broccoli to serve with Orange Beef (page 133), or you could roll by your local Chinese joint, ask them if they'd please make you some plain extra-crunchy steamed florets, and spend an extra half hour with the people you invited over for dinner.

CHAPTER ONE

Snacks

Perilla Leaf Bites with Bacon-Tamarind Caramel

If I ran the type of restaurant where waiters in suits presented each diner with an *amuse-bouche*, I'd make sure everyone who sat down got one of these. That's because each perilla leaf wrap is the perfect introduction to my food in just one bite: an intense mouthful that's herbaceous, sweet, sour, salty, bitter, chewy, and crunchy all at once. In fact, the wrap is so emblematic of what I do that if you don't like it, you should probably just give this cookbook away. I won't be mad at you.

Preheat the oven or toaster oven to 350°F. Spread the coconut flakes on a baking sheet in one layer and toast in the oven, shaking occasionally, just until they're very light golden brown and crunchy, about 2 minutes.

Heat the oil in a small pan over medium-high heat until it smokes lightly. Add the dried shrimp and cook, stirring frequently, until they're crisp all the way through and golden brown, 2 to 3 minutes. Transfer to paper towels to drain.

Arrange the perilla leaves on a platter. To each one, add ¼ teaspoon of caramel (it helps to use a lightly oiled spoon, so the caramel doesn't stick), ¼ teaspoon of the peanuts, one slice of chile, one sliver of lime, one flake of coconut, and one dried shrimp. Tell your friends to eat each leaf in one bite.

Makes 24

24 large unsweetened coconut flakes

2 tablespoons vegetable oil

24 medium dried shrimp

24 fresh perilla leaves (see Perilla Leaves, below)

2 tablespoons Bacon-Tamarind Caramel (page 190), at room temperature

2 tablespoons roughly chopped unsalted roasted peanuts

24 thin slices fresh red Thai chile (including seeds)

⅛ lime, cut into 24 (¼-inch) pieces (including rind)

Perilla Leaves

This dish is my take on *miang kam*, a one-bite Thai snack in which ingredients like dried shrimp, chiles, and peanuts are wrapped in pungent betel leaf. Instead of betel leaf, I use the slightly easier-to-find perilla leaf, a jagged-edged fresh herb that tastes like what would happen if mint, licorice, and betel leaves all got freaky. It comes in different varieties, but they're all good for this dish. The herb goes by *shiso* in Japanese grocery stores, sesame leaves in Korean ones (even though they're not really sesame leaves), and *tia to* in Vietnamese ones. Actually, the herb grows in Brooklyn and I see mad Koreans coming out of Prospect Park with bags filled with it. If you're having trouble finding *shiso,* you could even do some urban foraging and ask at a few local Japanese restaurants if you can buy some from them. It's worked for me.

Crispy Sushi Rice with Yuzu Guacamole and Ham

Serves
4 to 8

SPECIAL EQUIPMENT
Parchment paper

FOR THE SUSHI RICE
¼ cup unseasoned rice vinegar

½ teaspoon granulated sugar

¼ teaspoon hon dashi powder or chicken bouillon

¼ teaspoon kosher salt

2 cups warm cooked short-grain white rice, preferably from your local Japanese restaurant

A drizzle of vegetable oil

FOR THE GUAC
2 medium Hass avocados, halved and pitted

2 teaspoons kosher salt

2 to 3 tablespoons bottled yuzu juice, or fresh Key lime or Meyer lemon juice

2 tablespoons seeded, diced (¼ inch) tomato

1 tablespoon finely chopped jalapeño chile (including seeds)

1 tablespoon diced (¼ inch) red onion

1 tablespoon finely chopped cilantro (thin stems and leaves)

1 medium garlic clove, very finely chopped

Continued, opposite

When I lived on Manhattan's Lower East Side, I used to hit up this Dominican restaurant across the street, one of those steam table joints where you'd roll up and point at what you wanted—roasted pork, fried pork belly, beans. Whatever you ordered came on top of fluffy white rice that a lady would spoon from a giant pot, and with two slices of avocado. But there was also this separate bowl of rice set aside on the counter, like it was special. Turns out it was.

Dominicans call it *concón*, Puerto Ricans call it *pegao*, and the Spanish call it *socarrat*. The fact that there are words in multiple languages for the layer of crispy, chewy rice that gets stuck to the bottom of the pot should tell you how dope it is. Now, where I come from, if you cook rice that has a layer like this, you screwed up. So I was skeptical at first. But I got so obsessed with it that I started trying to find a way to make rice that was all crispy layer. After I did came the fun part—deciding what to do with it. That's when things got weird.

Rice got me thinking sushi, so I vinegared the grains before crisping them up, then deglazed the pan with soy sauce. Those two slices of avocado got me thinking avocado rolls and then about guacamole. The ham was a total fat-kid move: I spotted a piece of Spanish ham in the kitchen, as red as raw tuna, and popped that on top. Come to think of it, tuna tartare on top would be great, too.

MAKE THE SUSHI RICE

Combine the vinegar, sugar, hon dashi, and salt in a small pan, set it over low heat, and cook, stirring, just until the sugar and salt dissolve, about 30 seconds. Pour the mixture into a medium mixing bowl, add the cooked rice, and stir gently but well, breaking up lumps and making sure not to smash the grains.

Line your smallest baking sheet with parchment paper and rub the paper with a drizzle of oil. Add the rice to one side and use wet fingers to gently press the rice to form an approximately 1-inch-thick layer with straight sides (the rice will probably cover only a portion of the sheet). Fold the parchment over the rice and use another baking sheet that fits into the first one or your hands to firmly press the rice to a ¾-inch-thick layer. Let the rice fully cool, about 30 minutes. Cut the rice into approximately 16 (3- by 1-inch) strips, or really whatever size you want.

MAKE THE GUAC

Scoop the avocado into a bowl, add the salt and 2 tablespoons of the yuzu juice, then stir and mash until fairly smooth. Add the remaining ingredients and stir gently but well. Season to taste with additional juice and salt.

FINISH THE DISH

Pour enough vegetable oil into a large, heavy skillet to reach a depth of about ⅛ inch. Heat the skillet over high heat until the oil smokes lightly and add half of the rice strips in a single layer with a little space separating them. Cook, flipping them once, until both sides are golden brown and crispy, about 2 minutes per side. Use a slotted spatula to transfer the strips to paper towels to drain. Cook the remaining strips, then transfer them to the towels as well. Pour out any oil remaining in the pan.

Add the butter to the skillet and let it melt and froth. Add the rice strips back to the skillet and cook, swirling, for a few seconds. Add the soy sauce, let it bubble, and swirl the mixture once or twice, just until the bottoms are coated in the sauce but not soggy, about 15 seconds.

Use the slotted spatula to transfer them to a platter, leaving any liquid behind. Top the strips with the guacamole, then the ham, chile slices, and nori. Eat.

TO FINISH THE DISH

About ½ cup vegetable oil

2 tablespoons unsalted butter

2 tablespoons reduced-sodium soy sauce

8 or so thin slices prosciutto, serrano ham, or similar American ham, halved

1 teaspoon thinly sliced moderately spicy fresh red chile (including seeds), such as Fresno, or more to taste

1 sheet nori seaweed, halved and cut into ⅛-inch-wide strips

Pepperoni-Pizza "Very Warm" Pockets

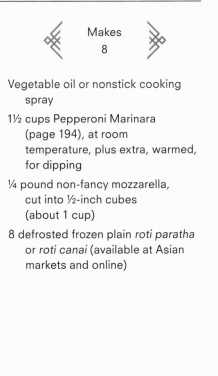

Makes
8

Vegetable oil or nonstick cooking
spray

1½ cups Pepperoni Marinara
(page 194), at room
temperature, plus extra, warmed,
for dipping

¼ pound non-fancy mozzarella,
cut into ½-inch cubes
(about 1 cup)

8 defrosted frozen plain *roti paratha*
or *roti canai* (available at Asian
markets and online)

You may front like you never liked Hot Pockets. But if you grew up in
the '80s, you know you did. When you eat junk food long enough, you
start to get snobby about it. After downing mad Hot Pockets, I learned
that if I cooked them in the oven the crust would turn out crispier and
that the best variety by far was pepperoni pizza.

Then one day, I didn't like Hot Pockets, even the pepperoni pizza
ones. For a while, I was stuck in this weird place where I had affection
for certain foods but no longer liked eating them. So I set out to improve
the Hot Pocket—since I'm legally obligated to change the trademarked

name, I'll call mine "Very Warm" Pockets—but not by so much that it became something else and I lost what the sixth grader in me had loved. The result might be my greatest achievement to date as a cook.

I hope it goes without saying that you shouldn't get all bougie with the cheese and pepperoni for this recipe. If you're at a store where the staff pronounce mozzarella the Italian way, then you should probably go somewhere else. Not only would the expensive stuff get drowned out by all the other flavors, but it wouldn't melt in the nostalgic stretchy way.

Preheat the oven to 450°F and lightly oil or spray one very large or two medium baking sheets. Combine the 1½ cups of marinara and the mozzarella in a bowl and stir well.

Form one pocket at a time: Keep the roti between the plastic squares it comes in (the roti is very sticky) and put it on the counter. Use your palm to stretch the roti slightly, starting in the center and applying gentle pressure as you move toward the edges.

Peel off the top layer of plastic and spoon ¼ cup of the marinara mixture in the center of the roti. Holding the two corners of the plastic square that are closest to you, fold the roti over the filling to form a semicircle, gently forcing the air out but keeping the filling in. If a little filling seeps out, just wipe it off with a paper towel. Firmly press the rounded edge of the roti to create a seal. Repeat with the remaining marinara mixture and roti.

Put the pockets on the baking sheet, leaving some space around each one. Use a sharp knife to make three slashes through the top of each (so they don't burst in the oven), cutting through the roti layer and leaving ½ inch or so separating the slashes. You can bake them right away, keep them covered in the fridge for up to 12 hours, or freeze them (see Note).

Brush the tops with a very thin layer of vegetable oil or coat with cooking spray. Bake until the outsides are golden brown and puffy, 10 to 15 minutes. Let them cool slightly before you eat and serve with extra marinara alongside for dipping.

NOTE: To freeze the unbaked pockets, put them uncovered on a plate in the freezer just until frozen, then transfer to bags with parchment paper separating the hot pockets. Freeze for up to 3 months. Bake the frozen pockets in a 350°F oven for 15 minutes, until they're thawed. Brush the tops with oil, raise the oven heat to 450°F, and bake until golden, about 8 minutes more.

Hot pocket [haht **pok**-it]; VERB
To encase in flaky dough; to successfully employ store-bought roti; to create a hot meal without a big deal: *Why make quiche when you can hot pocket an omelet?*

Kung Pao Chicken Wings

Makes about
20 wings

SPECIAL EQUIPMENT
Deep-fry thermometer

FOR MARINATING
AND FRYING THE WINGS

2 pounds medium-size chicken
wing drumettes and flats
(about 20 total)

½ cup low-fat plain yogurt
(not Greek)

Vegetable oil for deep frying

2 cups Asian white rice flour
(not sticky rice flour)

⅓ cup Thai or Vietnamese fish
sauce

TO FINISH THE WINGS

3 tablespoons vegetable oil

1 teaspoon Szechuan
peppercorns, ground

6 Asian dried red chiles

¼ cup coarsely chopped unsalted
roasted peanuts

1 cup Kung Pao Sauce (page 187)

¼ cup thinly sliced scallion greens

¾ cup loosely packed roughly
chopped cilantro (thin stems
and leaves)

1 cup Buttermilk Ranch (page 199) or
bottled Ranch

I'm definitely not the first person to rethink the Buffalo wing, but I'd put my take up against anyone else's. After a double batter and double deep fry—it's much easier than it sounds—I toss the wings in sweet-tangy sauce modeled on kung pao chicken, or at least the Sichuan classic as loosely interpreted by a Filipino kid from Chi-Town. Blue cheese sauce gets the ax in favor of homemade buttermilk Ranch, because Ranch is king.

And I've said it before and I'll say it again, if frying at home freaks you out or if you're feeling lazy, hit up Popeyes and kung pao–ify their extra-spicy wings.

MARINATE THE WINGS

Combine the chicken and yogurt in a large bowl and toss to coat the chicken well. Cover and let the chicken marinate in the fridge for at least 12 hours or up to 3 days (the longer the better).

BATTER AND FRY THE WINGS

About an hour before you're ready to eat, pour enough oil into a wide pot to reach a depth of about 3 inches. Set the pot over medium-high heat and bring the oil to 275°F (use a deep-fry thermometer). Meanwhile, combine the rice flour, fish sauce, and 1 cup water in a large mixing bowl and stir very well until the mixture is well combined and has no lumps.

Line a baking sheet with paper towels. You're going to cook the chicken in two batches to avoid crowding the oil. Add the first batch of chicken pieces to the batter and toss to coat well. Gently shake the pieces to let any excess batter drip off and add them to the oil. Fry, stirring and turning them over occasionally, until they're light golden brown and crispy but not quite cooked through, 8 to 10 minutes. Transfer the pieces to the paper towel–lined sheet. Batter and fry the remaining chicken. Reserve the batter and the oil.

BATTER AND FRY THE WINGS AGAIN

Set a rack over a baking sheet and use a mesh sieve to remove any stray fry from the oil. Set the pot over high heat and bring the oil to 350°F. Working in batches again, add the chicken to the batter, toss to coat, shake the pieces gently, and fry again, stirring, until they're deep golden brown, crispy, and fully cooked, about 5 minutes. Transfer the pieces to the rack as they're cooked.

FINISH THE WINGS

Combine the oil, ground peppercorns, and dried chiles in a wide (at least 12 inches), heavy skillet. Heat the skillet over very high heat until the oil sizzles, then add the wings and peanuts. Cook, frequently tossing the wings with tongs, until you can smell the peanuts, about 1 minute.

Pour the kung pao sauce into the skillet, toss the wings really well to coat them in the sauce, then add the scallions and cilantro. Let the sauce bubble furiously until it reduces slightly to form a glaze that coats the wings, 1 to 2 minutes. Toss the wings well once more and transfer them to a platter.

Eat alongside a bowl of the Ranch dressing.

Saigon Crepes with Shrimp, Ham, and Herbs

Makes
3 crepes

FOR THE BATTER

1½ cups Asian white rice flour
(not sticky rice flour)

½ cup well-shaken coconut milk

1½ teaspoons Thai or Vietnamese
fish sauce

2¼ teaspoons turmeric powder

Generous ¼ teaspoon kosher salt

FOR THE SHRIMP

1 lemon, halved

½ pound medium shrimp, peeled
and deveined

FOR THE CREPES

6 tablespoons vegetable oil

¾ cup loosely packed very thinly
sliced red onion

1 tablespoon thinly sliced
moderately spicy fresh red chile
(including seeds), such as Fresno

1½ cups loosely packed fresh mung
bean sprouts

2 cups loosely packed arugula

½ cup loosely packed very roughly
chopped cilantro (thin stems
and leaves)

½ cup loosely packed mint leaves

½ cup loosely packed Thai or
regular basil leaves

6 thin slices prosciutto, serrano
ham, or similar American ham

About 1 cup Vietnamese Dipping
Sauce (Nuoc Cham), opposite

My version of *banh xeo*, the Vietnamese crepe you eat wrapped in lettuce leaves and dunked into a salty-sweet dipping sauce, is a little less DIY than the original (I stick the greenery inside the crepe). That way, you can eat it like a giant taco. I also hit it with ham, because that's how I like my French crepes. Otherwise, the dopeness of the original is intact—the addictive crispy-chewy texture of the turmeric-spiked rice flour batter, the contrasting crunch of slightly wilted bean sprouts, and the fresh blast of herbs.

MAKE THE BATTER

Combine the batter ingredients and 1 cup plus 2 tablespoons water in a mixing bowl and stir until you have a completely smooth batter. Set aside for at least 30 minutes or up to 2 hours. Stir well right before you start cooking.

POACH THE SHRIMP

Bring 1 quart water to a boil in a medium pot, squeeze the lemon into the water, and add the halves to the pot. Add the shrimp and immediately turn off the heat. When the shrimp are just cooked through, 3 to 5 minutes, scoop them out, let them cool slightly, and cut each into a few pieces.

MAKE THE CREPES

Make the test crepe (see Note). Next, make three crepes, one at a time: Heat a 10-inch skillet (preferably stainless steel and *not* nonstick) over medium to medium-high heat. Add 1 tablespoon of the oil and swirl the pan to coat the bottom and about ½ inch up the sides. When it smokes lightly, move the pan off the heat, add ½ cup of the batter, and quickly swirl the pan to coat the bottom and about ½ inch up the sides. Return the pan to the heat and cook without messing with the crepe at all until the edges look thin and lacy, about 1 minute.

Scatter on ¼ cup of the onion and 1 teaspoon of the chile, then ½ cup of the bean sprouts and one-third of the shrimp. Cook, without messing with anything, until the crepe's edges lift from the skillet, about 2 minutes more. Gently lift one edge and add another 1 tablespoon oil, tipping the pan so the oil flows underneath the crepe. Cook for another 30 seconds, then carefully but firmly shake the pan so the crepe releases from the skillet and moves around without breaking. (If the crepe doesn't release, carefully work a spatula underneath to help it.)

Add about a third of the arugula, herbs, and ham to one side of the crepe (so you'll have an easier time folding it over later). Keep cooking, occasionally and carefully peeking underneath, until the bottom is crispy with brown spots, about 1 minute more. Turn off the heat.

Use the spatula to fold the emptier half of the crepe over the other half, press lightly so it stays folded, and transfer the crepe to a plate. Drizzle on about ⅓ cup of the sauce. Serve immediately, then get to work on the next one.

———— ◦◦◇◦◦ ————

NOTE: Like all crepes, the first one is never as good as the fourth. That's why my recipe gives you enough batter to make a test crepe. The key to making the crepes is finding your stove's sweet spot. Start by heating the pan over somewhere between medium and medium-high heat, and then, as instructed, adding the oil and the batter. Next, let the crepe cook, without messing with it, for 3 minutes. If the crepe doesn't release from the pan easily, cook the remaining crepes with slightly higher heat. If the crepe has blackish spots, cook the remaining crepes with slightly lower heat. You'll get the hang of it.

Another couple tips: Have your ingredients organized before you turn on the stove, and do not mess with the batter too much once you've added it to the pan—let it do its thing.

Vietnamese Dipping Sauce (Nuoc Cham)

Makes about 1½ cups

¼ cup fresh lime juice

¼ cup Thai or Vietnamese fish sauce

¼ cup superfine sugar

1 teaspoon finely chopped garlic

1 teaspoon thinly sliced fresh red Thai chiles (including seeds), or to taste

Combine all the ingredients with ¾ cup water in a container with a lid and shake until the sugar has dissolved. The sauce keeps for up to 5 days in the fridge.

Filipino Sausage Sliders

I'll pound regular burger sliders all day, but the Filipino in me would rather eat these pork patties seasoned with soy sauce, chile oil, and a little sugar. Basically, they're casing-less *longaniza*, a sausage I grew up eating as often as white boys ate hot dogs. My mom browned it in a pan to serve with eggs or fried rice on the daily. She never squished it between soft, sweet buns, slicked it with vinegary mayo, or topped it with pickled shallots, but damn if that's not the shit right there.

If you can't find a butcher who will grind meat to order, buy ground pork belly or the fattiest stuff you can. I'm definitely not someone who stresses about authenticity, but I couldn't bring myself to leave out the annatto seeds in this recipe, which contribute nothing but color. To me, a sausage is not *longaniza* without that reddish hue.

MAKE THE SAUSAGE

Combine the oil and annatto seeds in a very small pan and set over high heat. Tip the pan so the oil and seeds collect at one side and the oil more or less submerges the seeds. Cook until the oil looks bright red, 1 to 2 minutes. Let it fully cool in the pan, then strain, discarding the seeds.

Combine the remaining sausage ingredients in a large bowl, add the oil, and use your hands to mix everything just until the ingredients are well distributed. Overmix and your sausage will be tough. Let the mixture sit for at least 1 hour or keep in the fridge for up to 24 hours.

MAKE THE SLIDERS

Preheat the oven to 350°F. Using about ¼ cup of the sausage mixture for each, form 12 round ½-inch-thick patties.

Arrange the rolls cut sides up in one layer on a baking sheet and toast in the oven until the cut sides are light golden and the insides are still soft, about 2 minutes. Meanwhile, heat the oil in a large ovenproof skillet over medium heat until it shimmers. Add the patties and cook, flipping once, until they're brown on both sides, about 2 minutes per side. Transfer the skillet to the oven and bake until the sausage is cooked through, about 3 minutes.

Spread as much mayo as you'd like on both the roll tops and bottoms. Put as much as you want of the pickled shallots on the roll bottoms. Top with the sausage patties, cover with the roll tops, and eat.

Makes
12 sliders

FOR THE SAUSAGE

1 tablespoon plus 1 teaspoon vegetable oil

¾ teaspoon annatto seeds (aka achiote seeds; available at Latin markets)

1 pound lean boneless pork shoulder, coarsely ground by your butcher

6 ounces pork fatback, coarsely ground by your butcher

1 tablespoon Worcestershire sauce

2 teaspoons reduced-sodium soy sauce

1½ teaspoons kosher salt

1½ teaspoons granulated sugar

½ teaspoon garlic powder

½ teaspoon Asian chile oil

½ teaspoon ground paprika

½ teaspoon ground black pepper

FOR THE SLIDERS

12 small, soft sweet rolls such as Hawaiian buns or potato rolls, split open

2 tablespoons vegetable oil

Garlic-Vinegar Mayo (page 193)

Pickled Shallots (page 204)

Marinated Shiitake Sliders

Whenever I need to make a dish vegetarian, I look to shiitake mushrooms, which pack some of the umami flavor and texture of meat. Roasted, then marinated in soy sauce, ginger, and sesame oil, they make a slider "patty" that satisfies even the most carnivorous customers. The mushrooms themselves also go great on Nasi Lemak–Style Coconut Grits (page 61).

Makes
12 sliders

**FOR THE MUSHROOMS
AND MARINADE**

12 fresh thick shiitake mushroom caps or 24 thin caps (about 6 ounces)

3 tablespoons vegetable oil

¼ teaspoon finely chopped garlic

¼ teaspoon kosher salt

½ cup reduced-sodium soy sauce

1 tablespoon Asian sesame oil

1½ teaspoons finely chopped fresh ginger

1½ teaspoons granulated sugar

1½ teaspoons chicken bouillon, optional

FOR THE SLIDERS

12 small, soft sweet rolls such as Hawaiian buns or potato rolls, split open

Garlic-Vinegar Mayo (page 193)

Pickled Shallots (page 204)

ROAST AND MARINATE THE MUSHROOMS

Preheat the oven to 400°F. Combine the mushrooms, oil, garlic, and salt in a mixing bowl and toss well to coat the mushrooms. Spread them out on a baking sheet in one layer and roast until fully tender and golden brown, 5 to 8 minutes, depending on the size.

While they're roasting, make the marinade: In the same bowl, combine the remaining ingredients along with ½ cup water and stir well.

Add the hot mushrooms to the marinade and toss. Let them sit for at least 2 hours or in the fridge for up to a day.

MAKE THE SLIDERS

Preheat the oven to 350°F.

Remove the mushrooms from the marinade (reserve it in case you want to make the dish again within the next 5 days). Heat the mushrooms in the microwave or on a baking sheet in the oven just until they're hot.

Arrange the rolls cut sides up in one layer on a baking sheet and toast in the oven just until the cut sides are light golden and the insides are still soft, about 2 minutes.

Spread as much mayo as you'd like on both the roll tops and bottoms. Put as much as you want of the pickled shallots on the roll bottoms. Top with one very large mushroom cap or two smaller ones, cover with the roll tops, and eat.

Lobster Salad Sliders with Chile Mayo

Some modern culinary trends deserve to die: foams and froths, the sauce swoosh, garnishing with stuff that's so tiny you need tweezers to plate it. But chile mayo needs to be resurrected. I don't care how played out people think it is, we need to get in the DeLorean and retrieve that stuff, *Back to the Future* style, from the '90s. My chile mayo—flavored with Sriracha, brightened by lemon juice, and umami-boosted by chile bean paste—turns chunks of lobster (or crab or shrimp, for that matter) into the seafood salad that dreams are made of. I eat it with potato chips when I'm feeling extra-classy.

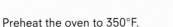

Preheat the oven to 350°F.

Combine the mayo, bean paste, Sriracha, lemon juice, and sesame oil in a bowl and stir really well. Add the lobster, stir to coat it well, then stir in the scallions and cilantro.

Arrange the rolls cut sides up in one layer on a baking sheet. Toast in the oven just until the cut sides are light golden and the insides are still soft, about 2 minutes.

Make sandwiches and eat.

 Makes 8 sliders

½ cup mayo

1 tablespoon Chinese chile bean paste (aka *toban djan*), such as the Lee Kum Kee brand

1½ teaspoons Sriracha

1 teaspoon fresh lemon juice

¼ teaspoon Asian sesame oil

10 ounces cooked lobster meat (from two 1½-pound lobsters), chopped into bite-size chunks (2 cups)

1 generous tablespoon thinly sliced scallions

1 generous tablespoon cilantro leaves

8 small, soft sweet rolls such as Hawaiian buns or potato rolls, split open

Bao-ed Lobster in Warm Chile Butter

I have no loyalties when it comes to lobster rolls. If you pile sweet chunks of crustacean on a bun, I'm sold. Yet there's something about the Connecticut style—warm, buttery lobster as opposed to the chilled mayo-coated Maine style—that gets me particularly amped. Purists, look away: I use scallion, cilantro, and Sriracha in my version. For anyone who thinks Sriracha is played out, I dare you to taste what happens when it gets mellowed with butter and brightened with lemon juice. Chinese steamed *bao* buns provide a slightly sweet, doughy backdrop similar to the classic split-top bun.

Right before you serve, arrange the buns on a plate, cover them with damp paper towels, and microwave, flipping once, about 1 minute.

Melt the butter in a small saucepan over medium-low heat and stir in the Sriracha, chile flakes, and ½ teaspoon salt. Reduce the heat to low, add the lobster, and stir occasionally just until the lobster is hot all the way through, 1 to 2 minutes. Take the pot off the heat and stir in the lemon juice, scallions, and cilantro. Season to taste with more salt and lemon juice. Cover to keep it warm.

Remove the buns from the parchment and put them on a plate. Use a slotted spoon to transfer the lobster meat to the *bao* buns, spoon on as much of the sauce as you'd like, and eat.

 Makes
6 buns

6 fresh or frozen Chinese buns (aka *gua bao*, folded buns, or steamed sandwiches)

1 stick (¼ pound) unsalted butter, cut into several pieces

¼ cup Sriracha

½ teaspoon red chile flakes

½ teaspoon kosher salt, plus more for seasoning

10 ounces cooked lobster meat (from two 1½-pound lobsters), chopped into bite-size chunks (2 cups)

1 generous tablespoon fresh lemon juice

1 generous tablespoon thinly sliced scallions

1 generous tablespoon loosely packed cilantro leaves

Bao [bou]; VERB
To use pillowy Chinese bread to transform anything into a sandwich; to make one more likely to eat something exotic; to make trendy: *Even though it's delicious, people might not try Filipino sausage unless we* bao *it.*

Crispy Moo Shu Beef Tartare Sandwiches

When the French serve beef raw, people call it old-school elegance and pay up the nose. When Asians do it, people bug out like someone just tried to serve them rattlesnake. So if you must, think of this as steak tartare, just with mayo and kimchi instead of egg yolk and cornichons. I sandwich the mixture in between moo shu pancakes brushed with sweet sauce and charred until crispy to provide a whiff of the Korean BBQ spot.

Wrap the steak in plastic wrap and put it in the freezer until it's frozen at the edges, about 1 hour. Meanwhile, preheat a grill pan over high heat. Lightly season the reserved fat with salt and grill it, flipping occasionally, until it's well charred, 5 to 8 minutes. Let it cool.

Take the meat from the freezer, thinly slice it, cut the slices into thin strips, then cut those into very small pieces (about ⅛ to 1⁄16 inch). Mince enough of the grilled fat to give you 3 tablespoons. In a small mixing bowl, combine the chopped steak, minced fat, kimchi, kimchi liquid, scallions, mayo, soy sauce, shallot, sesame oil, garlic, white pepper, and salt to taste. Stir well.

Spread 1 teaspoon eel sauce on one side of each pancake. Spray the same grill pan with nonstick spray and heat over medium-high heat. Add the pancakes sauce side down, in batches if necessary. Cook, rotating them 90 degrees halfway through, until they have crosshatched char marks, 1 to 2 minutes. Flip the pancakes and cook until they're light golden brown on the bottom and brittle, about 1 minute more. Let them cool slightly and break them into irregular, approximately 3-inch shards.

Make sandwiches with the tartare mixture, jalapeño slices, and pancake shards, sauce side out. Eat.

Makes about
20
mini sandwiches

1 (10-ounce) rib eye steak, very large pockets of fat trimmed and reserved

Kosher salt

3 tablespoons finely chopped drained cabbage kimchi, plus 1 tablespoon kimchi liquid

3 tablespoons thinly sliced scallion greens

2 tablespoons mayo

1 tablespoon plus 1 teaspoon reduced-sodium soy sauce

1 tablespoon finely chopped shallot

½ teaspoon Asian sesame oil

⅛ teaspoon finely chopped garlic

Pinch ground white pepper

1 tablespoon plus 1 teaspoon Japanese eel sauce (aka *unagi* sushi sauce)

Nonstick cooking spray

4 (8-inch) moo shu pancakes or flour tortillas

1 small jalapeño chile, very thinly sliced (including seeds)

Authenticity

I like to say my food is proudly inauthentic. My pad thai is made with bacon and fried oysters. My lo mein features roast chicken, rosemary, sage, and thyme. But saying that authenticity is overrated doesn't go far enough. Authenticity is a slippery concept. Just when you think you've got a handle on it, it's gone.

At Pork Slope, I make my version of one of the most delicious dishes on the planet—a dish that also happens to be one of the most hated on. I'm talking about hard tacos. While mine don't come straight from the bright-yellow Old El Paso kit, they still provide all the classic components: the crunchy corn shells and seasoned ground beef, the shredded cheddar and iceberg lettuce, the sour cream.

Now, lots of people look down on these for being "inauthentic." My question is: What's so bad about not being authentic? Sure, you probably won't see these in Michoacán or Oaxaca. But you will see tostadas (nothing more than crunchy fried corn tortillas). You will see *picadillo*, tasty ground meat that occasionally ends up in tacos. And you'll definitely see all sorts of food topped with cheese (Cotija, queso fresco, you name it), Mexican *crema* (which is barely different from sour cream), and shredded lettuce. In other words, hard tacos are like the Filipino food my mom cooked back in the day: the flavors you remember made from the ingredients you've got.

That's not all. When you look a little closer at Mexican food—and Asian food and all food, really—even the stuff that seems authentic reveals itself: The frying of tortillas to make tostadas, the olives you see in typical *picadillo*, and the techniques used for cheese making all came, for better or for worse, from European conquerors. Cilantro and lime—the two most Mexican-seeming ingredients after chiles—came from Asia. In other words, the what's-authentic rabbit hole is not one you want to go down.

Even if there's no such thing as authenticity, there are certain dishes that become so significant in our hungry imaginations that we want to protect them from corruption. These are typically dishes with master practitioners, cooks who have spent years devoted to making them great. Take sushi. There are guys in Japan (Jiro-*san*, what up!) who have spent decades perfecting the craft of blowing people's minds with just fish and rice. You can either think of the spicy tuna roll as a second-rate fake or you can embrace it as a different and delicious invention. The same is true for so much food. Chicago-style deep-dish pizza is a different animal than New York–style pizza, which is a different animal than the pies you'd get in Naples. The chorizo tacos with corn tortillas in Mexico City are different from the grilled beef tacos with flour tortillas in Sonora and the hard tacos at Pork Slope. You can be a hater or you can eat and enjoy it all.

Authentic Nachos

If you're the type who doesn't eat steak unless it's dry-aged rib eye, or who messes with tomatoes only in peak summer, these nachos are for you. When I make nachos today—for friends or customers at Pork Slope—I give them the same love that Daniel Boulud lavishes on foie gras. I treat them with the same reverence that Eric Ripert gives to sea urchin.

Not that I don't still eat down-and-dirty nachos. Back in the day, my boys and I would take a break from playing Street Fighter II at our favorite hot dog spot to hit 7-Eleven. We'd fill the paper rafts meant to hold the tortilla chips to the brim with chili and cheese, straight from the pump-action faucets. Dude at the counter would get so pissed. I haven't stooped that low in a long time, though at 3 a.m., I'll admit that just about any nachos hit the spot.

Making next-level nachos, though, means getting each element right. The chips should be the best you can find. The chili has to be good enough to impress on its own. The cheese sauce has to K.O. the flavor of squirt-on stuff, but it's also got to mimic its velvety texture. The worst mistake people make is building a big-ass pile of chips, because then the ones on the bottom get no love. I like to scatter the chips in approximately one layer on a big plate or parchment paper–lined baking sheet, then Michel Bras the hell out of them. Bras was the French chef who pioneered the style of plating where food looks like no one plated it at all—it just fell from the heavens. In other words, make it rain sour cream and jalapeño.

MAKE THE CHEESE SAUCE

Melt the butter in a small pot over medium-high heat. Stir in the flour and cook, stirring frequently, until the flour is no longer raw (the pasty mixture should not turn any shade of brown), about 2 minutes. Add the milk about a quarter at a time, stirring to break up lumps. Bring the mixture to a steady simmer and cook just until it thickens enough to barely coat the back of a spoon, 5 to 8 minutes. Stir in the cheeses, Sriracha, Frank's, salt, and pepper and simmer just until the cheeses melt and the flavors come together, about 3 minutes. Season to taste with salt and hot sauce, cover, and keep warm.

MAKE THE NACHOS

Spread the tortilla chips in a layer no more than two chips deep on one or two large platters. Pour the cheese sauce evenly over the chips (topping cheese-first insulates the chips and keeps them from getting soggy too quickly). Do the same with the chili, then make it rain the remaining ingredients. Eat.

Serves
6 to 10

FOR THE CHEESE SAUCE

3 tablespoons unsalted butter

3 tablespoons all-purpose flour

3 cups whole milk, warmed

¾ cup shredded American cheese

¾ cup shredded sharp cheddar cheese

¾ cup shredded Parmesan

2 teaspoons Sriracha

2 teaspoons Frank's RedHot sauce

2 teaspoons kosher salt

¾ teaspoon ground black pepper

FOR THE NACHOS

1-pound bag tortilla chips (about 16 cups)

2 generous cups of your favorite chili or Beef and Bean Chili (page 193), hot

½ cup finely chopped white onion

½ cup diced (¼ inch) fresh tomato

½ cup thinly sliced fresh jalapeño chiles (including seeds) or sliced drained canned pickled jalapeños

½ cup sour cream

½ cup roughly chopped cilantro (thin stems and leaves)

CHAPTER TWO

Breakfast

Buttered-Toast Ramen with Bacon and Eggs

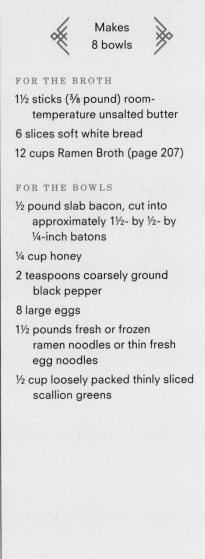

Makes
8 bowls

FOR THE BROTH

1½ sticks (⅜ pound) room-
temperature unsalted butter

6 slices soft white bread

12 cups Ramen Broth (page 207)

FOR THE BOWLS

½ pound slab bacon, cut into
approximately 1½- by ½- by
¼-inch batons

¼ cup honey

2 teaspoons coarsely ground
black pepper

8 large eggs

1½ pounds fresh or frozen
ramen noodles or thin fresh
egg noodles

½ cup loosely packed thinly sliced
scallion greens

My first real taste of American breakfast came at night. After eve-
nings of high school–style wilding out, my boys and I would hit up the
24-hour diner, where whatever you ordered, no matter how massive the
portion, came with a stack of toast. Somehow, it wasn't the over-easy
eggs, sausages, or hash browns, but that toast that became emblematic
of American breakfast for me. The scrape of the knife as you buttered
it, the smell of dairy melting on warm bread.

Even though my restaurant Talde is far from an omelet-your-way
kind of joint, I knew toast had to make an appearance on the brunch

menu. So why not in ramen, my favorite breakfast food? And *boom*, a new staple was born: perfectly chewy noodles doused in a broth infused with the flavor of buttered toast. Bacon and soft-boiled egg are the obvious extras.

MAKE THE BROTH

Preheat the oven to 400°F. Rub the butter on both sides of the bread, and arrange the bread in one layer on a rimmed baking sheet, leaving any extra butter in pieces on the bread. Bake, turning the pan and flipping the slices occasionally, until the bread has absorbed the butter and is crisp like toast and deep golden brown all over, about 15 minutes.

Meanwhile, bring the broth to a gentle simmer in a medium pot. When the bread is ready, add the slices to the broth and increase the heat to bring it to a boil. Turn off the heat and let the bread steep in the broth for 15 minutes. Strain the broth through a sieve, stirring and smooshing the solids to get as much liquid as you can. Pour the broth back into the pot and keep it hot while you finish the ramen. The broth keeps for up to 2 hours; stir well before serving.

FINISH THE DISH

Put the bacon in a skillet, set it over medium-high heat, and let it sizzle, stirring occasionally, until it's crisp and golden, about 10 minutes. Use a slotted spoon to transfer the bacon to paper towels to drain. Pour out all but a slick of fat in the pan, reserving the rest for another purpose. Combine the honey and black pepper in the skillet, set it over medium-high heat, and let the honey bubble. Add the bacon and cook, stirring frequently, until it's coated in a sticky glaze, 3 to 5 minutes. Set aside.

Bring a large pot of water to a boil and prepare a large bowl of icy water. Carefully add the eggs and cook for 6 minutes (set a timer). Transfer the eggs to the icy water (keep the water boiling) until they're just cool enough to handle. Peel them, halve them, and set aside.

Cook the noodles in the boiling water according to the package instructions until al dente. Drain in a colander and run under water to rinse off some starch and cool the noodles. Shake to drain them very well and divide among 8 bowls along with the eggs, bacon, and scallions. Ladle the broth into each bowl, gently agitate the noodles with a fork or chopsticks to keep them from clumping, and eat.

Shrimp Toast with Sausage Gravy and Fried Eggs

Serves
4 to 8

FOR THE SHRIMP TOAST

At least ½ cup vegetable oil

2 tablespoons thinly sliced scallions (white and light green parts only)

1 tablespoon finely chopped shallot

1 teaspoon finely chopped garlic

1 teaspoon finely chopped fresh red Thai chiles (including seeds)

1½ pounds medium shrimp, peeled and deveined, shells reserved for the gravy (below)

½ cup well-shaken coconut milk

2 tablespoons Thai or Vietnamese fish sauce

¼ teaspoon kosher salt, plus extra for seasoning

8 (½-inch-thick) slices Chinese white bread or other soft white bread, crusts removed

FOR THE DISH

1½ cups Chinese-Sausage Gravy (page 197), warmed gently

4 to 8 fried eggs, however you like them, cooked at the last minute

Nothing takes me back like the pu pu platter. You remember: You went to the Chinese spot with your family and before the plates of egg foo yung and shrimp with lobster sauce, you got that massive tray (outfitted with a mini-hibachi grill) of spareribs, egg rolls, beef skewers, and—my favorite—shrimp toast. I especially loved the texture—a thin layer of crunch encasing an awesomely dense crustacean mousse—but as a kid I was mystified: This tastes like shrimp, but I don't see any. I liked that.

Even before I opened Talde, I knew I had to resurrect my old favorite. The "toast" in the name always makes me think of breakfast. And whenever I think breakfast, I start craving that white sausage gravy that you see on biscuits in the South. As it turns out, the gravy and shrimp toast go together like Kim and Kanye. Right before we opened Talde, when we were constantly cooking but barely eating, I found Kyle, my sous chef at the time, squatting at his station with two slabs of shrimp toast sandwiching a fried egg. We had just finalized the menu, but as soon as I saw him, I knew the dish deserved a fried egg on top. The result is best consumed in the morning, afternoon, evening, or middle of the night.

MAKE THE SHRIMP TOAST

Heat 2 tablespoons of the oil in a medium pan over medium heat until it shimmers. Add the scallions, shallot, garlic, and chiles and cook, stirring occasionally, until the shallots are translucent but not colored, about 2 minutes. Take the pan off the heat and let the mixture cool slightly.

Combine the shallot mixture with the shrimp, coconut milk, fish sauce, and salt in a food processor and pulse to a fairly smooth paste (think whitefish salad). You'll have about 3 cups of paste. You can store it in the fridge for up to 2 days.

Preheat the oven to 400°F and very lightly oil a large baking sheet. Spread the shrimp paste on the bread slices in an even layer that goes all the way to the edges; lightly season the layer with salt.

Cook the shrimp toast in batches. For each batch, heat 3 tablespoons oil in a large well-seasoned or nonstick skillet over medium heat until it shimmers. Add 3 or 4 of the bread slices—whatever fits in your skillet—shrimp side down and cook until golden brown, about 3 minutes. Flip the slices with a spatula, cook for 15 seconds or so, then transfer the slices, bread side down, to the prepared baking sheet.

After you've browned all of the shrimp toasts, transfer them to the oven and bake just until the shrimp mixture is cooked through (it'll be opaque) and the bread is golden brown and crispy on the bottom, 3 to 5 minutes.

FINISH THE DISH

Cut each slice of shrimp toast diagonally into four triangles and eat with the sausage gravy and fried eggs.

Corncakes with Ham and Coconut–Brown Butter Syrup

I'll always have a soft spot for pancakes. Ever since I was a kid, even before I worked my first restaurant gig as a host at a Chicago pancake house, I understood pancakes to be the all-American breakfast that I wanted so badly after too many straight mornings of salty fish and fried rice. Yet even when I was eating pancakes, I couldn't shake my affection for a savory start to the day. Asians don't get down with sweets in the morning the way Americans do. That's why these pancakes walk the line between sweet and savory, with ham and syrup joining forces. The corn plays switch hitter—to Americans it's considered savory despite its sweetness, though in Asia it's more likely to end up in dessert. Props to my chef de cuisine at Talde, Andrew Del Vecchio, aka Big Boy, for showing me how to make the illest corn pancakes.

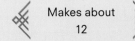

Preheat the oven to 200°F. Put a large plate or baking sheet in there, so you have a place to keep finished pancakes warm while you make the rest.

Melt 1 tablespoon of the butter in a small pan over medium heat. Add the corn and cook, stirring occasionally, until the kernels are cooked but still crunchy, 1 to 2 minutes. Season with ½ teaspoon of the salt.

Combine the eggs, milk, buttermilk, sugar, and vanilla extract in a large mixing bowl and whisk vigorously until the sugar has dissolved. In a separate bowl, combine the flour, cornmeal, baking powder, baking soda, and the remaining ½ teaspoon salt, and stir well. Add half of the liquid mixture to the dry mixture, stir briefly, then add the remaining liquid mixture and stir gently but well, just until the batter is fairly smooth with pea-size lumps of flour. Embrace the lumps. They lead to fluffier pancakes. Gently stir in the corn. Let the batter sit at room temperature for 30 minutes to let the glutens relax, which will give you better pancakes.

Heat a well-seasoned griddle or very large skillet over medium heat until it's good and hot. Add a tablespoon of butter and spread it all over the griddle. Work in batches to make about three or four pancakes at a time (use about ½ cup of batter per pancake), adding just enough butter between batches to coat the griddle and transferring the finished pancakes to the plate in the oven. Cook until the bottoms are deep brown (I don't like mine light golden), the edges look dry, and bubbles form on top, 3 to 4 minutes. Use a spatula to flip them and cook just until they're cooked through, 1 to 2 minutes more.

Do it up: pancake, syrup, ham, and repeat until you can barely fit your mouth around it.

Makes about 12

- 1 tablespoon unsalted butter, plus about 2 tablespoons extra for the griddle
- ¾ cup corn kernels (from about 1 large ear)
- 1 teaspoon kosher salt
- 2 large eggs, lightly beaten
- 1½ cups whole milk
- 1 cup well-shaken buttermilk
- ½ cup granulated sugar
- ¼ teaspoon vanilla extract
- 2¼ cups all-purpose flour
- ¾ cup cornmeal
- 1 tablespoon baking powder
- 1½ teaspoons baking soda
- Coconut–Brown Butter Syrup (page 201) or maple syrup, warmed, for serving
- 24 thin slices (about ½ pound) prosciutto, serrano ham, or similar American ham

Apple Pancakes with Five-Spice and Coconut–Brown Butter Syrup

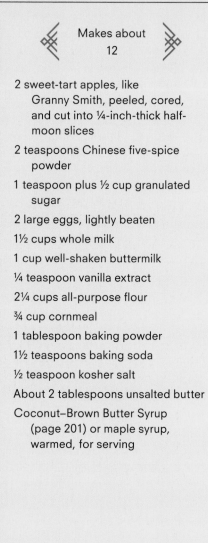

Makes about
12

2 sweet-tart apples, like
    Granny Smith, peeled, cored,
    and cut into ¼-inch-thick half-
    moon slices

2 teaspoons Chinese five-spice
    powder

1 teaspoon plus ½ cup granulated
    sugar

2 large eggs, lightly beaten

1½ cups whole milk

1 cup well-shaken buttermilk

¼ teaspoon vanilla extract

2¼ cups all-purpose flour

¾ cup cornmeal

1 tablespoon baking powder

1½ teaspoons baking soda

½ teaspoon kosher salt

About 2 tablespoons unsalted butter

Coconut–Brown Butter Syrup
    (page 201) or maple syrup,
    warmed, for serving

Apple pancakes are the first dish I ever cooked and my first form of culinary rebellion. I was nine years old, scrawny, and just over four feet tall. Mom had made *sinigang*—again. I was usually down with this tamarind-based Filipino soup. Sometimes, though, I'd get tired of it, like white kids probably get tired of yet another meat loaf. "I'm not eating that," I told her. "I want apple pancakes." Apple pancakes might be the polar opposite of fish-head *sinigang*. Mom wasn't having any of my shit: "If you want pancakes, make them yourself." So I did. I dug around the kitchen cabinets until I found the Aunt Jemima pancake mix we'd had for more than a decade. It was a strange sight in a pantry filled with shrimp paste, fish sauce, and tamarind pulp. I'm still not sure why we even had it, but knowing Mom, I'm sure it had been on sale.

Things didn't go well. Today, though, I'm a better cook and these fluffy pancakes topped with five-spice-spiked apple might even convince my mom to go a morning without eating fish. Especially if she doesn't sleep on the coconut–brown butter syrup.

When you're cooking the pancakes, remember not to flip them too early, the mistake I always make. You need a certain amount of patience to cook pancakes, and that's not something I have. I'm still trying to find a way to cook them in a blazing-hot wok. Your best bet is a nonstick electric griddle, which provides reliably even heat and means you can forget that stuff about the first pancake being the ugliest. A well-seasoned cast-iron griddle does the trick, too.

Preheat the oven to 200°F. Put a large plate or baking sheet in there, so you have a place to keep the finished pancakes warm while you make the rest. Toss the apple slices with the five-spice powder and 1 teaspoon sugar in a bowl.

Combine the ½ cup sugar, eggs, milk, buttermilk, and vanilla extract in a large mixing bowl and whisk vigorously until the sugar has dissolved. In a separate bowl, combine the flour, cornmeal, baking powder, baking soda, and salt and stir well. Add half of the liquid mixture to the dry mixture, stir briefly, then add the remaining liquid mixture and stir gently but well, just until the batter is fairly smooth with pea-size lumps of flour. Embrace the lumps. They lead to fluffier pancakes. Let the batter sit at room temperature for 30 minutes to let the glutens relax, which will give you better pancakes.

Heat a well-seasoned griddle or very large skillet over medium heat until it's good and hot. Add a tablespoon of butter and spread it all over the griddle. Work in batches to make about three or four pancakes at a time (use about ½ cup batter per pancake), adding just enough butter between batches to coat the griddle and transferring the finished pancakes to the plate in the oven.

Cook until bubbles form at the edges of the pancakes, about 30 seconds, then add four or five apple slices to each one, pressing the slices gently so they sink in a little. Keep cooking until the bottoms are deep brown (I don't like mine light golden), the edges look dry, and bubbles form on top, about 3 minutes. Use a spatula to flip them and cook just until they're cooked through, 1 to 2 minutes more. Serve them in a stack, drizzle with syrup, and eat.

The Bodega

My first bodega was on 31st Avenue, in Astoria, Queens, a couple blocks from my first New York apartment. Narrow, dingy, and dimly lit, my bodega didn't look like much. None of them do. Somehow, though, it seemed to have everything you'd ever need, as much stuff as the vast, air-conditioned chain stores I had frequented in Chicago. Actually, my bodega sold even more stuff. Besides the necessary products—shampoo, Tums, Twix, etc.—it had my favorite Japanese brand of cold green tea, leather cowboy belts, Jesus candles, and a shockingly good selection of beer. Near the front, perched on a milk crate, was a big-ass steamy pot of something.

It's not that New York doesn't have plenty of Duane Reades and other stores with automatic sliding doors and corny music; it's that, in New York, bodegas still seem to outnumber them. It's not that you can't find bodegas in L.A. or Boston or Austin; it's that, in New York, they become a part of your daily life. I'd never experienced anything quite like it. I was used to making bi-weekly trips to a store or two to stock up on the stuff I needed. Once I moved to New York, morning or night, whatever I needed was always a three-minute walk away. You can't hoard supplies when you've only got 500 square feet, so the bodega became an extension of my apartment, an urban closet.

I've lived in the city for more than a decade, in six or seven different apartments, and I've never lived more than a few blocks from a bodega, which I inevitably start calling "my bodega." While you're definitely never the only customer, you do come so often that you end up feeling a sense of ownership. It becomes part of your community and you become part of its. In the chains in Chicago, I never got to know the always-changing roster of pre-adults who took my money, even though they all wore name tags. In New York, I got to know the characters in my bodega through osmosis: You are always around and so are they. You know that the lady who wears crazy jeans always orders her coffee "light and sweet," the New York slang for a little coffee with your milk and sugar. You know the dudes who come through to buy single cigarettes and beer way too early in the day. And in that amazing way big cities let you stay anonymous, you never have to interact beyond the occasional nod of recognition.

At first glance, every bodega looks more or less the same. The differences reveal themselves when one of them becomes yours. Occasionally, they reflect the ethnicity of the owners. My first bodega, for example, sold tamales (which I discovered when I got the courage to open that giant pot) and the Mexican ice pops called *paletas* in flavors like pineapple and lime. When I lived on Second Avenue and Ninth Street, my bodega was Korean-owned and stocked tons of fresh fruit, seaweed snacks, and kimchi.

Near my place on Allen and Delancey, a Tunisian guy ran my bodega. He didn't sell harissa or anything, but he was always dressed to impress—an ascot, newspaper-boy hat, circular specs, and suspenders so the chubby dude's slacks didn't drop. Every morning when I came in for a breakfast sandwich, he and I would talk about Tunisia, how he'd hook me up if I ever visited. He reminded me in some ways of my parents. For second-generation immigrants like me and my friends, running a store for a living, serving dumbasses like me and my friends, would have felt like a failure, like we weren't living up to our potential. My Tunisian friend, however, was clearly proud of his job and rightly so. He was making it in a new country, building a life for his kids in the hope that when they got older, they'd feel as entitled as we did.

Like all bodegas, his survived on volume and markup. The first time you grab a box of cereal, take it to the register, and learn it costs $8, you bug out. That's insane! That's robbery! What do you take me for? But spend enough time in the city and you make peace with it. The moment typically comes at around 2 a.m., when you stumble by drunk and realize you can buy Gatorade, toilet paper, and an eight-pack of D batteries without going even a block out of your way. You made a contract with this city when you moved here. You pay ridiculous rents and the city provides everything you could want, all day and all night. You accept the fleecing, enjoy the spoils, and respect the hustle.

Sausage, Egg, and Cheese Fried Rice

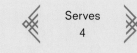

Serves
4

The sausage, egg, and cheese on a roll is one of those iconic New York foods that, unlike pizza slices, bagels, and dirty-water dogs, you only really get to know if you live here. In that way, it's like the bodega itself. In fact, the moment I felt like I'd become a real New Yorker was the night I rolled into my bodega and the guy behind the counter finished my order for me. I go, "Sausage, egg, and cheese…" And before I could finish, he chimes in "…salt, pepper, extra ketchup."

The sandwich, along with its brother, the bacon, egg, and cheese, is generally known as a breakfast sandwich, even though you can order it anytime. I mostly ate it at night on the way back from going out after my shift. It helped me maintain my girlish figure. It became a daily part of my diet the way my mom's fried rice once was. For me, combining the two wasn't a stretch—I just swapped one carb for another. You won't believe how good it is until you try it.

My recipe is just a jumping-off point. At Talde, I use Filipino *longaniza* as the sausage, but any flavorful variety works. You could go Mexican with chorizo and then do Chihuahua cheese instead of American. You could use hot Italian and throw in some bell peppers with the onion and swap in provolone. The only rules are: (1) You've got to have hot sauce or something to cut the richness, and (2) Lord help you if you let American cheese cool. It melts like no other, but when it gets cold, it's like silly putty.

3 tablespoons vegetable oil

½ pound raw sausage, such as *longaniza* (see page 34), breakfast, chorizo, or Italian, casings removed if necessary

½ cup diced (¼ inch) red onion

4 large eggs, lightly beaten

4 cups cooked jasmine rice or Chinese takeout white rice, preferably day-old

4 thin slices yellow American cheese, torn in half

2 teaspoons kosher salt

1 teaspoon ground white pepper

2 tablespoons thinly sliced scallions

Dale's "Homemade" Hot Sauce (page 187) or Garlic-Chile Vinegar (page 186), to taste

Heat 2 tablespoons of the oil in a large, wide, heavy skillet over medium-high heat until it shimmers. Add the sausage and cook, stirring occasionally and breaking up chunks, until it's cooked through, about 5 minutes. Stir in the onion and cook, stirring occasionally, until it's translucent, about 3 minutes.

Beat the eggs with the remaining 1 tablespoon oil. Push the sausage mixture to one side of the skillet and add the egg mixture to the other. Let the egg cook without stirring just until it begins to set around the edges, about 15 seconds. Drag a spoon or spatula through the eggs to move them around as they cook (but don't scramble them) for about 15 seconds more, then stir everything together and cook, stirring frequently, just until the egg has fully set. Increase the heat to high, then add the rice, cheese, salt, and pepper. Cook, stirring and flipping the ingredients constantly and breaking up any rice clumps, until the rice is hot and the cheese has fully melted, 2 to 3 minutes. Stir in the scallions. Eat immediately with the hot sauce or vinegar.

Nasi Lemak–Style Coconut Grits

I grew up without breakfast. It's not that Mom never fed me in the morning. It's that for her, like many Asians, there's no clear line between morning and evening foods. The morning meal meant essentially the same food you had the night before. A great example, though not something Mom made, is *nasi lemak*, the Malaysian breakfast of champions. The dish of coconut rice surrounded by things like hard-boiled eggs, cucumber slices, and fish couldn't be more different from French toast and bacon. At Talde, I take the concept and run with it, subbing grits cooked in coconut milk for the rice and encircling them with small portions of some of the same dishes on my dinner menu. At home, the savory, rich, aromatic grits make a great canvas for leftovers of dishes from this book—or roast chicken, sautéed greens, or whatever else is hanging out in your fridge.

Combine the coconut milk, milk, and 2 teaspoons salt in a small pot and bring to a boil over high heat. Add the grits about a quarter at a time, stirring constantly. Let the liquid come back to a boil, stirring, then reduce the heat to maintain a very gentle simmer. Cook, stirring almost constantly, or occasionally if you're lazy (the more you stir, the creamier the grits will be), until they're fully cooked, 15 to 20 minutes.

Stir in the hot water, cook for another minute, then remove from the heat and stir in the butter until it has completely melted. The mixture will be loose (not stiff), like a proper risotto. Season to taste with salt. Covered in the pot, the grits will stay warm for up to 30 minutes.

Eat the grits with as many and as much of the garnishes as you want.

Serves
4

FOR THE COCONUT GRITS

1 (14-ounce) can well-shaken
    coconut milk

2¼ cups whole milk

2 teaspoons kosher salt,
    plus extra for seasoning

1 cup stone-ground yellow grits

½ cup hot water

2 tablespoons unsalted butter

FOR THE TOPPINGS
(PICK A FEW)

Leftover braised pork shank
    (see Red-Cooking Pork Shank
    with Crisp Rice Noodles,
    page 90), warm

Leftover Short Rib Kare-Kare
    (page 129), warm

Leftover marinated shiitake
    mushrooms (see Marinated
    Shiitake Sliders, page 35), warm

Store-bought kimchi or Cauliflower
    Kimchi (page 205), drained

Pickled Shallots (page 204)

Thinly sliced cucumbers

Hard- or soft-boiled eggs

XO sauce or sambal

Banana "Yogurt" with Fruit Salad and Spiced Honey

This dish is inspired by my boy and fellow *Top Chef* contestant Rich-y Blais. And by "inspired by," I mean straight "ripped off from." During a vegan challenge on the show, he blew my dome by using bananas and tofu to make something that tasted like yogurt but better. Eat it however you want, but I like to serve it with whatever fruits are in season dressed with honey infused with a few spices.

Serves
6 to 8

MAKE THE "YOGURT"

Preheat the oven to 450°F. Make one long cut through the skin (but not into the flesh) of each banana. Rub the bananas with the oil to coat them well, put them on a foil-lined baking sheet, and bake until the peels are black and the flesh is very soft, 15 to 20 minutes. Let the bananas cool slightly. Peel the bananas, discard the peels, and put the bananas in a blender.

Meanwhile, combine the sugar and ⅓ cup water in a small pan. Bring the mixture to a boil over high heat, then reduce the heat and cook at a very gentle simmer just until the sugar fully dissolves, about 1 minute.

Pour the sugar syrup into the blender along with the tofu, juice, and vanilla extract. Blend until very smooth. Pour the mixture into a bowl, cover with plastic wrap, and press the wrap onto the surface to prevent discoloration. Keep in the fridge until well chilled but no longer than 3 hours.

MAKE THE FRUIT SALAD

Combine the honey, lemon zest and juice, cardamom, star anise, and chile in a small pan. Bring the mixture to a boil over medium-high heat, swirling occasionally, then turn off the heat and let the mixture steep for at least 5 minutes or up to 1 hour. Use a spoon to scoop out and discard the spices and chile. Combine the seasonal fruit and honey mixture in a bowl and gently toss to coat.

FINISH THE DISH

Just before you're ready to eat, spread the "yogurt" on a large platter, then top with the fruit, salt, granola, and basil.

FOR THE "YOGURT"

2 ripe peel-on bananas

2 teaspoons vegetable oil

⅓ cup granulated sugar

½ pound drained silken tofu

¼ cup bottled yuzu juice or mixture of 1 tablespoon plus 1 teaspoon each fresh lemon, lime, and orange juices

1 teaspoon vanilla extract

FOR THE FRUIT SALAD

¼ cup honey

1½ teaspoons finely grated lemon zest

2 tablespoons fresh lemon juice

3 cardamom pods, smashed with a knife

1 star anise

1 Asian dried red chile

6 cups mixed seasonal fruit

TO FINISH THE DISH

Flaky sea salt

1 cup of your favorite granola

About 12 Thai basil leaves, torn at the last minute

Chicken Wings and Waffles

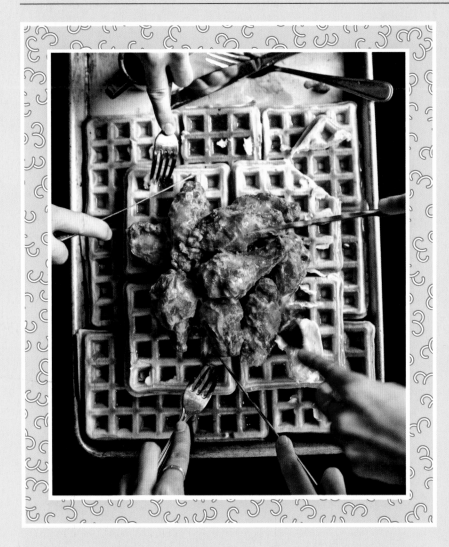

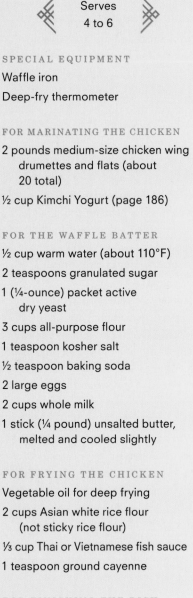

Serves
4 to 6

SPECIAL EQUIPMENT
Waffle iron
Deep-fry thermometer

FOR MARINATING THE CHICKEN
2 pounds medium-size chicken wing
    drumettes and flats (about
    20 total)
½ cup Kimchi Yogurt (page 186)

FOR THE WAFFLE BATTER
½ cup warm water (about 110°F)
2 teaspoons granulated sugar
1 (¼-ounce) packet active
    dry yeast
3 cups all-purpose flour
1 teaspoon kosher salt
½ teaspoon baking soda
2 large eggs
2 cups whole milk
1 stick (¼ pound) unsalted butter,
    melted and cooled slightly

FOR FRYING THE CHICKEN
Vegetable oil for deep frying
2 cups Asian white rice flour
    (not sticky rice flour)
⅓ cup Thai or Vietnamese fish sauce
1 teaspoon ground cayenne

FOR FINISHING THE DISH
Nonstick cooking spray, if necessary
1 cup Kimchi Yogurt (page 186)
Coconut–Brown Butter Syrup
    (page 201) or maple syrup, warmed

This is the second most-ordered dish, after Buttered-Toast Ramen (page 48), on Talde's brunch menu. And I can take only partial credit: People just go nuts for the combination of crunchy, salty fried chicken and waffles, no matter who makes it. Yet I like to think that my version would get props even from connoisseurs of the genre.

I treat my bird in the Korean style, double frying for extra crunch and coating it in sauce for extra flavor. (Remember, though, that you can always cheat and buy wings from Popeyes.) The waffle is textbook: light, crispy, and drizzled with syrup to achieve the sweet-savory collision that makes the dish so popular.

MARINATE THE CHICKEN

Combine the chicken and kimchi yogurt in a large bowl and toss to coat the chicken well. Cover and let the chicken marinate in the fridge for at least 12 hours or up to 3 days (the longer the better).

MAKE THE WAFFLE BATTER

Combine the warm water, sugar, and yeast in a small bowl, stir well, and leave in a warm place until it looks frothy, about 5 minutes. Meanwhile, combine the flour, salt, and baking soda in a large mixing bowl and stir well. In a medium bowl, lightly beat the eggs, add the milk and butter, and stir well.

Stir the yeast mixture into the milk mixture. Briefly stir this mixture into the flour mixture, about a quarter at a time, then stir just until you have a very thick, very lumpy batter. Cover the bowl and keep the batter in the fridge (the batter will get even thicker) for at least 3 hours or up to 12 hours. The waffles will be more flavorful and crispier the longer you let the yeast do its thing.

BATTER AND FRY THE CHICKEN

Bring the chicken to room temperature. You're going to fry the chicken twice and in several batches to avoid crowding the oil.

About an hour before you're ready to eat, pour enough oil into a large pot to reach a depth of about 3 inches. Set the pot over medium-high heat and bring the oil to 275°F (use a deep-fry thermometer). Meanwhile, combine the rice flour, fish sauce, cayenne, and 1 cup water in a large mixing bowl and stir until the mixture is well combined and has no lumps.

Line a baking sheet with paper towels. Add the first batch of chicken pieces to the batter and toss to coat well. Gently shake the pieces to let any excess batter drip off and add them to the oil. Fry, turning them over occasionally, until they're light golden brown and crispy but not quite cooked through, about 8 minutes. Transfer the pieces to the paper towel–lined baking sheet and fry the remaining chicken. Reserve the batter and the oil.

COOK THE WAFFLES

Preheat the oven to 200°F.

Preheat a waffle iron (if possible, on the second-darkest setting) and, if necessary, spray with nonstick cooking spray. Pour about ¾ cup of the waffle batter onto the iron (the amount will vary according to the machine), spreading it a bit. Cook until golden brown, crispy, and cooked through, 4 to 6 minutes. Transfer the waffles directly onto the oven rack to keep them warm while you make the rest.

FINISH THE DISH

Set a rack over a baking sheet and use a skimmer to remove any stray fry from the oil. Set the pot over high heat and bring the oil to 325°F. Working in batches again, add the chicken to the batter, toss to coat, shake the pieces gently, and fry again until they're deep golden brown, crispy, and fully cooked, 4 to 5 minutes. Transfer the pieces to the rack as they're cooked and put the baking sheet in the oven to keep the chicken warm.

Toss the chicken well in a large bowl with the kimchi yogurt. Waffles, chicken, syrup. Eat.

Tater Tots with Sriracha Ketchup

There was a hot minute when "Tater Tots" appeared, with the quotes around them, on menus at nice restaurants. Winking chefs were reimagining the school lunch staple, making the tots themselves and tricking them out with duck confit and salmon roe. I appreciated these shout-outs, because growing up I straight-up loved the little shredded potato nuggets, crispy on the outside and creamy in the middle. But I was always kind of disappointed, too. In their effort to improve the taters, these chefs fiddled with the idea of the dish until it became something different altogether. I realized that I didn't want "Tater Tots"—I wanted the real thing. So when Tater Tots hit the brunch menu at Talde, they were straight from the bag you get in the frozen foods section of the supermarket, un-defrosted and dumped straight into hot oil. (Don't even get me started on the blasphemy that is baked Tater Tots.) My only twist is the ketchup: I add a little spice and umami, but just enough to elevate the sauce, not to change it. If you can't taste the ketchup, then you're not having Tater Tots.

MAKE THE SAUCE
Combine the sauce ingredients and stir well. The sauce keeps in an airtight container in the fridge for up to 1 month.

MAKE THE TOTS
Preheat the oven to 200°F and line a baking sheet with paper towels.

Pour enough oil into a large pot to reach a depth of about 3 inches. Set the pot over high heat and bring the oil to 350°F (use a deep-fry thermometer). Working in several batches to avoid crowding the oil, carefully add the Tater Tots to the oil (use a splatter guard, because those with ice crystals will splatter) and fry until they're golden brown on the outside and hot and creamy in the middle, 3 to 5 minutes per batch. Use a spider to transfer them to the prepared baking sheet to drain. Lightly season immediately with salt and keep the baking sheet in the oven while you fry the rest.

Eat right away with a bowl of the sauce for dipping.

Serves
6 to 8

SPECIAL EQUIPMENT
Deep-fry thermometer
Splatter guard
Spider

FOR THE SAUCE
½ cup ketchup
1½ tablespoons Sriracha
1 teaspoon Ranch seasoning
powder, such as the Hidden
Valley brand
½ teaspoon finely grated
fresh ginger

FOR THE TOTS
Vegetable oil for deep frying
1 (32-ounce) bag frozen Ore-Ida
Tater Tots (not defrosted)
Kosher salt

CHAPTER THREE

Rice, Dumplings, and Noodles

Crab Fried Rice with Jalapeño Aioli

My theory on fried rice is this: If a couple of ingredients taste good together in some dish, odds are they'll taste dope in fried rice, too. Like crab and jalapeño. That's my jam. And because Asians have probably been tossing sweet chunks of crabmeat with rice in a wok since the Han dynasty, all I had to figure out was the best way to add the chile. The answer hit me when I was thinking about another one of the world's best rice dishes: paella. To their great credit, Spanish cooks serve aioli with just about everything, including paella. Boom, I thought, I'd hit the fried rice with jalapeño aioli, a dead-simple emulsion of vegetable oil, egg yolks, and chile—with a little fish sauce thrown in to rep my people.

Serves
4

¼ cup finely chopped shallots

¼ cup diced (about ¼ inch) celery

2 tablespoons thinly sliced drained canned pickled jalapeños (including seeds)

2 teaspoons kosher salt

¼ teaspoon ground white pepper

3 tablespoons vegetable oil

4 large eggs, lightly beaten

4 cups cooked jasmine rice or Chinese takeout white rice, preferably day-old

¼ pound fresh lump crabmeat, picked over for bits of shell

¼ cup Jalapeño Aioli (page 186)

Handful very roughly chopped cilantro (thin stems and leaves)

1 tablespoon red tobiko (flying-fish roe), optional

1 tablespoon black tobiko (flying-fish roe), optional

1 lime, cut into wedges

Combine the shallots, celery, pickled jalapeños, salt, and white pepper in a small container and set aside.

Heat 2 tablespoons of the oil in a wide, large heavy skillet over medium-high heat until it begins to smoke. Lightly beat the eggs with the remaining 1 tablespoon oil, then add to the skillet. Let the eggs cook, without stirring, just until they begin to set around the edges, about 15 seconds. Drag a spoon or spatula through the eggs to move them around as they cook (but don't scramble them) until they're nearly set but not colored, about 15 seconds more.

Push the eggs to one side of the skillet and add the shallot mixture to the other side. Let the shallot mixture cook for 10 seconds, then stir it and the eggs together and cook, stirring constantly and breaking up the eggs, until very aromatic, about 30 seconds.

Add the rice and cook, stirring and flipping the ingredients constantly and breaking up any rice clumps, just until the rice is hot, about 2 minutes. Add the crab and cook, stirring well, for another 30 seconds.

Spoon half of the aioli onto a large plate, spread it out a little, then add the fried rice. Sprinkle on the cilantro and both types of tobiko (if using), then drizzle on the remaining aioli. Eat right away with lime wedges on the side.

"Egg Foo Yung" Fried Rice with Shrimp

My favorite part of fried rice is the eggs. I used to beg my mom to add extra whenever she made fried rice, so I could get my fill of those fatty yellow curds. When I started making the dish myself, I used so much egg that the result reminded me of egg foo yung. And no, I don't mean the O.G. version of egg foo yung, which was probably an elegantly runny dish closer to custard and studded with seafood and other ingredients fit for royalty. I'm talking about the version most of us know from our local beef-and-broccoli slinger. You know, a hard-cooked omelet-like object coated in brown sauce so full of cornstarch it barely moves. This egg foo yung, delicious in its own right, is yet another love child of China and America. My fried rice is also an eggy bastard. And since I'm the daddy, I nix the brown sauce and add fresh shrimp.

Combine the cilantro, shallot, dried shrimp (if using), chile, sugar, pepper, and 1 teaspoon of the salt in a small container and set aside.

Heat 2 tablespoons of the oil in a wide, large heavy skillet over medium-high heat until it begins to smoke. Add the raw shrimp, season with the remaining ¼ teaspoon salt, and cook, flipping them over once, until they're just cooked through, about 3 minutes. Transfer to a plate, leaving the oil behind.

Increase the heat to very high until the oil begins to smoke. Beat the eggs with the remaining 1 tablespoon oil, then add to the skillet. Let the eggs cook without stirring just until they begin to set around the edges, about 5 seconds. Drag a spoon or spatula through the eggs to move them around as they cook (but don't scramble them) until they're nearly set but not colored, about 15 seconds more.

Push the eggs to one side of the skillet and add the cilantro mixture to the other side. Let them cook for 10 seconds, then stir it all together and cook, stirring constantly and breaking up the eggs, until very aromatic, about 30 seconds. Add the rice, bean sprouts, and fish sauce and cook, stirring and flipping the ingredients constantly and breaking up any rice clumps, until the rice is hot through, the grains are soft, and there are no more clumps, about 3 minutes. Add the cooked shrimp, toss, and cook just until they're warm, another minute or so. Season to taste with more fish sauce. Transfer the fried rice to bowls and top with the fried shallots. Eat.

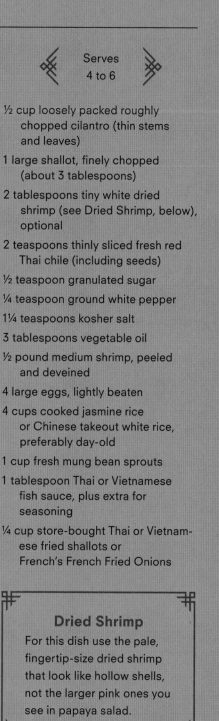

Serves
4 to 6

½ cup loosely packed roughly chopped cilantro (thin stems and leaves)

1 large shallot, finely chopped (about 3 tablespoons)

2 tablespoons tiny white dried shrimp (see Dried Shrimp, below), optional

2 teaspoons thinly sliced fresh red Thai chile (including seeds)

½ teaspoon granulated sugar

¼ teaspoon ground white pepper

1¼ teaspoons kosher salt

3 tablespoons vegetable oil

½ pound medium shrimp, peeled and deveined

4 large eggs, lightly beaten

4 cups cooked jasmine rice or Chinese takeout white rice, preferably day-old

1 cup fresh mung bean sprouts

1 tablespoon Thai or Vietnamese fish sauce, plus extra for seasoning

¼ cup store-bought Thai or Vietnamese fried shallots or French's French Fried Onions

Dried Shrimp

For this dish use the pale, fingertip-size dried shrimp that look like hollow shells, not the larger pink ones you see in papaya salad.

The Wok

I rolled into my first job in a Chinese kitchen with all the swagger in the world. The Cantonese guy who ran the kitchen asked if I'd ever worked a wok. No, I said, but since I could fillet 30 fish, reduce 20 pounds of onions to perfect cubes, and make 10 gallons of meringue, all without breaking a sweat, I figured I could handle a bowl-shaped skillet. So he dumped 2 cups of raw rice in a wok set on a round platform and told me to toss the rice until I could do it without any grains escaping the high sides. Two weeks later, I was still at it.

The problem was, I had to toss the rice in the wok without lifting the underside from the platform, known as a wok ring. In a real cooking situation, lifting the wok would mean losing the heat that shoots like that of a rocket thruster up the wok's sides. Consistent high heat, after all, is essential to the technique of stir-frying. I was also forbidden from generating any sound louder than a barely audible *shh, shh, shh* as I tossed the rice. This, I was told, would teach me finesse.

Once I finally mastered raw rice, I moved on to egg. Typically the first ingredient that goes in the hot oil when making traditional fried rice, egg presents its own challenges. The goal is to keep the egg "young"—that is, soft and colorless instead of rubbery and brown. In fact, I was told, nothing I put in the wok should get any color. This notion went against the brown-equals-flavor tenet of French cooking. I had to learn to choose the right heat level and to move the egg *constantly*, so it wouldn't scorch. The wok burner still had to be ridiculously hot—otherwise, the egg would stick—but not too ridiculously hot. I didn't realize that. On my first try, I cranked the heat all the way up to prevent sticking. Not only did the egg burn instantly, but the wok itself caught on fire.

I ultimately got the hang of it, but my struggles taught me that Asian cooking operates under a different physics than the European techniques I learned in culinary school. Put even a culinary demi-god like Thomas Keller on a concave piece of almost paper-thin carbon steel riding a jet flame and bad things will happen. This is one reason why most of the recipes in this book don't call for a wok. Another is, Who has a wok burner at home? Without the BTUs I have in the kitchen at Talde, I wouldn't mess with real-deal stir-frying either.

For the purposes of this book, you can make great stir-fries in a wide heavy skillet set over really high heat. The skillet retains heat, unlike lightweight woks, so that when you add ingredients, the cooking temperature doesn't dip too much.

Fried Dirty Rice with Chicken Andouille

My first bite of dirty rice felt weirdly familiar. After my second bite, I was onto these Cajuns: I was eating the Deep South's version of fried rice. Instead of resurrecting leftover grains with oil, egg, and a hot wok, Cajun cooks used chicken livers (which give it that "dirty" look) and a skillet. Instead of ginger and garlic, they rocked green bell pepper, celery, and onion. When I merge the two, I double down on chicken, making a quick, no-casing chicken andouille, then finishing the rice last-minute with chicken liver mousse.

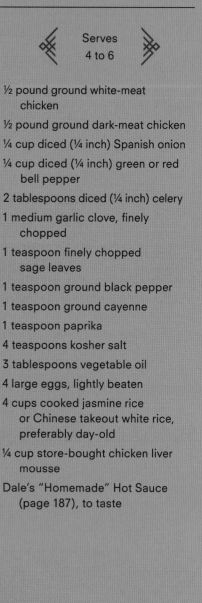

½ pound ground white-meat chicken

½ pound ground dark-meat chicken

¼ cup diced (¼ inch) Spanish onion

¼ cup diced (¼ inch) green or red bell pepper

2 tablespoons diced (¼ inch) celery

1 medium garlic clove, finely chopped

1 teaspoon finely chopped sage leaves

1 teaspoon ground black pepper

1 teaspoon ground cayenne

1 teaspoon paprika

4 teaspoons kosher salt

3 tablespoons vegetable oil

4 large eggs, lightly beaten

4 cups cooked jasmine rice or Chinese takeout white rice, preferably day-old

¼ cup store-bought chicken liver mousse

Dale's "Homemade" Hot Sauce (page 187), to taste

Combine the ground chicken, onion, bell pepper, celery, garlic, sage, black pepper, cayenne, paprika, and 2 teaspoons of the salt in a medium mixing bowl. Mix really well with your hands until everything is well distributed.

Heat 2 tablespoons of the oil in a large, wide heavy skillet over high heat until it smokes lightly. Add the chicken mixture and cook, frequently stirring and breaking up chunks, until it's cooked through and lightly browned, about 5 minutes.

Beat the eggs with the remaining 1 tablespoon oil. Push the chicken mixture to one side of the skillet and add the egg mixture to the other. Let the egg cook without stirring just until it begins to set around the edges, about 5 seconds. Stir in the sausage and cook, stirring frequently, just until the egg has fully set, about 15 seconds more.

Dump in the rice and the remaining 2 teaspoons of salt and cook, constantly stirring, scraping the skillet, and breaking up clumps, until the rice is hot, the grains are soft, and there are no more clumps, 3 to 5 minutes. Take the pan off the heat and stir in the chicken liver mousse until it melts. Transfer the fried rice, including any brown bits stuck to the skillet, to a large plate and eat with the hot sauce on the side.

Dim Sum–Style Sticky Rice
with Braised Bacon

At good dim sum spots you need to be on your game. Waiters pushing carts come along three times a minute, trying to drop yet another order of *char siu bao* (fluffy buns crammed with sweet pork) on your table—especially if you've got round eyes. You have to be able to ice grill the waiter, like "Back up, homie." Not that you'd mind another *char siu bao*, but you're also trying to save room for sticky rice with bacon.

Often wrapped in lotus leaf, the bundle of springy grains is studded with braised bacon (typically the superfirm and dark version sold in slabs at Chinese markets) and glistening from the porky cooking liquid. It's not as flashy as dumplings or egg custard tarts, but it's just as flip-your-shit good. At home, you can skip the wrapper altogether and serve it as a side dish or pop a fried egg over each portion and call it breakfast.

Stir together the bacon, oyster sauce, soy sauce, Shaoxing wine, sugar, garlic, ginger, and 1 cup water in a medium pot with a lid. The liquid should just about cover the bacon. Cover the pot, set it over high heat, and bring the liquid to a boil. Reduce the heat to maintain a gentle simmer and cook, covered, until the bacon is very tender but not falling apart, about 30 minutes. Keep it warm if you're using it right away or let it cool and store in a covered container in the fridge for up to a week.

Heat the bacon mixture in a large pot until it's hot, then cover and set aside over very low heat.

Fill a medium pot with an inch or so of water and bring it to a boil. Drain the rice well in a large fine-mesh strainer (or a colander lined with cheesecloth) that will rest in the pot but not make contact with the water. Spread the rice (up the sides, if necessary) to form a more or less even 1/2-inch layer, set it in the pot, and cover with a lid or foil. Steam just until the rice is fully cooked, chewy with a slight bite, 7 to 8 minutes.

Dump the rice into the pot with the bacon and stir (gently so you don't smash the grains) until there are no clumps and all the rice is coated in the liquid. Cover the pot, turn off the heat, and let the mixture sit for 10 minutes so the rice can absorb some of the flavorful liquid. Eat right away.

Serves
4 to 8

½ pound Chinese bacon (skin removed) or regular slab bacon, cut into about ½-inch cubes (about 1½ cups)

½ cup oyster sauce

2 tablespoons reduced-sodium soy sauce

1½ tablespoons Shaoxing wine, dry sherry, or bourbon

1 tablespoon granulated sugar

1 tablespoon finely chopped garlic

1 tablespoon finely chopped fresh ginger

2½ cups uncooked sticky rice, soaked overnight in enough water to cover

NOTE: At the restaurant, we take the extra steps of letting the finished rice and bacon cool, wrapping them in banana leaves, and then steaming. The leaf adds a little extra flavor and gives you a baller presentation. To do this at home, cut fresh or defrosted frozen banana leaves in twelve 5-inch squares. Wipe them clean with paper towels and arrange them shiny sides down. Put ½ cup of the rice mixture in a low mound in the center of each square, then roll the leaf to form a cylinder, leaving the sides open. You can keep them in the fridge for up to 2 days. When you're ready to eat them, steam or microwave on medium until hot.

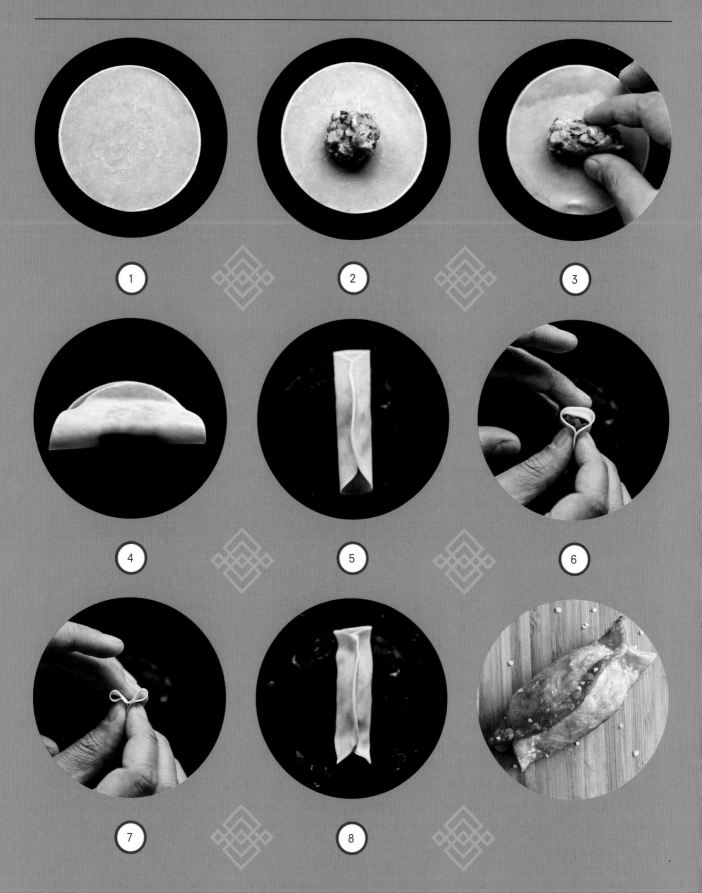

Pretzel Pork-and-Chive Dumplings

I'd never seen a pretzel made until I worked in the soy-scented kitchen at Buddakan, of all places. My boy Brian Ray, a fellow cook, had finished prep early and figured he'd make some soft pretzels for the hell of it. Basically, he made a simple dough, formed it into pretzels, blanched them in water mixed with lye, brushed them with egg wash, and baked them. Some coarse salt and it was on. I ate about seven of them. But instead of making pretzels myself, all I could think about was what other foods I could pretzel-ify. Then it hit me. Ten minutes later, we were applying all the steps that make pretzels taste like pretzels—the blanching, the egg wash, the salt—to pork dumplings. Now Talde regulars would riot if we took them off the menu.

MAKE THE FILLING

Heat the oil in a medium pan over medium-high heat, add the chives, and cook, stirring, just until they're wilted and very fragrant, 1 to 2 minutes. Let them cool slightly. Combine the pork in a mixing bowl with the chives and remaining filling ingredients. Mix gently but thoroughly with your hands until everything is well distributed. Don't overmix or the filling will be too dense.

FORM THE DUMPLINGS

Line a large baking sheet with parchment paper. Fill a small bowl with water. Form the dumplings one at a time, keeping the yet-to-be-used wonton wrappers under a damp towel. (1) Put a dumpling wrapper on the work surface. (2) Add a slightly mounded tablespoon of the pork mixture to the center. (3) Dip your finger into the water and use it to moisten the edge of the wrapper, then pinch and slightly flatten the filling to form a log shape. (4) Fold the wrapper to form a semi-circle. (5) Firmly press the two edges together, leaving both sides open. (6) Holding the pinched edge with one hand, invert the dumpling. (7) Use the other hand to push the rounded bottom of an open end so it meets the pinched edge and very firmly pinch those closed. Force out the air from the pocket you created, then do the same to close the other open end. Make sure all the edges are tightly sealed; if two edges won't seal, try moistening the edges with a little more water. (8) Transfer the dumpling to the prepared baking sheet and repeat the process with the remaining filling and wrappers.

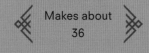

Makes about 36

SPECIAL EQUIPMENT

Food-safe brush

Parchment paper

FOR THE FILLING

2 tablespoons vegetable oil

¾ cup thinly sliced chives, preferably Chinese chives (flat, like blades of grass)

1½ pounds fresh pork belly, ground by your butcher, or other fatty ground pork, cold

1 tablespoon finely chopped fresh ginger

1 tablespoon reduced-sodium soy sauce

1 tablespoon Asian sesame oil

1 teaspoon potato starch or cornstarch

1 teaspoon kosher salt

1 teaspoon granulated sugar

1 teaspoon chicken bouillon

½ teaspoon ground white pepper

FOR FORMING AND PAR-COOKING THE DUMPLINGS

36 wonton wrappers (round), preferably "Shanghai style"

4 quarts water

3 tablespoons baking soda

3 egg yolks, beaten

1 stick (¼ pound) unsalted butter, melted

Continued

PAR-COOK THE DUMPLINGS

This step gives the dumplings that pretzel-like chew and aroma. Combine the water and baking soda in a large pot and bring to a boil over high heat. Line a large baking sheet or plate with parchment paper.

Working in three batches, boil the dumplings until their filling springs back when you squeeze it, 4 to 5 minutes. Use a slotted spoon to transfer the dumplings to the prepared baking sheet as they're done.

Brush the dumplings all over with the egg yolk (or drizzle and rub with a spoon to coat), then do the same with the melted butter. Let the dumplings sit for at least 2 hours or in the fridge, uncovered, for a day or two. The longer the better.

FINISH THE DUMPLINGS

Preheat the oven to 200°F. Put a paper towel–lined baking sheet in there, so you have a place to keep finished dumplings warm while you make the rest.

Cook the dumplings in several batches to avoid crowding the skillet: Heat a large, heavy skillet over medium-high heat and add enough oil to reach a depth of about ¼ inch. As soon as the oil shimmers, arrange some of the dumplings in a single layer, leaving some breathing room between them. Cook, using tongs to turn them occasionally, until you see golden-brown blisters on all three sides, about 5 minutes total. Sprinkle on about 1 tablespoon of the pretzel salt, toss, and transfer the dumplings to the oven to keep them warm. Add enough oil to maintain the ¼-inch depth, let it shimmer, and repeat with the remaining dumplings and salt.

Eat right away with a bowl of the tahini mustard sauce.

FOR FINISHING THE DUMPLINGS

About 1 cup vegetable oil for shallow frying

¼ cup pretzel salt

1 cup Tahini Mustard Sauce (page 190)

Shrimp-Brrl Shumai

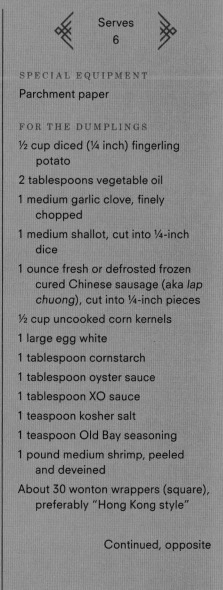

Serves
6

SPECIAL EQUIPMENT
Parchment paper

FOR THE DUMPLINGS

½ cup diced (¼ inch) fingerling
potato

2 tablespoons vegetable oil

1 medium garlic clove, finely
chopped

1 medium shallot, cut into ¼-inch
dice

1 ounce fresh or defrosted frozen
cured Chinese sausage (aka *lap
chuong*), cut into ¼-inch pieces

½ cup uncooked corn kernels

1 large egg white

1 tablespoon cornstarch

1 tablespoon oyster sauce

1 tablespoon XO sauce

1 teaspoon kosher salt

1 teaspoon Old Bay seasoning

1 pound medium shrimp, peeled
and deveined

About 30 wonton wrappers (square),
preferably "Hong Kong style"

Continued, opposite

If you've spent some time down south, you know about the shrimp brrl (pronounced "boil" up north), the dump-onto-newspaper dinner of crawfish or shrimp, potatoes, corn, and sausage simmered in a vat of spicy liquid. I'm not the first Asian to get in on the action. On the Gulf Coast, which is ground zero for boils, many seafood spots are run by Vietnamese immigrants, so sometimes you spot fusions like crawfish fried rice. But you won't spot this riff on the boil down there, unless someone's been biting my ideas.

MAKE THE DUMPLING FILLING

Put the potato in a medium saucepan, add enough water to cover, and bring to a boil over high heat. Reduce the heat and simmer gently until the potato is just tender, about 3 minutes. Drain well, transfer to a medium mixing bowl, and wipe out the saucepan.

Combine the oil, garlic, shallot, and Chinese sausage in the pan, set it over high heat, and cook, stirring, until the shallot and garlic are deep brown, about 3 minutes. Scrape the mixture into the mixing bowl. Set the pan back on the heat, add the corn kernels, and cook, stirring, just until they're no longer raw, about 1 minute. Transfer the corn to the mixing bowl, let the contents cool slightly, then add the egg white, cornstarch, oyster sauce, XO sauce, salt, and Old Bay.

Smash a quarter of the shrimp with the flat of a large knife, then finely chop them. Cut the remaining shrimp into approximately ¾-inch pieces. Add the shrimp to the bowl and use your hands to mix everything together really well. Don't be gentle.

FORM THE DUMPLINGS

Line a baking sheet with parchment paper. Fill a small bowl with water. Form the dumplings one at a time, keeping the yet-to-be-used wonton wrappers under a damp towel: Add a slightly mounded tablespoon of the shrimp mixture to the center of one dumpling wrapper. Dip your finger into the water and use it to moisten the edge of the wrapper. Gather the edges of the wrapper around the filling to form a purse that's open at the top. With one hand, loop your index finger and thumb around the purse just below the opening and squeeze lightly until the dumpling holds its shape and is still open at the top. With the other hand, press lightly to flatten the bottom then push lightly to flatten the filling on top. Transfer the dumpling to the prepared baking sheet and repeat the process with the remaining filling and wrappers.

The dumplings keep covered in the fridge for up to 1 day and in the freezer for up to 1 month. To freeze, arrange the dumplings on a plate in one layer, put it in the freezer until they're frozen, then transfer the dumplings to a resealable freezer bag.

MAKE THE BOIL

Pour enough water into a wide (at least 12 inches) skillet with a lid to reach a depth of ¼ inch or so. Bring it to a boil over high heat, add the dumplings open side up, then cover and cook just until the dumplings are cooked through (the visible filling will be pinkish and opaque), about 5 minutes. Transfer the dumplings to a plate, discard the water, and wipe out the pan.

Add the butter to the pan and melt over medium-high heat. Add the shallots and chiles, and cook, stirring, until the shallots turn golden at the edges, about 5 minutes. Add the sliced potatoes, corn rounds, and Chinese sausage, stir, and add the beer and Old Bay. Cook at a boil for 3 minutes, stir in the shrimp, and keep cooking until the beer reduces by about half, the potatoes are tender, and the shrimp are fully cooked, about 2 minutes more. Pour in ½ cup water, bring to a boil, then add the dumplings and cover the pot. Cook just until they're warmed through, about 30 seconds.

Take the pan off the heat. Squeeze on just enough lemon juice to brighten the flavors. Baste the dumplings with the pan liquid, then sprinkle on the cilantro and scallions and bring the pan to the table. Eat.

FOR THE BOIL

1 stick (¼ pound) unsalted butter, cut into chunks

4 large shallots (about ½ pound), cut into ¼-inch-thick rounds

8 Asian dried red chiles

4 large fingerling potatoes, cut into ¼-inch-thick rounds

4 small ears corn, shucked, cut into 1-inch-thick rounds

Scant 3 ounces fresh or defrosted frozen cured Chinese sausage (aka *lap chuong*), cut into ¼-inch-thick rounds

1 (12-ounce) bottle light-colored beer

1 tablespoon plus 2 teaspoons Old Bay seasoning, plus extra for sprinkling

6 medium shrimp, peeled and deveined

1 lemon, halved

½ cup loosely packed cilantro leaves

¼ cup thinly sliced scallion greens

Wonton Noodle Soup

My mom made the best wonton soup. What made it taste even better was that she only occasionally blessed us with its presence. The slick pork-filled dumplings in rich broth made an appearance on special occasions like Thanksgiving—and whenever Mom felt like eating it. I will never try to compete with her wonton soup–making skills, but I do pay homage in my own way. I look to ramen broth, which delivers a similarly gelatinous body as her Chinese-style pork stock, and instigate some starch-on-starch action, letting noodles swim with the dumplings. Asians get down like this all the time: When I was growing up, rice and noodles often shared the same plate. But I'm not going to hate if you just use wontons.

Serves
4

6 cups Ramen Broth (page 207)

4 large eggs

25 Pork Wontons (page 101)

¾ pound fresh or frozen ramen noodles (see page 212) or thin fresh egg noodles

2 tightly packed cups roughly chopped kale, broccoli rabe, or another bitter green (thick stems removed)

¼ cup thinly sliced scallion greens

Bring the broth to a bare simmer in a medium pot.

Bring a large pot of water to a boil and prepare a large bowl of icy water. Carefully add the eggs and cook for 6 minutes (set a timer). Transfer the eggs to the icy water (keep the water boiling) until they're just cool enough to handle. Peel, halve, and set aside.

Add the wontons to the boiling water and cook just until the skins are fully tender and the filling is cooked through, about 3 minutes. (Try one; that's why you made 25 instead of 24.) Gently scoop out the finished wontons with a strainer (keep the water boiling), drain them well, and transfer them in a single layer to a large plate.

Add the noodles and bitter greens to the boiling water and cook according to the package instructions until the noodles are al dente. Drain the noodles and greens in a colander and rinse them under running water to remove some starch and cool the noodles. Shake to drain very well.

Divide the noodles and greens among 4 bowls, then add the eggs, wontons, and scallions. Ladle the broth into each bowl, gently agitate the noodles with a fork or chopsticks to prevent them from clumping, and eat.

Roast-Chicken-Dinner Lo Mein

I'd like to officially induct lo mein into the American comfort food Hall of Fame. The slick, salty noodles we all slurp from white paper takeout containers are no less American than mac and cheese or spaghetti and meatballs—and probably just as easy to find. Since lo mein has already morphed so far from its Chinese origins, I'm cool going even further. I fuse it with another comfort-food staple, the roast chicken, just as I do with Roast-Chicken-Dinner Ramen (page 84). Lo mein is no stranger to chicken, carrots, and celery, but when you add herbs like thyme and rosemary and leave the vegetables in fat batons meant to mimic the chunks you might find in the roasting pan, the dish tastes familiar and different at the same time. I finish the whole thing with chicken liver mousse in order to drive home the chicken flavor and to make a dish known for being cheap feel luxurious.

Bring a large pot of water to a boil, add the noodles, and cook until they're tender but still chewy, about 3 minutes for fresh noodles and about 6 minutes for dried. Drain them, run under cold water, then drain well again. (If you want to do this more than 10 minutes in advance, toss the noodles with 1 tablespoon vegetable oil to prevent clumping.)

Combine the stock, dashi powder, and bouillon in a bowl, stir until the powders dissolve, and set aside.

Heat the oil in a large heavy skillet over high heat until it smokes lightly. Add the carrots, celery, onion, and garlic and cook, stirring and tossing frequently, until the carrots and celery are lightly browned, about 3 minutes.

Add the noodles, chicken stock mixture, chicken, oyster sauce, Shaoxing wine, half the parsley, half the thyme, half the tarragon, the sage, and the rosemary. Cook, stirring and tossing frequently, until the carrot and celery are tender with a slight crunch and the chicken and noodles are hot, 3 to 5 minutes.

Turn off the heat, add the mousse, and toss until it melts. Gradually add water to loosen the sauce, if necessary. Add the lemon juice and remaining parsley, thyme, and tarragon, toss again, and eat.

Serves 4 to 6

4 cups fresh lo mein noodles, or ½ pound dried thin Chinese egg noodles

½ cup low-sodium chicken stock or roasted chicken stock (see the Note on page 85)

1½ teaspoons hon dashi powder

1½ teaspoons chicken bouillon

2 tablespoons vegetable oil

2 medium carrots, peeled and cut into approximately 3- by ½-inch batons

2 large stalks celery, cut into approximately 3- by ½-inch batons

½ cup loosely packed thinly sliced red onion

1 medium garlic clove, thinly sliced

1 small roasted chicken, store-bought or homemade, meat pulled into bite-size pieces

3 tablespoons oyster sauce

3 tablespoons Shaoxing wine, dry sherry, or bourbon

¼ cup roughly chopped flat-leaf parsley (thin stems and leaves)

1 heaping tablespoon thyme leaves

2 teaspoons roughly chopped tarragon leaves

1 teaspoon roughly chopped sage leaves

½ teaspoon roughly chopped rosemary leaves

¼ cup store-bought chicken liver mousse

2 tablespoons fresh lemon juice

Roast-Chicken-Dinner Ramen

Serves 4

FOR THE BROTH

6 cups low-sodium chicken stock (see Note)

3 tablespoons reduced-sodium soy sauce

1½ tablespoons kosher salt

1 tablespoon hon dashi powder

1½ teaspoons chicken bouillon

¾ teaspoon granulated sugar

3 sprigs flat-leaf parsley

1 large sprig fresh thyme

1 large sage leaf

FOR THE DISH

¼ cup plus 2 tablespoons vegetable oil

½ cup diced (¼ inch) Spanish onion

½ cup diced (¼ inch) carrot

½ cup diced (¼ inch) celery

1 medium garlic clove, smashed and peeled

1 teaspoon finely chopped thyme leaves

1 teaspoon finely chopped flat-leaf parsley

1 teaspoon finely chopped sage

1 teaspoon finely chopped rosemary leaves

1 pound fresh or frozen ramen noodles or thin fresh egg noodles

½ warm roasted chicken, store-bought or homemade, breast meat sliced, leg and thigh meat pulled (bones reserved, see Note)

½ cup thinly sliced scallions

1 tablespoon plus 1 teaspoon fresh lemon juice

A good roast chicken is one of the best things you can put in your mouth. And ramen? It should officially replace chicken noodle soup as the most comforting food on earth. Together, they make magic: the undeniably awesome aroma of a bird roasted with garlic, thyme, and sage infused into an umami-packed broth teeming with addictively chewy noodles. Because the dish is essentially just a really good chicken soup, I'd happily eat it with any noodle, from the proper ramen I recommend to thin Chinese wheat noodles, Japanese udon, or fresh fettucine. Even elbow macaroni would hit the spot.

MAKE THE BROTH

Combine the stock, soy sauce, salt, dashi powder, chicken bouillon, and sugar in a medium pot. Twist the herbs in your hands to bruise them slightly, add them to the pot, and set it over high heat. Bring to a boil, then reduce the heat and very gently simmer for 10 minutes. Scoop out and discard the herbs. Keep the broth hot over low heat or keep it in the fridge for up to 2 days.

FINISH THE DISH

Heat 2 tablespoons of the oil in a medium pan over high heat until it begins to smoke. Add the onion, carrot, and celery and cook, stirring frequently, until the vegetables are browned at the edges and the carrot is tender with a slight crunch, 5 to 8 minutes. Transfer to a bowl and set aside.

Combine the remaining ¼ cup oil and the garlic in the same pan, set it over high heat, and cook, flipping the garlic once, until it's deep golden brown on both sides, about 3 minutes. Discard the garlic and let the oil cool fully. Stir in the thyme, parsley, sage, and rosemary.

Bring a large pot of water to a boil. Cook the noodles in the boiling water according to the package instructions until al dente. Drain in a colander and rinse under running water to remove some starch and cool them. Shake to drain them very well, then divide among 4 bowls along with the chicken and scallions.

Increase the heat to bring the broth to a boil, then turn off the heat. Stir in the carrot mixture, herb oil, lemon juice, and more salt to taste. Divide the broth among the bowls, gently agitate the noodles with a fork or chopsticks to prevent them from clumping, and eat.

NOTE: This dish gets even better when you use roasted chicken stock instead of regular stock. There are a million recipes for it out there, so I won't add another here. But I will offer a shortcut: Once you strip the meat from the rotisserie chicken you need for this recipe, reserve the bones, drizzle them with oil, and roast in a single layer on a baking sheet in a 350°F oven until they're golden to mahogany brown. Add the roasted bones to a pot with the regular chicken stock and bring the stock to a simmer. Let it simmer gently with the bones for half an hour or so, strain, then proceed with the recipe.

Tom Kha Lobster with Noodles, Corn, and Potato

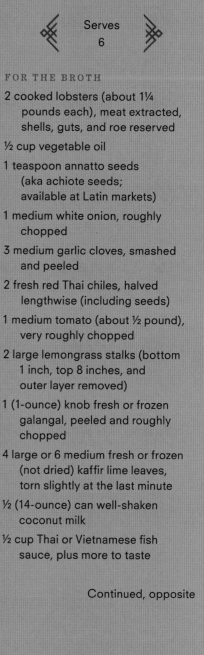

Serves
6

FOR THE BROTH

2 cooked lobsters (about 1¼
  pounds each), meat extracted,
  shells, guts, and roe reserved

½ cup vegetable oil

1 teaspoon annatto seeds
  (aka achiote seeds;
  available at Latin markets)

1 medium white onion, roughly
  chopped

3 medium garlic cloves, smashed
  and peeled

2 fresh red Thai chiles, halved
  lengthwise (including seeds)

1 medium tomato (about ½ pound),
  very roughly chopped

2 large lemongrass stalks (bottom
  1 inch, top 8 inches, and
  outer layer removed)

1 (1-ounce) knob fresh or frozen
  galangal, peeled and roughly
  chopped

4 large or 6 medium fresh or frozen
  (not dried) kaffir lime leaves,
  torn slightly at the last minute

½ (14-ounce) can well-shaken
  coconut milk

½ cup Thai or Vietnamese fish
  sauce, plus more to taste

Continued, opposite

Tom kha gai, the lime-spiked coconut soup that has become a universally beloved Thai takeout classic, was just begging for an upgrade. So instead of *gai* ("chicken" in Thai), I go for lobster, mining the shells (plus the guts and roe) for a flavorful broth and rocking big chunks of lobster in a lime- and coconut-spiked soup. Because red-edged flesh in milky white broth looks exactly like something you'd slurp out of Styrofoam bowls on the New England coast, I complete the chowder picture with sweet corn and potato. Noodles make each bowl a meal.

MAKE THE BROTH

Preheat the oven to 500°F. Pull off the legs and heads from the lobster bodies. Separate the head shell from the insides of the head, pull off and discard the feathery gills (they're bitter), and put the shells (including the legs and insides of the head) on a baking sheet. Roast in the oven without any oil until the shells turn a deep red color and smell like lobster, about 10 minutes for the shells and a little longer for the insides of the head.

Combine the oil and annatto seeds in a large pot, set it over medium-high heat, and cook until the oil turns deep red, about 2 minutes. Add the onion, garlic, and chiles and cook, stirring often, until they're aromatic, about 2 minutes. Add the tomato, lower the heat to medium, and cook, stirring and mushing the tomato, until it softens, about 5 minutes. Turn off the heat.

Push the contents of the pot to one side, add the lobster shells and insides, and use a potato masher or sturdy spoon to smash them into pieces (the smaller the better). Turn the heat back to high and add 2 quarts water. Bruise the lemongrass by smashing it with a pestle or heavy pan and cut it into ½-inch pieces. Add the lemongrass, galangal, and kaffir lime leaves to the pot, bring the water to a strong simmer, and cook, stirring occasionally, for 10 minutes or so. Add the coconut milk, simmer for 5 minutes, then add the fish sauce and simmer for another 2 or 3 minutes. Strain the mixture into a new pot, stirring and smashing the solids to extract as much liquid as you can. (The broth keeps in airtight containers for up to 2 days.)

FINISH THE SOUP

Bring a large pot of water to a boil, add the noodles, and cook just until they're fully cooked, about 30 seconds. Drain really well.

Add the coconut milk to the broth in the pot and bring to a gentle simmer. Add the bean sprouts, corn, potatoes, herbs, and lime juice. Cook just until the corn is no longer raw, about 2 minutes. Cut the reserved lobster meat into bite-size pieces, add to the soup, and cook just until it's warmed through. Season generously with more fish sauce and lime juice to taste.

Divide the noodles among 6 bowls, ladle on the soup, and eat.

FOR THE SOUP

1 (1-pound) bag semi-dried thin rice noodles (called *banh pho*; look in the refrigerated section at Asian markets)

½ (14-ounce) can well-shaken coconut milk

2 cups loosely packed fresh mung bean sprouts

1 cup raw corn kernels

6 ounces fingerling potatoes, boiled and sliced into ¼-inch-thick rounds (about 1 cup)

Handful Thai basil leaves

Handful very roughly chopped cilantro (thin stems and leaves)

¼ cup fresh lime juice, plus more to taste

Phot Roast

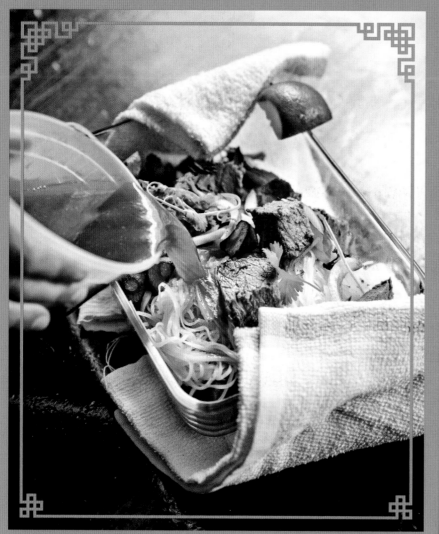

**Makes
4 bowls**

SPECIAL EQUIPMENT
Cheesecloth

FOR THE SOUP

1 large skin-on Spanish onion
  (about 1 pound), halved
  lengthwise

1 (2-ounce) skin-on knob ginger,
  halved lengthwise

2 medium garlic cloves, peeled

2 star anise

2 cloves

2 teaspoons black peppercorns

2 cardamom pods

2 cinnamon sticks

2 tablespoons vegetable oil

1½ pounds beef chuck, cut into
  1½-inch pieces

1 tablespoon kosher salt

1 teaspoon ground black pepper

1 tablespoon granulated sugar

2 tablespoons tomato paste

4 cups low-sodium beef stock

3 tablespoons Thai or Vietnamese
  fish sauce, plus more to taste

1 large carrot (about ½ pound),
  peeled and cut into ½-inch
  chunks

¼ pound waxy potatoes, cut into
  ½-inch chunks

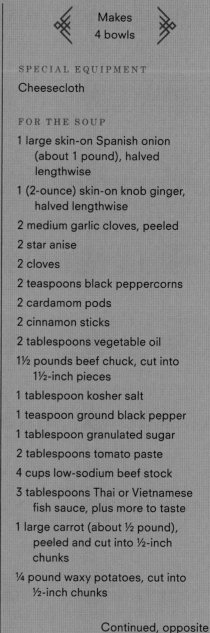

Continued, opposite

I have a problem. I really, really like noodle soup. Practically every vaguely soupy dish I eat makes me think how much better it could be if it were served in a bowl with noodles and some chopsticks. This mash-up came to me the last time I ate pot roast, that old New England standard that's delicious but, let's be honest, needs to raise its game. My brain went straight to another beefy dish: pho, the Vietnamese soup that sports a rich stock made from beef bones cooked for hours. I skip the homemade stock and borrow seasonings—like star anise and cinnamon, charred onions and ginger—from pho to inject new life into the American stew. The only real holdovers are the potatoes and carrots, which soak up the flavor of the cooking liquid and somehow fit right in among the rice noodles. The lime, hoisin, Sriracha, and fish sauce on the side, which you see at Vietnamese restaurants in the U.S., allow everyone to season his or her own bowl to taste.

MAKE THE SOUP

Turn a stovetop burner to high. Using tongs, set the onion and ginger, cut sides down, directly over the flame, and let those sides almost completely blacken, about 5 minutes. Stick the garlic cloves on the tines of a fork and hold the garlic over the flame until it blackens on both sides, about 3 minutes.

Roughly chop the onion. Put the onion, ginger, garlic, star anise, cloves, peppercorns, cardamom, and cinnamon on a double layer of cheesecloth, gather the edges to form a tight bundle, and secure it with kitchen twine or a strip of cheesecloth.

Heat the oil in a medium pot over medium-high heat until it shimmers. Toss the beef with the salt and pepper. Brown the beef in two batches, turning over the pieces occasionally until well browned on all sides, and transfer to a plate. Return both batches to the pot, sprinkle on the sugar, and cook, tossing occasionally, for about 1 minute. Add the tomato paste, stir well, and cook, stirring, until the tomato paste has lost its rawness, about 2 minutes. Pour in the stock, fish sauce, and 2 cups of water, increase the heat, and bring the liquid to a strong simmer, scraping the bottom of the pot occasionally.

Add the spice bundle to the pot so it's more or less submerged. Cover the pot, reduce the heat to maintain a gentle simmer, and cook until the beef is very tender but not falling apart, about 1½ hours. About 30 minutes before the beef is done, stir in the carrot and potatoes.

Remove the cheesecloth bundle, using tongs to squeeze it gently over the pot, then discard. Aggressively season to taste with fish sauce. Keep it warm over very low heat. It keeps for a few days in the fridge.

FINISH THE DISH

Bring a large pot of water to a boil, add the noodles, and cook according to the package instructions until fully tender but not mushy. Drain well. Divide the noodles, cilantro, basil, and red onion among 4 large bowls. Bring the soup to a simmer, then divide it among the bowls. Stir and serve with the lime, hoisin, Sriracha, and extra fish sauce on the side so people can season their bowls.

FOR THE DISH

12 ounces semi-dried thin rice noodles (called *banh pho*; look in the refrigerated section at Asian markets), or 8 ounces dried rice noodles, soaked in water for 10 minutes

1 cup loosely packed very roughly chopped cilantro (thin stems and leaves)

1 cup loosely packed Thai basil leaves

¼ cup very thinly sliced red onion

ON THE SIDE

Lime wedges

Hoisin sauce

Sriracha

Thai or Vietnamese fish sauce

Red-Cooking Pork Shank with Crisp Rice Noodles

It's easier to mess with food when it isn't your own. Like, I have adobo running through my veins. That makes the vinegar-and-garlic-bombed Filipino stew hard for me to corrupt. I feel my mom looking over my shoulder. But I will bastardize the hell out of some pastrami. I will do weird stuff to dumplings all day long. And I will do what I do in this dish. I take Chinese-style stewed pork and serve it with wide rice noodles, even though it always goes on rice. I'm sure some drunk Chinese dude has done this late one night. But I bet you no one has rolled the noodle into a big spiral, crisped it in a hot pan, and hit it with butter.

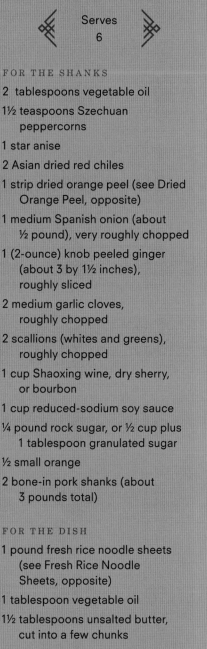

Serves
6

FOR THE SHANKS

2 tablespoons vegetable oil

1½ teaspoons Szechuan peppercorns

1 star anise

2 Asian dried red chiles

1 strip dried orange peel (see Dried Orange Peel, opposite)

1 medium Spanish onion (about ½ pound), very roughly chopped

1 (2-ounce) knob peeled ginger (about 3 by 1½ inches), roughly sliced

2 medium garlic cloves, roughly chopped

2 scallions (whites and greens), roughly chopped

1 cup Shaoxing wine, dry sherry, or bourbon

1 cup reduced-sodium soy sauce

¼ pound rock sugar, or ½ cup plus 1 tablespoon granulated sugar

½ small orange

2 bone-in pork shanks (about 3 pounds total)

FOR THE DISH

1 pound fresh rice noodle sheets (see Fresh Rice Noodle Sheets, opposite)

1 tablespoon vegetable oil

1½ tablespoons unsalted butter, cut into a few chunks

½ cup thinly sliced radish

Continued, opposite

COOK THE SHANKS

Heat the oil in a wide, deep oven-safe pot with a lid over very high heat. Open a window and turn on a fan. When the oil smokes, add the Szechuan peppercorns, star anise, chiles, and orange peel and cook, stirring constantly, until very aromatic, about 20 seconds. Add the onion, ginger, garlic, and scallions and cook, stirring occasionally, until the onion is translucent and (ideally, if your pot gets hot enough) slightly charred, 5 to 7 minutes.

Pour in the Shaoxing wine, let it bubble a little, and then add the soy sauce, sugar, and 1½ cups water. Squeeze the orange half over the mixture then add it to the pot. Bring the mixture to a boil and add the shanks side by side. Cover the pot, reduce the heat to maintain a gentle simmer, and cook covered until the meat is falling off the bone, 2½ to 3 hours.

Carefully transfer the shanks to a plate. Strain the cooking liquid through a sieve into a large bowl or pot, pressing the solids to extract as much liquid as you can. Discard the solids. Pull the meat from the shanks in bite-size chunks, discard the bones, and toss the meat into the liquid. Keep the meat warm.

This dish is even better a few days after you cook it. Let the pork cool in the liquid, cover, and store in the fridge for up to 5 days. Gently reheat it when you're ready to eat.

FINISH THE DISH

Carefully unfold the noodle sheets, and cut six neat strips that are each approximately 18 inches long and 1½ inches wide, reserving any remaining noodle for another purpose. Make two neat stacks, with three strips per stack, then carefully roll each stack the long way to form a big spiral.

Heat the oil in a wide cast-iron skillet over high heat until it begins to smoke. Add the noodle spirals flat sides down and cook, flipping them once with a spatula, until both sides are light brown, about 2 minutes total. Add the butter to the skillet and cook, swirling the pan, until the undersides of the spirals are golden brown and crispy, about 1 minute more.

Spoon the stewed meat mixture onto a large plate or platter and top with the spirals, golden brown side up. Scatter the radishes and pickled mustard greens on each plate and add hot sauce to taste. Eat.

½ cup drained and roughly chopped pickled mustard greens, store-bought and soaked for 20 minutes or homemade (page 206)

Dale's "Homemade" Hot Sauce (page 187) or your favorite hot sauce

---

Dried Orange Peel

You can buy dried orange peel at any Chinese grocery store or you can make it yourself: Cut the peel into 4- by ¾-inch strips and trim off as much of the white pith as you can. Spread the strips in a single layer on a plate with a little room between them, and leave them uncovered until they're brittle and start to curl, 2 or 3 days.

Fresh Rice Noodle Sheets

For this recipe, you need to find super-fresh sheets (not pre-cut into ribbons) of rice noodle and use them within a day, keeping them in a cool place (but not in the fridge) overnight if need be. Older noodles, including the sheets in the refrigerated section of a market, just won't cut it because they're typically too brittle to roll into spirals. You'll find the fresh sheets in your city's Chinatown, typically at shops dedicated to making and selling fresh rice noodles (aka *chow fun*). If you're getting stressed out reading this, just forget the noodles and serve the shanks over white rice.

Pad Thai with Bacon

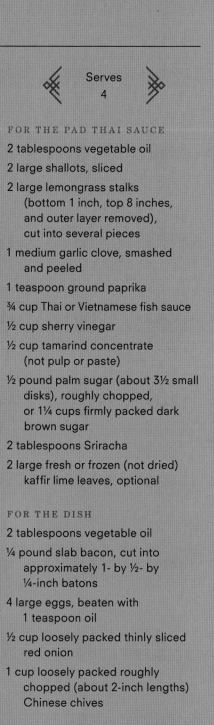

Serves
4

FOR THE PAD THAI SAUCE

2 tablespoons vegetable oil

2 large shallots, sliced

2 large lemongrass stalks
(bottom 1 inch, top 8 inches,
and outer layer removed),
cut into several pieces

1 medium garlic clove, smashed
and peeled

1 teaspoon ground paprika

¾ cup Thai or Vietnamese fish sauce

½ cup sherry vinegar

½ cup tamarind concentrate
(not pulp or paste)

½ pound palm sugar (about 3½ small
disks), roughly chopped,
or 1¼ cups firmly packed dark
brown sugar

2 tablespoons Sriracha

2 large fresh or frozen (not dried)
kaffir lime leaves, optional

FOR THE DISH

2 tablespoons vegetable oil

¼ pound slab bacon, cut into
approximately 1- by ½- by
¼-inch batons

4 large eggs, beaten with
1 teaspoon oil

½ cup loosely packed thinly sliced
red onion

1 cup loosely packed roughly
chopped (about 2-inch lengths)
Chinese chives

Continued, opposite

My pad thai is about as authentic as Taco Bell's 7-Layer Crunchwrap. But then again, so is the pad thai we all grew up eating from takeout containers. Entrepreneurial immigrant cooks transformed the simple noodle stir-fry to appeal to the American palate. Now it's the saucy, sweet face of Thai cuisine in the U.S. And since Thais have about a thousand other noodle dishes to choose from, I'd bet Americans today eat more pad thai than Thai people do. I know I eat it every chance I get. Even mediocre versions taste kind of good—or at least they do reheated around 3 a.m., or for bleary-eyed brunch the next morning.

Actually, my version started as an attempt at a brunch dish. I was hungover. I wanted a Bacon, Egg, and Cheese—or at least pork, egg, fat, and starch. And that's exactly what pad thai is. I borrow the best elements from American-style pad thai and include a few shout-outs to the American South: flash-fried oysters and bacon—not such a stretch considering that in Thailand vendors cook the noodles in pork fat. Shit, I almost went traditional by accident.

Don't be put off by the long list of ingredients—collecting them all is the only time-consuming part of this recipe—or the frying of the oysters. You can leave them out or, if you're craving aquatic life, toss in 8 or so medium shelled and deveined shrimp when you add the onions. Actually, you can be flexible with just about any ingredient but the sauce and noodles, and still get a great result.

MAKE THE SAUCE

Combine the oil, shallots, lemongrass, and garlic in a medium pot over medium-high heat and cook, stirring frequently, until very aromatic, about 3 minutes. Add the paprika and cook, stirring constantly, until aromatic, about 30 seconds. Add 1 cup water and the rest of the sauce ingredients, bring the mixture to a gentle simmer, and cook, breaking up the palm sugar, until the sugar has melted and the flavors have melded, about 15 minutes. Strain, discarding the solids. You'll have about 3 cups of sauce. It keeps for up to 1 month in the fridge.

MAKE THE DISH

Combine the oil and bacon in a wide (at least 12-inch) heavy skillet, set it over medium-high heat, and let it sizzle, stirring occasionally, until the bacon is crisp and golden, about 10 minutes. Use a slotted spoon to transfer the bacon to paper towels to drain. Pour out all but ¼ cup of the fat from the pan.

Turn the heat to very high. Add the eggs to the pan and let them cook without stirring until they're just set at the edges, about 15 seconds. Push the eggs to one side of the skillet, then add the onion, chives, salted radish, dried chiles, and bacon to the other side. Wait another 15 seconds and flip the egg onto the other ingredients (no need to be neat about it).

Push everything to one side and add the noodles to the other side. Spread them out and cook, without stirring, until they wilt slightly, about 45 seconds. Then stir and flip the ingredients, breaking the eggs into bite-size pieces. Cook without stirring until the bottom of the eggs has browned slightly, about 1½ minutes. Then add half the carrots and bean sprouts along with a pinch of the cilantro and Thai basil, stir well, and evenly pour in 1½ cups of the pad thai sauce. (Reserve the rest to use another day.) Cook, without stirring, until the noodles have fully absorbed the sauce and are fully tender, about 2 minutes.

Add half the peanuts, stir, and transfer the pad thai to a large plate. Top with the cabbage and the remaining carrots, bean sprouts, herbs, and peanuts, squeeze on the lime, and eat.

2 tablespoons finely chopped Thai salted or preserved radish (available at Asian markets or online)

6 Asian dried red chiles

Scant ½ pound dried thin, flat rice noodles (aka pad thai or *banh pho*), soaked in cold water for about 1 hour

1 cup carrot matchsticks (about 2 by ⅛ inch)

1 cup fresh mung bean sprouts

½ cup loosely packed very roughly chopped cilantro (thin stems and leaves)

½ cup loosely packed Thai basil leaves

½ cup roughly chopped unsalted roasted peanuts

½ cup thinly sliced red cabbage

1 lime, halved

IF YOU'RE DOWN TO DEEP-FRY OYSTERS

Just before you serve the pad Thai, pour enough vegetable oil in a medium pot to reach a 2-inch depth and set it over high heat. Put ½ cup white rice flour in a bowl, add 12 drained shucked oysters, and toss to coat them in a thin layer of flour. When the oil registers 375°F on a deep-fry thermometer, carefully add the oysters to the oil and cook just until crispy and light golden brown, 30 seconds to 1 minute.

MSG

My mom's cupboard always contained a bag of mysterious white crystals. I knew whatever was in the bag was a fairly important weapon in her arsenal, because it sat up front next to the salt and pepper, not in back with the nutmeg and allspice. But I never thought much of it, even when I learned it was MSG. My guess is that most people reading this book have a negative opinion of MSG (or monosodium glutamate). That's only natural, since over the years, MSG has been accused of everything from causing headaches to autism. It's all bullshit.

I'm definitely no scientist. But scientific research has repeatedly cleared it of all charges. MSG is a form of glutamic acid. The main difference between glutamic acid and MSG is that the first occurs naturally and the second doesn't. But chemically, they're exactly the same. When either one hits your tongue, it generates the taste sensation known as *umami*—distinct from salty, sweet, sour, and bitter, and sometimes translated as "damn that's good." High content of glutamic acid is the reason approximately one million foods taste amazing: Tomatoes, anchovies, and seaweed, for example, all have it. It's why cooks use miso paste, fish sauce, oyster sauce, and Parmesan.

Still, MSG's reputation lives on. I blame two factors. (1) Once you hear that a food is bad for you, the notion is hard to shake. Not so long ago, people thought eggs were terrible for you. Now we know better, but old guys everywhere still settle for egg whites—just to be sure. And (2) We're all a little racist. You know how when people get sick from eating, they typically blame it on the Chinese or Thai food they had for dinner, even though

the salad bar they hit up for lunch is just as likely to be the culprit? Shit, I'm Asian and I still sometimes do that. Part of this is fear of the unknown. Part of it is lingering prejudice. The same kind that causes diners to happily pay double digits for a dish of tagliatelle while sneering at bowls of rice noodles that break the 10-buck barrier. The same kind that keeps fools joking about what animal the meat in your lo mein came from.

The takeaway is this: MSG is fine in moderation, just like eggs, butter, and booze. The real argument should be over how much to use. My mom mainly used the crystals in dishes that didn't already contain a ton of soy sauce, oyster sauce, vinegar, and other natural sources. She'd sprinkle a little, like magic dust, in *picadillo*, ground beef with garlic, potatoes, and peas. The MSG brought out the beefy flavor without adding saltiness. She was on one end of the spectrum. At the other are cooks who lean on it like a crutch, putting it in everything *instead* of using the natural ingredients and techniques that create great flavor. Without the real stuff, the fake stuff is all you taste.

I fall somewhere in the middle. That's why you'll see chicken bouillon and hon dashi powder, both basically MSG by another name, in many of the ingredient lists in this book. Sometimes I've made them optional, but I encourage you to try them. If you make my Kimchi Yogurt (page 186), for instance, with and without the addition of bouillon, you'll notice that the more MSG-rich version tastes even more exciting and complex. You'll find yourself sensing the individual spices as well as a surge in the sauce's overall impact. Some might not approve, but I'm about food tasting good. Period.

Cold Soba Noodles with Dashi, Sesame, and Vegetables

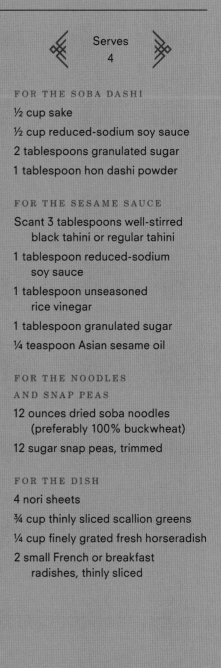

Serves
4

FOR THE SOBA DASHI

½ cup sake

½ cup reduced-sodium soy sauce

2 tablespoons granulated sugar

1 tablespoon hon dashi powder

FOR THE SESAME SAUCE

Scant 3 tablespoons well-stirred
black tahini or regular tahini

1 tablespoon reduced-sodium
soy sauce

1 tablespoon unseasoned
rice vinegar

1 tablespoon granulated sugar

¼ teaspoon Asian sesame oil

**FOR THE NOODLES
AND SNAP PEAS**

12 ounces dried soba noodles
(preferably 100% buckwheat)

12 sugar snap peas, trimmed

FOR THE DISH

4 nori sheets

¾ cup thinly sliced scallion greens

¼ cup finely grated fresh horseradish

2 small French or breakfast
radishes, thinly sliced

I was noodle deprived during the four frantic months I spent toiling to open the New York City outpost of the Morimoto Empire. After work, I was a zombie. By the time I made it up the stairs of my four-story walkup on the Lower East Side, the only noodles I had the energy to make were instant ramen, dumped into a bowl and cooked with what I'd argue was the hottest tap water in Manhattan. When we finally got the place open, some of the Japanese guys in the kitchen made soba for family meal. It was summer, so they chilled the buckwheat noodles and plunked a few ice cubes in the dipping sauce. Some chopped scallions, a little grated wasabi, and that was lunch. A few slurps later, I was amazed at how satisfying such a spare dish could be when expert hands crafted the main components—the chewy handmade noodles and smoky dashi. In less-practiced hands, like mine and yours, even store-bought soba and shortcut soba dashi can blow minds with a few extra touches. I dare you to serve it on a giant slab of ice.

MAKE THE SOBA DASHI

Pour the sake into a small pan and bring to a boil over high heat. Pour the sake into a medium bowl, add the soy sauce, sugar, dashi powder, and 1 cup water, and stir until the sugar and dashi powder dissolve. Cover and chill in the fridge until it's cold. It keeps in the fridge for up to 3 days.

MAKE THE SESAME SAUCE

Combine the tahini, soy sauce, rice vinegar, sugar, and sesame oil in a medium bowl and stir until the sugar dissolves. It keeps in the fridge for up to 3 days.

COOK THE NOODLES AND SNAP PEAS

Bring a large pot of water to a boil. Add the noodles and cook according to the package instructions, stirring occasionally, until the noodles are al dente. About 1 minute before they're done, add the snap peas. Meanwhile, prepare a big bowl of icy water. Drain the noodles and peas, dump them into the icy water, stir, then drain them really well. Cut the snap peas in half.

FINISH THE DISH

Turn a stovetop burner to medium low. One by one, wave the nori sheets just above the flame until they're aromatic and crispy, 15 to 20 seconds per sheet. Cut the sheets into thin 2- to 3-inch strips.

Divide the noodles and snap peas among 4 wide bowls. Add about ½ cup of the soba dashi to each, and top with the scallions, horseradish, radishes, nori strips, and a tablespoon dollop of the sesame sauce. Tell your friends to stir before they eat.

Chang Fun Noodles with Vegetables and Soy Vinegar

Makes about
20 small rolls

SPECIAL EQUIPMENT

1 approximately 12-inch skillet
with a lid

1 sturdy plate (about 8 inches in
diameter not counting the lip)
that will fit inside the skillet
with room to spare

FOR THE SOY VINEGAR

½ cup reduced-sodium soy sauce

2 tablespoons sherry vinegar

2 teaspoons granulated sugar

FOR THE CHANG FUN NOODLES
AND FILLING

1½ cups tapioca starch

1 cup Asian white rice flour
(not sticky rice flour)

1 tablespoon vegetable oil

1½ teaspoons turmeric powder

½ teaspoon kosher salt

Nonstick cooking spray

¼ pound fresh shiitake mushrooms,
stems removed, caps cut into
¼-inch pieces (about 1 cup)

¼ cup thinly sliced moderately
spicy fresh red chile (including
seeds), such as Fresno

¼ cup thinly sliced scallion greens

If you've gone out to dim sum, you've probably eaten something that's
a lot like this dish: warm sheets of slick, chewy rice noodle rolled into
a cylinder and studded with shrimp or pork. You've pointed to it and
watched as a waiter in a suit pours on soy sauce tableside. With that
kind of service, you could be at a fine-dining establishment, if it weren't
for the screaming kids and the lazy Susan.

What's going to blow your mind is that you can make the noodle
rolls from scratch. I know it blew mine. Typically when I want to serve
fresh rice noodles at my restaurants, I hit up my girl in Chinatown

who makes them all day every day and sells them for less than a dollar a pound. These noodles, though, have to be cooked an hour or so before you eat them. So I spent some time on YouTube watching people make them and came up with a method that works every time. It takes some practice to get good at, but even your early attempts will turn out pretty damn good.

MAKE THE SOY VINEGAR

Combine the soy sauce, sherry vinegar, and sugar along with ¼ cup plus 2 tablespoons water in a small bowl and stir until the sugar dissolves. Set aside.

MAKE THE CHANG FUN BATTER

Combine the tapioca starch, rice flour, vegetable oil, turmeric, and salt along with 2 cups water in a medium mixing bowl and whisk until totally smooth. Let the batter rest for 30 minutes or so.

MAKE THE NOODLE ROLLS

You're going to make the noodle rolls one at a time, transfer them to a baking sheet, and cover with plastic wrap while you make the rest. The noodles should be served at room temperature, so keep the baking sheet in a warm place so they don't get cold.

Heat a medium pot of water until hot (to use for refilling the skillet as you steam the noodle rolls). Pour enough water into the 12-inch skillet to reach a depth of ½ inch. Make three tight aluminum foil balls that are each about 1 inch in diameter. Put the foil balls in the skillet to serve as a platform for the plate. Bring the water to a boil.

For each roll, spray the surface of the plate with nonstick spray, stir the batter well, and pour on just enough batter to cover the surface (about 5 tablespoons). Carefully set the plate on the balls in the skillet, pressing gently so the plate lies flat and steady.

Cover the skillet and steam just until the edges have set (they'll look a shade or so darker), 1 to 2 minutes. Sprinkle on about 1 generous tablespoon of the mushrooms and 1 teaspoon each of the chiles and scallions, then cover and steam until the batter has fully set, 4 to 5 minutes. Turn off the heat.

Use tongs and an oven mitt to carefully transfer the plate to a work surface. If you see any excess water, dab it with paper towels. Run a spoon around the edges of the noodle to help them lift from the plate, let it cool slightly, and carefully roll the circle into a loose cylinder. (If as you roll it, you notice that the underside looks cracked, that means it's not quite done. Lay it flat again and steam, covered, for another 30 seconds or so.) Cut the roll in half crosswise, then transfer to the baking sheet and cover with plastic wrap.

Wipe the plate clean and spray with nonstick spray. Stir the batter well, and make the next roll. Occasionally, add more hot water to maintain about ½-inch depth.

SERVE THE ROLLS

When you've made all the rolls, transfer them to plates or a platter and spoon on the soy vinegar, about 1 tablespoon per roll. Eat.

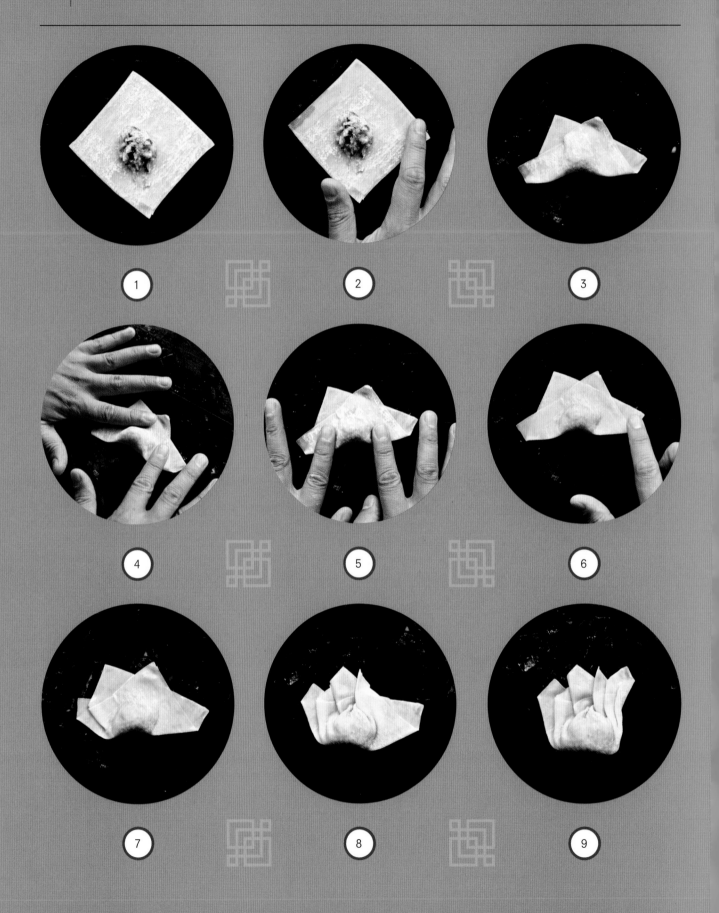

Pork Wontons

As making dumplings go, it doesn't get any easier than forming wontons. They don't require intricate folds or anything. And once you get good at them, you can start playing with the filling, like going half chopped shrimp and half ground pork belly. Serve the boiled dumplings in Wonton Noodle Soup (page 82) or more simply, in bowls splashed with reduced-sodium soy sauce, drizzled with Asian chile oil, and sprinkled with chopped scallions, and you're good to go. Feel free to make them in advance, and freeze the suckers. When you're ready to eat, drop them, frozen or fresh, straight into boiling water and cook just until the skins are fully tender and the filling is cooked through, 3 to 4 minutes.

MAKE THE FILLING

Heat the oil in a small pan over medium-high heat, add the chives, and cook, stirring, just until they're wilted and very fragrant, about 2 minutes. Let them cool. Combine the pork in a mixing bowl with the chives and remaining filling ingredients. Mix gently but thoroughly with your hands until everything is well distributed. Don't overmix or the filling will be too dense.

FORM THE WONTONS

Line a large baking sheet with parchment paper. Fill a small bowl with water. Form the dumplings one at a time, keeping the yet-to-be-used wonton wrappers under a damp towel.

(1) Position a wonton wrapper so a corner faces you and add a scant 2 teaspoons of the pork mixture to the center. (2) Dip your finger into the water and use it to moisten the edge of the wrapper. (3) Fold the corner over the filling so that it bisects one of the sides and overlaps the edge by about ¼ inch. (4, 5) Force out the air from the pocket you created, then press firmly so the wrapper adheres where it meets. (6) Position the wonton so that the longest side faces you. (7, 8, 9) Gather the bottom two corners together, as if you were closing a wooden fan. Firmly press the top of the wonton so it holds its shape. Put the wonton on the prepared baking sheet. Repeat the process with the remaining filling and wrappers, keeping the wontons covered loosely with damp paper towels.

Covered with plastic wrap, the wontons keep in the fridge for up to 2 days. They keep in the freezer for up to 3 months. To freeze, keep them uncovered in a single layer on a plate or baking sheet until they're fully frozen, then transfer them to freezer bags.

Makes 25

SPECIAL EQUIPMENT
Parchment paper

FOR THE FILLING
Scant 1 tablespoon vegetable oil

¼ cup thinly sliced chives, preferably Chinese chives (flat, like blades of grass)

½ pound fresh pork belly, ground by your butcher, or other fatty ground pork, cold

1 teaspoon finely chopped fresh ginger

1 teaspoon reduced-sodium soy sauce

1 teaspoon Asian sesame oil

Generous ¼ teaspoon potato starch or cornstarch

¼ generous teaspoon kosher salt

¼ generous teaspoon granulated sugar

¼ generous teaspoon chicken bouillon

Scant ¼ teaspoon ground white pepper

25 wonton wrappers (square), preferably "Hong Kong style"

CHAPTER FOUR

Proteins

Korean Fried Chicken with Kimchi Yogurt, Fruit, and Mint

Serves
8 to 10

SPECIAL EQUIPMENT
Deep-fry thermometer

FOR THE CHICKEN
4½ pounds assorted chicken parts, such as boneless skin-on breasts and bone-in, skin-on thighs and wings (or all thighs, my favorite)

1 cup Kimchi Yogurt (page 186)

Vegetable oil for deep frying

4½ cups Asian white rice flour (not sticky rice flour)

⅔ cup Thai or Vietnamese fish sauce

2 teaspoons ground cayenne

FOR THE DISH
1 cup Kimchi Yogurt (page 186)

½ lime

2 cups seasonal fruit, such as halved grapes or cherries, or sliced peaches or apples

¼ cup loosely packed mint leaves, torn at the last minute

My take on the Korean fast-food staple lives halfway between Seoul and Buffalo, NY. Fried twice so it's twice as crispy, the rice flour–battered chicken (gluten-free, son!) roosts on a sauce that channels the spicy, creamy alchemy that happens when hot sauce meets blue cheese dressing. A little bit of sweet-tart fruit cuts through the richness of all that salt and fry, like celery sticks only wish they could.

The secret to the crunch is to batter twice and fry twice, which sounds complicated until you see that you only make one batter and use one pot of oil. If you don't feel like dealing with a pot of hot oil, make the kimchi yogurt and hit up Popeyes. Popeyes is the shit.

MARINATE THE CHICKEN

Combine the chicken and kimchi yogurt in a large bowl and toss to coat the chicken well. Cover and let the chicken marinate in the fridge for at least 24 hours or up to 5 days (the longer the better).

BATTER AND FRY THE CHICKEN

Bring the chicken to room temperature. You're going to cook the chicken twice and in several batches to avoid crowding the oil.

About an hour before you're ready to eat, pour enough oil into a large pot to reach a depth of about 3 inches. Set the pot over medium-high heat and bring the oil to 275°F (use a deep-fry thermometer). Meanwhile, combine the rice flour, fish sauce, cayenne, and 2 cups water in a large mixing bowl and stir very well until the mixture is well combined and has no lumps.

Line a baking sheet with paper towels. Add 3 or 4 pieces of chicken to the batter and toss to coat well. Gently shake the pieces to let any excess batter drip off and add them to the oil. They'll probably sink to the bottom at first, so move them around a bit to prevent them from sticking. Fry, turning them over occasionally and adjusting the heat to maintain the oil's temperature, until they're light golden brown and crispy but not quite cooked through, 8 to 10 minutes for drumsticks and wings and 10 to 12 minutes for breasts and thighs. (It's totally fine if some pieces of batter fall off during the first fry.) Transfer the pieces to the paper towel–lined baking sheet and fry the remaining chicken. Reserve the batter and the oil.

Set a rack over a baking sheet and use a skimmer to remove any stray fry from the oil. Set the pot over high heat and bring the oil to 325°F. Working in batches again, add the chicken to the batter, toss to coat, shake the pieces gently, and fry again until they're deep golden brown, crispy, and fully cooked, 4 to 5 minutes. Again, adjust the burner as necessary to keep the heat steady. Transfer the pieces to the rack as they're cooked.

FINISH THE DISH

Pour the kimchi yogurt onto a large platter or plates and add the chicken. Squeeze some lime over the fruit, then scatter the fruit and mint around the chicken. Eat.

Chicken Soong, Thai-Larb Style

I dated a few girls back in the day who just did not like Chinese restaurants. They weren't down with the brusque service, the weak tea, the innards. At that age, the only thing I liked more than tripe and liver was girls, so I splurged on Chinese that they wouldn't consider weird or dirty. I took them to a classy, sophisticated spot—P.F. Chang's, at the mall. The most elegant-seeming dish on the menu (remember, this was the '90s) was chicken soong, a mixture of ground chicken, mushrooms, and water chestnuts that you'd wrap in lettuce leaves. More than elegant, it felt fun. Today, the lettuce wrap might seem corny. I don't care. I'm trying to keep it alive. What I update is the chicken component, packing it with lemongrass and herbs so the flavor loosely resembles Thai larb.

Serves
6 to 8

1 pound coarsely ground dark-meat chicken (the coarser the better)

1 pound coarsely ground white-meat chicken (the coarser the better)

¼ cup finely chopped shallots

3 tablespoons thinly sliced scallion greens

3 heaping tablespoons roughly chopped cilantro (thin stems and leaves)

2 large lemongrass stalks (bottom 1 inch and top 8 inches removed, outer 2 layers removed), very finely chopped (about 3 tablespoons)

1 heaping tablespoon finely chopped fresh ginger

2 tablespoons oyster sauce

1 tablespoon Thai or Vietnamese fish sauce

1 tablespoon Asian sesame oil

1 tablespoon kosher salt

1 teaspoon granulated sugar

1 teaspoon red chile flakes

1 teaspoon ground white pepper

1 teaspoon potato starch or cornstarch

¼ cup vegetable oil

15 to 20 large iceberg, romaine, green, or other lettuce leaves

Vietnamese Dipping Sauce (Nuoc Cham), (page 33), optional

Combine all but the vegetable oil, lettuce leaves, and dipping sauce in a medium mixing bowl and mix well with your hands so everything is well distributed.

Heat half the oil in a large heavy skillet over medium-high heat until it shimmers. Add half the chicken mixture and cook, stirring, flipping, and breaking up clumps, until any liquid has evaporated and the chicken is cooked through and lightly browned in spots, 5 to 8 minutes. Transfer to a serving bowl. Add the remaining oil to the pan and cook the rest of the chicken mixture the same way. Use a slotted spoon to transfer the second batch to the bowl (leaving the fat behind) and stir well.

Serve with the lettuce leaves and dipping sauce alongside (if using) and let everyone get to wrapping and dipping.

McNuggets

When I was a toddler, my mom and dad sent me to live in the Philippines for three years. They stayed behind in Chicago and worked nonstop double shifts until they could afford to buy a small house for the whole family in the Ravenswood neighborhood of Chicago.

We lived in that house for several years until Mom and Dad moved us out to the 'burbs and rented out floors of the first house for extra money. This was long before the first floor of the rental became a sort of historic flophouse for me and my boys; it was where we ran a sad sort of Asian Fight Club, where we did mushrooms for the first time, where my nephew was conceived. But as kids, the house was where my brother, sister, and I were employed as weekend laborers by my parents. We swept, shoveled snow, mowed the lawn, all that shit. Like so many immigrant children who had it much easier than their parents did, I bitched and moaned about these chores. I would've much rather been chilling at home watching *Thundercats*, or outside playing ball.

On the weekly drive to the house to do work, we'd pass a McDonald's, and a particularly ill one at that, with a spiral slide and giant ball pit. The '80s were the chain's glory days. I was born a year before the dawn of the Happy Meal. I was born when that fat-ass Grimace and that fiend the Hamburglar both turned seven years old. By the time I was 15, Michael Jordan and Larry Bird were shooting it out for Mike's Big Mac, and I was already worshipping at its altar.

But there was a time when I had never been inside a McDonald's. Neither had my siblings. We would

share resigned looks as Mom sped past it. She was the enemy of pizza and burgers and tacos. Her stopping wasn't even a question. Only when Dad drove us did we have a chance. So we begged him whenever we got close. We could sense that he, too, wanted to stop. And one day he did.

I don't remember that first time at Mickey D's, probably because I've been so many times since. I do remember that by the time I had my first order of McNuggets, I was too old to really enjoy the ball pit. And I remember that the food tasted so good—or really, so *different* from the stuff Mom was making at home. Mom was ahead of the curve. She was dead-set against fast food and way into local produce. She knew where her bitter melon came from, because she picked it from her garden. Her food was so pure compared to the chicken-like substance encased in crumbs. Her food featured sharp flavors meant to be toned down by the white rice we always ate with it. In some strange way, though, the nuggets were familiar, bland in the comforting way rice is and a vehicle for the intense trio of condiments—BBQ, honey mustard, and sweet chile sauces.

I know it's become politically incorrect to admit, but to this day, I still get down with Mickey D's. When I do, I feel like I'm chasing the dragon, trying to experience again that early high of eating something I knew I shouldn't be and tasting the America I wanted badly to be a part of. I'm also trying to recapture that time with my dad, who worked 12-hour days and wasn't around as often as I wanted. I keep trying, but it never quite works.

Chicken Nugs

Now that my tastes have changed and I can cook, I've set about re-inventing McNuggets. I wanted to big-up the qualities I love about them and ditch those I don't. That means chunks of chicken breast; thighs are my favorite cut, but dark-meat nuggets would just be wrong. That also means a marinade of yogurt and hot sauce, a rice flour batter for extra crunch, and my take on the three must-have sauces.

MARINATE THE CHICKEN

Combine the yogurt, Frank's, and Sriracha in a medium mixing bowl and stir well. Add the chicken, stir to coat well, cover, and marinate in the fridge for at least 12 hours or up to 2 days (the longer the better).

BATTER AND FRY THE CHICKEN

Preheat the oven to 200°F. Pour enough oil into a large pot to reach a depth of about 3 inches. Set the pot over medium-high heat and bring the oil to 325°F (use a deep-fry thermometer).

Meanwhile, combine 2 cups of the rice flour with the salt, pepper, and 2 cups water in another medium mixing bowl and stir really well. Put the remaining 1 cup rice flour on a large plate. Work with a third of the chicken at a time: Remove the chicken from the marinade, then add the chicken to the plate with the rice flour and toss to coat in a thin layer. Transfer the chicken to the batter, toss well, shake gently, then carefully add the chicken to the oil.

Fry each batch, stirring occasionally, until deep golden brown and crispy, 3 to 4 minutes. Use a spider to transfer the nuggets to a paper towel–lined baking sheet, season immediately with salt, and keep them warm in the oven.

Break apart the nuggets, if necessary. Eat with bowls of the sauces for dipping.

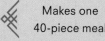
Makes one
40-piece meal

SPECIAL EQUIPMENT

Deep-fry thermometer
Spider

1 cup low-fat plain yogurt
(not Greek)

¼ cup Frank's RedHot sauce

¼ cup Sriracha

2 pounds boneless skinless breasts,
cut into approximately 1½-inch
pieces

Vegetable oil for deep frying

3 cups Asian white rice flour (not
sticky rice flour)

½ teaspoon kosher salt, plus extra
for seasoning

½ teaspoon ground black pepper

Chicken Nug Sauce Trio (page 188)

Burrito [buh-**ree**-toh]; VERB
To wrap in a tortilla, typically along with rice and beans; to bulk up; to make portable: *These chicken nuggets need to be burritoed so we can eat them in the car.*

Char Siu Pork with Apples, Peanuts, and Herbs

Even if you don't recognize the name, you know *char siu*. You've seen the glossy, reddish slabs of pork hanging from hooks in the windows of every Chinatown on earth. Sometimes, it is known as "barbecued pork," but I'll tell you, the process used to make it is the opposite of the low-and-slow cooking of southern barbecue. When I worked at Buddakan, we made *char siu* in a special oven-like contraption. The slabs of pork hung over jet burners in an insulated box that got so hot our fire-suppression system almost cracked. When that happens, the only thing you can do is run. At home, you can get a similar effect with a broiler, which not only keeps the meat juicy but also transforms the sugars in the marinade into something much more complex and exciting.

The tart, crunchy green apple salad served alongside provides a refreshing contrast in texture and flavor, and the tahini mustard dipping sauce is a more mellow stand-in for the tear-inducing Chinese mustard I used to dunk stuff in as a kid.

Serves
4 to 6

4 (½-pound) bone-in shoulder chops (½ to ¾ inch thick)

½ cup Char Siu Marinade (page 206)

Kosher salt

1 medium green apple, cored and very thinly sliced into half moons

1 tablespoon fresh lime juice, or more to taste

1 teaspoon Asian chile oil

½ cup roughly chopped unsalted roasted peanuts

½ cup loosely packed roughly chopped cilantro (thin stems and leaves)

½ cup loosely packed thinly sliced scallion greens

About 10 mint leaves, torn at the last minute

½ cup Tahini Mustard Sauce (page 190), for dipping, optional

Combine the pork in a bowl with the marinade and toss to coat the chops well. Cover the bowl and let the chops marinate in the fridge for at least 1 hour or up to 2 days.

Turn on the broiler and position the oven rack about 4 inches from the heat source. Season the chops on both sides with salt. Put the chops on a foil-lined baking sheet (or even better, on a rack on a foil-lined baking sheet) and broil until the edges and tops are almost black in patches and the meat is just cooked through, 8 to 10 minutes. Let them rest on a cutting board for about 5 minutes.

While the meat rests, combine the apple, lime juice, and chile oil in a medium mixing bowl and toss well. Add the peanuts, cilantro, scallions, and mint and toss briefly. Season to taste with more lime juice.

Cut the pork against the grain into approximately ¼-inch-thick slices, and transfer the slices to a platter. Serve with the apple salad and tahini mustard sauce (if using). Eat.

Root Beer–Glazed Pork Banh Mi with Bacon

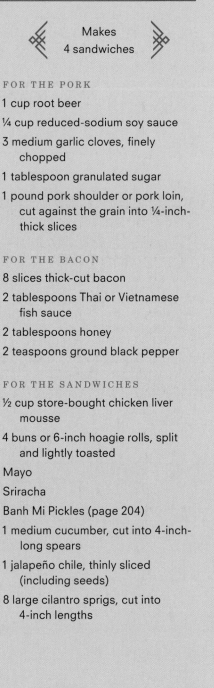

Makes
4 sandwiches

FOR THE PORK

1 cup root beer

¼ cup reduced-sodium soy sauce

3 medium garlic cloves, finely
    chopped

1 tablespoon granulated sugar

1 pound pork shoulder or pork loin,
    cut against the grain into ¼-inch-
    thick slices

FOR THE BACON

8 slices thick-cut bacon

2 tablespoons Thai or Vietnamese
    fish sauce

2 tablespoons honey

2 teaspoons ground black pepper

FOR THE SANDWICHES

½ cup store-bought chicken liver
    mousse

4 buns or 6-inch hoagie rolls, split
    and lightly toasted

Mayo

Sriracha

Banh Mi Pickles (page 204)

1 medium cucumber, cut into 4-inch-
    long spears

1 jalapeño chile, thinly sliced
    (including seeds)

8 large cilantro sprigs, cut into
    4-inch lengths

The banh mi got trendy. Several years back, it was on the cover of magazines. It headlined restaurants. It popped up on every menu from sea to shining sea. Of course, we all discovered the banh mi like Columbus discovered America: The Vietnamese had been on it since the French brought imperialism and the baguette. Still, when I stumbled on my first one, almost two decades ago in the Vietnamese-heavy Argyle neighborhood a few blocks from my 'hood in Chicago, I felt like I alone had unearthed a secret sandwich. I wondered why all sandwiches didn't contain sweet-tart pickled carrots and daikon, a crisp cucumber spear, cilantro, and hot green chile.

The weird thing about food trends is that enthusiasm eventually fizzles, even when the food warrants our continued devotion. I'll always champion the banh mi. This one features marinated pork in the style of Filipino *tocino*, or pork cured with Sprite or 7UP. (I use root beer, which tastes more complex.) The word *tocino* means "bacon" in Latin America, so I add that, too, plus a shmear of chicken liver mousse to big-up France—thanks for the colonization, homies!

To make thinly slicing the pork easier, put the pork in the freezer until it's frozen at the edges.

MARINATE THE PORK

Combine the root beer, soy sauce, garlic, and sugar in a medium mixing bowl and stir until the sugar dissolves. Add the pork slices so they're submerged, cover with plastic wrap, and marinate in the fridge for at least 24 hours or, even better, 2 or 3 days.

COOK THE BACON

Preheat the oven to 400°F. Add the bacon to a foil-lined baking sheet in one layer and bake in the oven until brown and crispy, about 15 minutes. Meanwhile, stir together the fish sauce, honey, and black pepper in a small bowl. When the bacon is done, pour most of the fat into a heatproof container and reserve it for another purpose. Pour the fish sauce mixture over the bacon and toss to coat the slices well. Continue baking just until the bacon is glossy and a shade darker, about 2 minutes more. Transfer to a plate.

COOK THE PORK

Preheat the oven to 500°F. Remove the pork slices from the marinade and pat them dry with paper towels. Put the slices on a foil-lined baking sheet (or even better, on a rack on a foil-lined baking sheet) and cook in the oven until the edges and bottoms are deep brown and the meat is just cooked through, about 10 minutes. Let them rest for a few minutes. Cut them, if necessary, to fit on the buns.

MAKE THE SANDWICHES

Spread the liver mousse on the bun bottoms, and mayo and Sriracha on the tops. Divide the pork and bacon among the buns, top with the other stuff, and get to it.

The Porky Melt

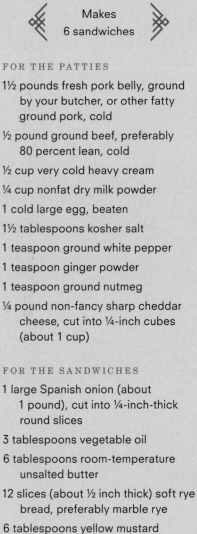

Makes
6 sandwiches

FOR THE PATTIES

1½ pounds fresh pork belly, ground
by your butcher, or other fatty
ground pork, cold

½ pound ground beef, preferably
80 percent lean, cold

½ cup very cold heavy cream

¼ cup nonfat dry milk powder

1 cold large egg, beaten

1½ tablespoons kosher salt

1 teaspoon ground white pepper

1 teaspoon ginger powder

1 teaspoon ground nutmeg

¼ pound non-fancy sharp cheddar
cheese, cut into ¼-inch cubes
(about 1 cup)

FOR THE SANDWICHES

1 large Spanish onion (about
1 pound), cut into ¼-inch-thick
round slices

3 tablespoons vegetable oil

6 tablespoons room-temperature
unsalted butter

12 slices (about ½ inch thick) soft rye
bread, preferably marble rye

6 tablespoons yellow mustard

When two giants like the patty melt and the Cheddar Wurst combine forces, the result forms like Voltron—all other sandwich royalty better watch the throne. The combo of rye bread, molten cheddar, and sweet griddled onions takes me back to the diner in Glenview, Illinois, where I lost my patty melt virginity. Instead of loosely packed beef, I make patties in the style of bratwurst, which reminds me of every non-Asian barbecue I ever attended in the Midwest. Props to Michael Ruhlman and Brian Polcyn for a kick-ass bratwurst recipe (their book, *Charcuterie*, is one of the greats). I hope y'all don't mind that I skip the casing and cheese it out.

⩕

MAKE THE PATTIES

Combine the pork, beef, cream, milk powder, egg, salt, and spices in a large mixing bowl. Use your hands to mix until the ingredients are well distributed, then mix and knead until the mixture looks sticky. You *want* to overmix slightly so the sausage will have some bounce to it. Add the cheese and mix again just until it's well distributed.

Form six ½-inch-thick oval patties that'll just about cover a slice of rye bread. Let them rest in the fridge for about 30 minutes before you cook them. Covered with plastic wrap, they keep in the fridge for up to 2 days.

COOK THE ONIONS AND PATTIES

Heat a wide heavy skillet over high heat until it begins to smoke. Toss the onion slices with 2 tablespoons of the oil in a bowl. Add half of the onions to the skillet in a single layer. Cook, without stirring but pressing them occasionally, until the onions begin to char on the bottom, 2 to 3 minutes, then stir and cook, stirring occasionally, until they're just translucent, about 2 minutes more. Transfer the onions to a bowl. Repeat with the remaining onions. Cover the bowl and set them aside. They'll cook further as they cool but should still have a slight crunch.

Wipe the skillet clean, set it over medium heat, and add the remaining tablespoon oil. When it shimmers, add half of the patties, leaving some space between them, and cook, flipping a few times, until both sides are well browned and the patties are cooked through, about 8 minutes. Transfer them to a plate and repeat with the remaining patties.

MAKE THE SANDWICHES

Meanwhile, butter one side of each slice of bread and turn the broiler to high. Arrange half of the bread on a baking sheet and broil 4 inches from the heat, buttered side up, until golden brown, about 3 minutes. Transfer the bread, buttered side down, to a plate and broil the remaining bread.

Make the sandwiches with the patties, onions, and mustard. Eat.

The Motherporker

By the way, don't sleep on the Motherporker variation (in the kitchen, we use a less polite name): The Porky Melt topped with sliced pickled jalapeños, a fried egg, and crispy bacon. It's awful for you. It's also perfect.

The Halal Cart

I'll always rep Chicago, but coming to New York was like coming to Mecca. I made my first pilgrimage in 2003, when I was chef de cuisine at a modern Chinese spot in Chicago called Opera. I decided to check out the restaurant scene and see if I wanted to move to New York to work.

Chicago wasn't no Podunk food town, though. At the time, the legendary Charlie Trotter (R.I.P.) had already been rocking it there for more than a decade. Chi-Town don Carrie Nahabedian, one of my mentors, can still ball with the best chefs in the game. Still, New York was *New York*. I was ready to have my mind blown. I went all out. I'm talking back-to-back tasting menus at Daniel and Jean-Georges, an incredible six-hour feast, most of which ended up on the tracks of the N train as I made my way back to Astoria, Queens, where I was crashing on a friend's couch.

Despite all this high-end dining, one of my most memorable meals from that trip was at a curbside cart. The friend I was staying with was going through some stuff with her boyfriend, so to escape the tension I spent a lot of time wandering the streets of Astoria. On 30th Street, I spotted a massive line of people and went over to investigate. I walked toward the front, wondering why anyone would wait on a line this long. And then I smelled it—a perfumed punch of cumin and coriander and onion and meat so all-encompassing that it was almost a physical presence. Everyone from New York knows this smell well. It stopped me in my tracks.

At the front of the line was a dinky silver structure no more than ten feet wide cluttered with squirt bottles, stacks of aluminum takeout containers, and a griddle full of yellow-tinged meat giving off mad steam. The burly dude who manned the griddle was moving a mile a minute, spooning, chopping, and squirting. I spent a few minutes just watching people order. No one ordered in full sentences—they were all so experienced that they communicated with words slammed together. "Mixed over rice. White. Extra red," said a woman. "Lamb, pita, extra pickles, extra white," said a guy. Each exchange of order and food happened so casually and mysteriously that it seemed like something illicit, like a drug deal. I wanted to order but I didn't know the code. So when I reached the front of the line, I played it safe: I pointed to the guy's foil package and said I'd have the same. I watched as the man who ran the cart used what looked like a dough scraper to separate a hill of lamb from the steaming mountain on the griddle, hack it up, and scoop it onto warm pita. Next, with a level of speed that could come only from years of daily practice, he tossed on pickles and, from a good three inches above, squirted it with two seconds of white sauce, then one second of red. The sweetness of the doughy pita and mysterious creaminess of the white sauce tamed the salty meat. The pickles and red sauce electrified the whole thing. It was so good that I didn't mind the stains I got on my shirt.

When I finally did move to New York, I ate at halal carts like it was my job. I absorbed the unspoken rules of the cart through trial and error. Rule #1: These dudes running the carts are busy, so order using as few words as possible. In other words, it's not "red sauce" and "white sauce," it's just "red" and "white." Rule #2: Never order anything that looks lonely. If there's only one kebab left, you can bet it's been sitting there for a long time. Rule #3: Don't ask for a cheeseburger even though there's a picture of one on the side of the cart. The response will almost always be "No." Since my first attempt, I've perfected my order, after finding out the hard way that too much red, with its vinegary sharpness, could wreck an entire large chicken over rice.

Vietnamese Halal Cart–Style Lamb Pitas

My version of the halal cart lamb sandwich delivers the pleasures of the real thing via an Asian detour. Easy pickled cabbage, white and red sauce, and pitas are all pretty much in line with the original. But then I go and rub tender lamb with spices that conjure Vietnamese pho and add an eggplant relish that exists halfway between the Mediterranean and Asia.

PICKLE THE CABBAGE
Combine the vinegar and sugar in a medium mixing bowl and stir to dissolve the sugar. Add the cabbage and press to more or less submerge it in the liquid, then cover and keep in the fridge for at least 4 hours or up to 1 day. Drain before using.

COOK THE LAMB
Preheat the oven to 400°F. Combine the sugar, salt, and all the spices in a small bowl and stir well. Put the lamb on a plate, drizzle on 1½ tablespoons of the fish sauce, and rub to coat the lamb well. Evenly sprinkle the spice mixture on all sides of the lamb, patting it to help the spices adhere.

Heat the oil in a heavy ovenproof skillet over medium-high heat until it shimmers. Sear the lamb on all sides until dark brown, about 5 minutes. Put the skillet in the oven and roast until the lamb is rare to medium rare, 8 to 10 minutes. Let the meat rest on a cutting board for 10 minutes, then thinly slice it against the grain and drizzle on the remaining fish sauce.

MAKE THE PITAS
Wrap the pitas in foil and warm in the oven for 3 to 5 minutes. Let everyone pile the cabbage, eggplant relish, lamb, white sauce, and hot sauce on their pita, fold it like a taco, and eat.

Makes
4 pitas

FOR THE PICKLED CABBAGE
1 cup unseasoned rice vinegar
2 tablespoons granulated sugar
2 cups thinly sliced red cabbage

FOR THE LAMB
1 teaspoon granulated sugar
½ teaspoon kosher salt
½ teaspoon onion powder
½ teaspoon garlic powder
½ teaspoon ground black pepper
½ teaspoon ginger powder
½ teaspoon fennel seeds, roughly chopped then coarsely crushed with flat of knife
Healthy pinch ground cinnamon
Healthy pinch ground clove
1 (1½-pound) piece of tender, boneless lamb, about 1 inch thick, such as leg steaks, lamb loin, lamb sirloin, or butterflied leg
2 tablespoons Thai or Vietnamese fish sauce
1 tablespoon vegetable oil

FOR THE PITAS
4 (8-inch) pocketless pitas
Eggplant Relish (page 161), at room temperature
Halal Cart–Style White Sauce (page 190)
Dale's "Homemade" Hot Sauce (page 187)

Grilled Kale Salad with Beets and Persimmon

Me? I'd much rather eat kale that's been stewed with pork. But not everyone out there is a fat kid at heart, especially not in Brooklyn, the epicenter of the Kale Salad. Though it takes many forms, the Kale Salad is almost always made with the raw green and its purpose is almost exclusively to make people feel like they're being healthy and therefore shouldn't feel bad about ordering the fried chicken, pork chop, or whatever else hits the table next. I can get with that logic, so Talde always has some wholesome, seasonally shifting version of the salad on its menu. (At Pork Slope, the bar my partners and I run, we serve the anti-kale salad, made with Ranch dressing, bacon, shredded cheddar, and crumbled potato chips.) The winter version here is probably my favorite. It demonstrates that as food trends go, the Kale Salad isn't so bad at all. In fact, with the right dressing, it can be kind of banging.

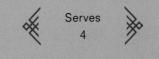

Serves
4

2 golf ball–size beets, peeled and very thinly sliced

½ cup Miso-Ponzu Dressing (page 198)

¼ cup unsalted roasted almonds

1 big bunch curly kale

2 tablespoons vegetable oil

1 teaspoon kosher salt

1 ripe fuyu persimmon, peeled and very thinly sliced

Combine the beets and 3 tablespoons of the dressing in a small bowl. Toss very well to coat and let them marinate at room temperature for at least an hour or, even better, overnight in the fridge.

Preheat the oven to 350°F. Spread the almonds in one layer on a small baking sheet or toaster oven tray and bake, shaking occasionally, until very fragrant, about 5 minutes. Set them aside to cool, then very roughly chop them.

Preheat a cast-iron griddle or prepare a grill to cook over high heat. Combine the kale, oil, and salt in a medium mixing bowl and toss really well. Add the kale leaves to the griddle in more or less one layer (cook in batches if you have to use a skillet) and cook, without flipping, just until the kale has spots of char on the underside, 30 seconds to 1 minute. Let the kale cool slightly, then use a knife to cut out the thick stems and chop the kale into bite-size pieces. You'll have about 4 cups.

Transfer the kale to a large mixing bowl. Pour in the remaining dressing and toss and scrunch the kale with your hands. Really beat it up. Add the beets, almonds, and persimmon, toss well, and serve on a big plate. Eat.

Pastrami-ed Roasted Beet Salad with Sour Cream, Horseradish, and Dill

For a solid decade it seemed like every last restaurant in America ran a beet salad. It was like the beet mafia made it illegal not to have one on your menu. So for a while I thought, "Hell no, I'm not serving one." But the truth is that I like beet salad. So I decided that instead of banishing it altogether, I'd make it my way. To me, beets don't bring to mind farm-to-table restaurants or Parisian brasseries. They get me thinking about the Jewish delis my brother and I used to hit up in Skokie, outside of Chicago, about borscht and horseradish and pastrami.

Preheat the oven to 350°F. Toss the beets with 2 tablespoons of the oil and 1 tablespoon of the salt in a bowl to coat well. Wrap the beets tightly in foil. Toss the bread with 1 teaspoon of the oil, then spread it out on a small baking sheet. Bake both in the oven until the croutons are crunchy all the way through, about 12 minutes, and the beets are tender, about 1 hour. Let the beets cool just to the touch in the foil, then peel with your hands. The skins should slip off. Cut the beets into irregular 1½-inch chunks.

In one bowl, stir together the sour cream, horseradish, finely chopped dill, and 1 teaspoon of the salt. In another, stir together the citrus juice, vinegar, sugar, the remaining ¼ teaspoon salt, and the remaining 2 tablespoons oil.

Toss the beets well with the citrus mixture and transfer to a large serving plate. Sprinkle on the pastrami spice, add the sour cream mixture in dollops, and sprinkle on the croutons and roughly chopped dill. Eat.

Serves
6 to 8

2½ pounds large beets (about 6)

¼ cup plus 1 teaspoon olive oil

1 tablespoon plus 1¼ teaspoons kosher salt

1 large slice rye or pumpernickel bread, cut into ½-inch cubes (about 1 cup)

1 cup sour cream

1 tablespoon finely grated fresh horseradish root

1 tablespoon finely chopped dill, plus ¼ cup very roughly chopped for garnish

2 tablespoons bottled yuzu juice, or fresh Meyer lemon or Key lime juice

2 tablespoons unseasoned rice vinegar

2 teaspoons granulated sugar

2 teaspoons Pastrami Spice (page 207)

Korean-Style Grilled Beef with Cauliflower Kimchi

The staff at San Soo Gab San in Chicago straight despised me and my boys. I have to say, though, that we earned their contempt, rolling in ten-deep after our shifts at various restaurants—loud, hungry, and smashed. You'd think they'd have gotten used to drunken fools. I mean, the place was open 24 hours and who else comes through at two in the morning?

They tolerated us, because we came with wads of cash from paydays at our jobs or from an occasional casino windfall. And we tolerated them for the real charcoal smoldering on each table and heaps of pricy-but-worth-it marinated slices of short rib. The idea at Korean BBQ spots is to grill the meat yourself, a novelty lost on guys who've just spent the last eight hours cooking lamb chops, so we had our friendly hosts do it for us. Then we'd wrap pieces of charred meat, kimchi, and *gochujang* (a sweet, spicy sauce made from fermented soybeans and chile) in lettuce leaves and knock the bundles back like shots of Patrón. This is my version, best made on a charcoal grill.

Combine the soy sauce, pineapple juice, onion, ginger, garlic, sesame oil, 1 tablespoon of the sugar, and 2 tablespoons water in a blender and blend until very smooth. Put the steak strips in a resealable bag with ¾ cup of the marinade, reserving the rest, and let them marinate in the fridge for at least 30 minutes or up to 2 hours.

Meanwhile, prepare a grill or grill pan to cook over high heat. Combine the *gochujang*, rice vinegar, and the remaining sugar in a very small saucepan, bring to a gentle simmer, and cook, stirring occasionally, until the sugar has dissolved, about 3 minutes. Scrape it into a small bowl.

Remove the steak strips from the marinade, discard the marinade, and wipe off most of the marinade with a paper towel. Thread the strips onto the skewers.

Rub a little oil on the grill grate or pan. Grill, turning over the skewers once, until the strips are deep brown and almost black in spots on each side and medium-rare inside, 2 to 4 minutes. As they grill, pour the remaining marinade in a bowl and occasionally brush it onto the strips.

Transfer the skewers to a platter and serve with the lettuce leaves, cauliflower kimchi, and cilantro alongside for wrapping, and the *gochujang* sauce for dipping.

Serves 4

SPECIAL EQUIPMENT

About 16 (8-inch) bamboo skewers, soaked in water for 30 minutes

A grill, preferably charcoal

½ cup reduced-sodium soy sauce

½ cup canned pineapple juice

½ medium Spanish onion (about ¼ pound), very roughly chopped

1 (½-ounce) knob peeled ginger (about 1½ by 1 inch)

1 medium garlic clove, peeled

1 tablespoon Asian sesame oil

3 tablespoons granulated sugar

1 (1-pound) boneless rib eye, frozen just until very firm and sliced against the grain into long, ¼-inch-thick strips

½ cup *gochujang* (Korean "hot pepper paste")

¼ cup unseasoned rice vinegar

Vegetable oil for the grill grate

15 to 20 large iceberg, romaine, green, or other lettuce leaves

Cauliflower Kimchi (page 205), drained

About 1 cup roughly chopped cilantro (thin stems and leaves)

Rib Eye Steak with Wasabi Salsa Verde

When I was served my first steak *au poivre*, I thought, "You got to be joking." I was 19, in my first year at the Culinary Institute of America, and in the school cafeteria. We ate what other students cooked, which, when all the newbies were taking Classics of French Cooking, meant some straight-from-the-textbook Escoffier shit, like cream of lettuce soup and steak *au poivre*. When that big-ass fillet hit the table, I swear I sat there waiting for someone to bring some greens and a big bowl of rice. That's how my mom would've done it. The rice was always the main event. Everything else was there to make the starch taste better. That much meat would've been enough for our whole family to share.

The only starch on the plate with my steak was in the form of three tiny *tournéed* potatoes, like a Chihuahua took a dump. This was also my first experience with medium-rare meat (Asians cook our meat hard). And the ridiculously rich sauce marked the first time I'd had cream that wasn't whipped and sprayed from a can. Still, I ate that whole steak. Then I found somewhere to lie down for a while.

It took me awhile to wrap my head around the idea of eating a meal that was all about steak. Now I can take down a whole rib eye, at least once in a while. It took me less time to get with rare meat, which is how most steaks deserve to be eaten. Only a few years ago did I convince my dad to try a steak that hadn't been, in the Filipino tradition, absolutely hammered and doused with so much soy and vinegar that it could've been goat for all he knew. This steak is the opposite: cooked to pink-centered perfection and dressed with just enough salsa verde to highlight the beefy flavor.

Whether you share it or house it is up to you.

Heat a wide heavy skillet over high heat until it's very hot. Rub a little oil on the surface. Pat the steak dry and generously season all over with salt and pepper.

Cook the steak in the skillet, flipping it once, until it's deep brown on both sides, about 8 minutes total. Reduce the heat to medium, add the butter to the skillet, and let it melt. Tip the pan so the butter pools and use a spoon to constantly baste the steak with the butter until the steak is medium rare, about 4 minutes more.

Transfer the steak to a cutting board to rest for 10 minutes, then cut along the bone to separate it from the steak. Don't even think about throwing the bone out—there will inevitably be dope meat and fat stuck to it that you'll want to gnaw at. Slice the steak against the grain into ⅓- to ½-inch-thick slices. Put the bone and steak on a big plate and drizzle on as much of the salsa verde as you want. Eat.

Serves
1 to 4

Vegetable oil

1 (1½-pound) bone-in rib eye (about 1½ inches thick), at room temperature

Kosher salt and ground black pepper

2 tablespoons unsalted butter, cut into several pieces

Wasabi Salsa Verde (page 192)

Black Pepper–Caramel Beef with Basil and Bean Sprouts

There's a whole category of savory Vietnamese dishes that rely on turning sugar into caramel, which keeps sauces from becoming too sweet. Pork often gets cooked for a while in caramel sauce, but because I'm an impatient cook, I use a budget version of the sauce to coat seared pieces of steak. Yet, even though my inspiration comes from the Far East, I can't hear "caramel" without thinking of the candies made with butter—I'm French-trained, after all—so I finish the sauce with dairy for a luxurious texture. Don't flinch at the amount of black pepper. It makes the dish.

MAKE THE SAUCE

Combine all the sauce ingredients in a medium saucepan along with ¼ cup plus 2 tablespoons water. Bring the mixture to a boil over high heat and cook, stirring occasionally, until it reduces just enough to coat the back of a spoon, 5 to 7 minutes. You'll have about 1½ cups. You need only 1 cup for this recipe; the sauce keeps in the fridge for up to 5 days and in the freezer for up to 3 months.

MAKE THE DISH

Combine the steak, egg whites, cornstarch, and salt in a bowl and toss with your hands to coat the beef well. Heat the oil in a wide cast-iron skillet over high heat until the oil begins to smoke. Add the beef in a single layer and cook without stirring until the bottom of the pieces turn golden brown, about 1 minute. Add the shallots, and cook, stirring occasionally, until the beef is cooked to medium rare, 2 to 3 minutes more. Transfer the contents of the skillet to a bowl.

Pour 1 cup of the sauce in the skillet and cook at a boil, stirring occasionally, until the sauce thickens to a syrupy texture. Dump the rib eye mixture into the sauce, add the bean sprouts, and stir until the sauce coats the beef, 30 seconds to 1 minute. Take the skillet off the heat, add the butter and basil, and stir until the butter has completely melted. Eat.

Serves
4

FOR THE SAUCE

⅓ cup granulated sugar

¼ cup Thai or Vietnamese fish sauce

¼ cup oyster sauce

¼ cup ketchup

¼ cup distilled white vinegar

2 tablespoons Worcestershire sauce

1 tablespoon ground black pepper

1½ teaspoons reduced-sodium soy sauce

1 medium garlic clove, finely chopped

FOR THE DISH

1 (1½-pound) boneless rib eye steak, very large pockets of fat trimmed, cut into 1-inch pieces

2 large egg whites

2 tablespoons cornstarch

¾ teaspoon kosher salt

¼ cup vegetable oil

1 cup thinly sliced shallots

2 cups fresh mung bean sprouts

4 tablespoons unsalted butter, cut into several pieces

1 cup loosely packed Thai basil leaves

FILIPINO
ADVISORY
EXPLICIT FLAVORS
This dish is too funky for most white people.

Short Rib Kare-Kare

Welcome to Filipino Christmas. There are screaming babies on your left, cases of Miller High Life on your right, and approximately four thousand people in the living room of whatever aunt, cousin, or sort-of cousin was willing to host that year. When I was a kid, I'd wait all year for this. It was my opportunity to eat my aunt Catalina's *kare-kare*.

Not that the other food wasn't dope, too. There was Mom's wonton soup, and her Christmas ham, lacquered with caramelized sugar and pineapple juice. Someone always brought *arroz valenciana*, a Filipino version of paella, yellow from turmeric rather than saffron and made with sticky rice, Chinese sausage, shrimp, and peas. I ate like a beast but always saved room for several servings of *kare-kare*, a classic Filipino stew rich with peanuts and funky from shrimp paste. Aunt Catalina reserved the stew for Christmastime, because it took a long time to make. She used oxtail and innards. I rock short ribs. The stew's so rich you might need some charred cabbage, eggplant, and long beans to go with it.

Preheat the oven to 350°F.

Combine the oil, annatto seeds, and turmeric in a large Dutch oven or oven-proof pot, set it over medium-high heat, and cook, stirring occasionally, until the oil is a reddish color, about 1 minute. Add the onion, ginger, garlic, and chiles and cook, stirring occasionally, until the onions are brown at the edges, about 5 minutes. Stir in the shrimp paste and sugar and cook, stirring, for about 3 minutes more. Use your hands to add the tomato, squeezing the pieces to release their juice. Cook, stirring occasionally and scraping the pot to release stuff that's stuck to it, until the tomatoes begin to fall apart, 5 to 7 minutes.

Stir in the coconut milk and vinegar, and let it come to a boil. Add the beef in a more or less even layer, tightly cover the pot, and cook in the oven until the beef is very tender but not falling apart (more like pot roast than pulled pork), about 3 hours.

Use a slotted spoon to transfer the beef to a plate and strain the liquid into a large bowl, discarding the solids. Return the liquid to the pot, set it over very low heat, whisk in the peanut butter until it's fully combined, and return the beef to the liquid. Season with salt (or even better, more shrimp paste) to taste, turn the heat to medium, bring the liquid to a simmer, stir well, then turn off the heat.

You can eat it right away—topped with the garlic-chile vinegar, cilantro stems, and toasted coconut flakes—but it's even better a few days after you cook it. Let the beef cool in the liquid, cover, and store it in the fridge. Gently reheat it when you're ready to eat.

Serves 8

3 tablespoons vegetable oil

1 teaspoon annatto seeds (aka achiote seeds; available at Latin markets)

½ teaspoon turmeric powder

1 medium Spanish onion (½ pound), very roughly chopped

1 (2-ounce) knob peeled ginger (about 4 by 1½ inches), roughly chopped

2 medium garlic cloves, smashed and peeled

2 fresh red Thai chiles, halved lengthwise (including seeds)

⅓ to ½ cup Shrimp Paste Soffrito (page 194), or well-stirred Barrio Fiesta brand spicy *ginisang bagoong*

2 tablespoons granulated sugar

1 medium tomato (about ½ pound), very roughly chopped

4 cups well-shaken coconut milk

¼ cup distilled white vinegar

5 pounds boneless beef short ribs (excess fat trimmed) or chuck roast, cut into approximately 3-inch pieces

5 tablespoons smooth peanut butter

Kosher salt

FOR SERVING

Garlic-Chile Vinegar (page 186)

Thinly sliced cilantro stems

Unsweetened coconut flakes, toasted

American Chinese Food

Whenever we went out to eat as a family—typically for someone's birthday—we went out for Chinese food. Specifically, we went to China Chef in Morton Grove. It had all the furnishings of a Chinese restaurant, including decor that practically screamed, "You are about to eat Chinese food!" There was the Oriental font on the sign, the Zodiac-themed place-mats, and a big fish tank with a few sad-looking fish that my nephew, a kid at the time but now 17, would track with his finger against the glass.

To the untrained eye, we must have looked like just another Asian family eating at an Asian restaurant. But to a kid who grew up almost exclusively on adobo, *sinigang*, and other Filipino dishes, the food at China Chef was as new and exciting as burritos and burgers.

With our mounds of white rice, we always got shrimp in black bean sauce and Mongolian beef, crispy strips of meat coated in sticky-sweet brown sauce served on a bed of deep-fried mung bean noodles. Mom would always order a vegetable, like steamed Chinese broccoli, that only she and Dad ate. If it was my birthday or my brother's, we got sweet and sour snapper, a whole deep-fried fish coated in cornstarch-rich electric-red sauce. Otherwise, Mom ordered steamed fish with ginger and soy sauce and my brother and I got sweet and sour pork. Notice that sweet and sour sauce had to be involved somehow; otherwise, we weren't really eating Chinese food.

Of course, we still weren't really eating Chinese food—or at least very little on our table would have been recognizable to people living in China, the massive country with more regional cuisines than Italy and France combined. Instead, we were eating a sort of caricature of Chinese food. Each dish—from chow mein to egg foo yung to General Tso's chicken—took root somewhere in China before it was distorted like words in an international game of telephone. When you eat kung pao chicken at a place like China Chef, you're eating what Chinese people think *you* think kung pao chicken is.

The reason is money. Give people food that appeals to their palates and they will pay. American Chinese food began by some shrewd immigrant cooks looking for a way to support their families, not for a way to showcase their culture. But decades later, the food they came up with has become a culture and cuisine of its own, and something that fools like me crave. Sometimes, I don't want Sichuan double-cooked pork or Cantonese winter melon soup, but egg rolls with duck sauce and moo shu pork. Same goes for other American creations. Sometimes you don't want one of those individual pizzas with perfect tomato sauce and a few blobs of mozzarella, but a slice that's as big as your head with enough cheese to kill a man. A few good shakes of dried oregano and chile flakes and you're good.

Orange Beef

In American-Chinese, as in any other cuisine, you see the good and the bad. Take orange beef, one of the greatest dishes that's ever headlined an $8.95 lunch special. I've never had the Sichuan original. But I know for damn sure that it doesn't rock gloppy, supersweet sauce or meat that's more batter than beef. Yet this exact version exists from Seattle to Sarasota with an appearance so similar that it looks like it was assembled on a factory conveyor belt. Making the dish at home is often easier than scouting out the increasingly rare rendition that features tender beef and a sauce that balances the proper heavy dose of sugar with acidity and a little bitterness from citrus peel. My major contribution to the genre is to use a more flavorful cut of beef (rib eye, because I ball that hard). Sometimes I rock charred orange wedges (slick them with oil and give them a few minutes in a hot skillet). What I will never change is the highly traditional plain steamed broccoli that is always served on the side.

MAKE THE SAUCE
Combine all the sauce ingredients in a medium skillet, bring the mixture to a boil over high heat, and cook, stirring occasionally, until it reduces by about half (to about 1½ cups) and it's just barely thick enough to coat the back of a metal spoon, about 10 minutes. Reserve ½ cup for the dish. The rest will keep in the fridge for up to 5 days or in the freezer for up to 3 months.

MAKE THE DISH
Combine the steak, egg white, cornstarch, and salt in a bowl and toss with your hands to coat the beef well. Heat the oil in a wide cast-iron skillet over high heat until the oil begins to smoke. Add the beef in one layer and cook without stirring until the bottoms of the pieces turn golden brown, about 1 minute. Flip the beef, add the red onion, scallion pieces, and dried chiles and cook, stirring occasionally, until the beef is cooked to medium rare, about 2 minutes more. Transfer the contents of the skillet to a plate.

Pour ½ cup of the orange sauce into the skillet, let it boil, and cook, stirring occasionally, just until the sauce thickens to a syrupy texture. Dump the rib eye mixture into the sauce and stir until the sauce coats the beef, 15 to 30 seconds. Take the skillet off the heat, stir in the orange zest and scallion greens, and transfer the dish to a plate with the broccoli. Eat.

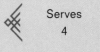
Serves
4

FOR THE SAUCE

1½ cups orange juice

½ cup unseasoned rice vinegar

½ cup granulated sugar

¼ cup reduced-sodium soy sauce

¼ cup Worcestershire sauce

2 tablespoons Thai or Vietnamese fish sauce

1½ teaspoons finely chopped fresh ginger

1½ teaspoons finely chopped garlic

1 fresh red Thai chile, thinly sliced (including seeds)

FOR THE DISH

1 (1-pound) boneless rib eye steak, very large pockets of fat trimmed, cut into 1-inch pieces

1 large egg white

1 tablespoon plus 1 teaspoon cornstarch

½ teaspoon kosher salt

¼ cup vegetable oil

½ cup sliced (about ½ inch thick) red onion

3 scallions, dark greens thinly sliced, the rest cut into 1½-inch pieces

2 Asian dried red chiles

1 tablespoon finely grated orange zest

2 cups steamed broccoli florets, preferably from your local Chinese restaurant (ask them to keep them crunchy)

Fish with Black-Bean Brown Butter

Bet you never thought brown butter could get better. Then one day, it did. Back in the day at Buddakan, we served a dope sauce made from a paste of fermented black beans thinned out with just a little stock. At Talde, I wanted to flaunt the flavor without freaking people out with its intensely salty funk. Then it hit me—I'd bribe them. With butter. I thought of the many fish I'd cooked à la meunière and decided to sneak in those black beans. Instead of headlining the dish, they lay in the cut, boosting the umami in the brown butter and clinging to the surface of the fish as you baste to give it a striking dark color.

Typically, delicate white-fleshed fish fillets rock this butter at Talde, but any briny, slightly sweet sea creature could, too—like lobster, crab, scallops, and even peel-and-eat shrimp.

Toss the edamame, orange zest, and cilantro together in a small bowl and set aside.

Season the fish fillets with salt. Put the potato starch on a plate. One by one, add the fillets and turn to coat them all over in a very thin layer, shaking to remove any excess.

Heat the vegetable oil in a wide, well-seasoned skillet over medium-high heat. If the fillets won't all fit without crowding, cook them in two batches. When the oil smokes lightly, add the fillets and cook until the first side is lightly browned, about 2 minutes. Carefully flip the fillets, add the butter to the skillet, and let it melt and bubble. Reduce the heat to medium. Use one hand to tilt the pan so the butter pools at one side and the other hand to spoon the butter mixture (and especially the dark solids) over the fillets. Occasionally un-tilt the skillet and let it rest on the heat for 10 seconds or so. Cook until the fillets are just cooked through and the tops have taken on a blackish color, about 4 minutes.

Take the skillet off the heat and pour on about 2 tablespoons of the lime juice. Use a slotted spatula to transfer the fish to a plate, leaving the butter behind. Spoon some of the dark solids in the skillet onto the fish, pour most of the butter into a bowl to use for another purpose, and return the fish to the pan. Add the remaining lime juice to the edamame mixture, toss well, and use it to top each fillet. Eat.

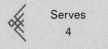

Serves
4

½ cup frozen shelled edamame, boiled in salted water until tender, about 5 minutes, then drained

1 tablespoon very thin strips orange zest

½ cup loosely packed roughly chopped cilantro (thin stems and leaves)

4 (6-ounce) skinless halibut, cod, or hake fillets (about ¾ inch thick)

Kosher salt

¼ cup potato starch or cornstarch

3 tablespoons vegetable oil

¾ cup Chinese Black-Bean Brown Butter (page 198)

3 tablespoons fresh lime juice

Salt and Pepper Porgies with
XO Tartar Sauce and Soy-Citrus Vinegar

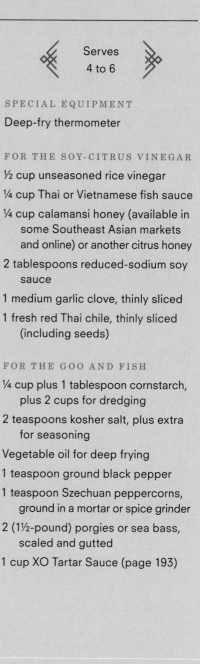

Serves
4 to 6

SPECIAL EQUIPMENT
Deep-fry thermometer

FOR THE SOY-CITRUS VINEGAR
½ cup unseasoned rice vinegar

¼ cup Thai or Vietnamese fish sauce

¼ cup calamansi honey (available in some Southeast Asian markets and online) or another citrus honey

2 tablespoons reduced-sodium soy sauce

1 medium garlic clove, thinly sliced

1 fresh red Thai chile, thinly sliced (including seeds)

FOR THE GOO AND FISH
¼ cup plus 1 tablespoon cornstarch, plus 2 cups for dredging

2 teaspoons kosher salt, plus extra for seasoning

Vegetable oil for deep frying

1 teaspoon ground black pepper

1 teaspoon Szechuan peppercorns, ground in a mortar or spice grinder

2 (1½-pound) porgies or sea bass, scaled and gutted

1 cup XO Tartar Sauce (page 193)

"Salt and pepper" is a masterpiece of the Chinese-menu-translation undersell. It's right up there with "red-cooking pork" and "orange beef." Because how are you supposed to know when you order salt and pepper shrimp that you're not just getting some plain-ass crustaceans, but shrimp encased in the thinnest, crispiest batter of all time?

I take the idea and run with it, battering and deep-frying whole fish (and I promise it's not as scary to do at home as it may sound) and serving it with tartar sauce and vinegar sauce—classic fish-and-chips condiments—done Chinese style. The bizarre batter is what makes the dish: Cornstarch and water combine to produce a magical goo, or if you want to get all food science-y, a hydrocolloid gel. Yet all you need to know is that the stuff fries to an impossibly light, lacy, translucent crust. R.I.P. Paul Wildermuth, who shared his batter with me when I worked with him at Opera in Chicago. He was a true cook, who died one night on the line.

MAKE THE SOY-CITRUS VINEGAR

Combine the vinegar, fish sauce, honey, soy sauce, garlic, and chile in a small bowl and stir well. Let the mixture sit for at least 1 hour at room temperature or for up to 3 days in the fridge (the longer the better).

MAKE THE GOO

Combine ¼ cup plus 1 tablespoon of the cornstarch and 1 teaspoon of the salt with 4 cups water in a medium pot and set it over high heat. Cook, frequently stirring and scraping the pan, just until it boils and melds into a thick, opaque goo. Transfer the goo to a large mixing bowl and let it cool, stirring occasionally to keep it smooth.

FRY THE FISH

Dump the remaining 2 cups cornstarch into a shallow baking dish. Pour enough oil into a wide pot or Dutch oven to reach a depth of about 3 inches. Set the pot over high heat and bring the oil to 375°F (use a deep-fry thermometer). Meanwhile, combine the remaining 1 teaspoon salt with the pepper and ground Szechuan peppercorns in a small bowl and mix well.

Arrange a rack over a baking sheet, put it near the pot, and preheat the oven to 200°F. Fry one fish at a time: Season one fish on both sides with salt, then add it to the goo and slather the goo thickly on both sides of the fish, making sure not to get any on the flesh at the belly. Add the fish to the bowl with the cornstarch and pat the cornstarch on the fish to form a thick layer on both sides and from head to tail.

Add the fish to the oil and fry, using tongs to carefully turn the fish over halfway through, until it's golden brown and crispy, 12 to 15 minutes. Transfer the fish to the rack and immediately season both sides with ¼ teaspoon or so of the Szechuan pepper mixture. Transfer the fish to the oven to keep warm while you batter and fry the second fish.

Serve the fish with the vinegar and tartar sauce in small bowls for dipping.

Singapore Chile Lobster

Serves
4

FOR THE CHILE SAUCE

½ cup vegetable oil

2 cups diced (¼ inch) shallots

3 large lemongrass stalks (bottom
1 inch, top 8 inches, and outer
2 layers removed), very finely
chopped (about ¼ cup)

2 tablespoons medium dried shrimp,
roughly chopped

1 tablespoon finely chopped fresh
ginger

1 tablespoon finely chopped garlic

4 fresh red Thai chiles, thinly sliced
(including seeds)

½ cup unseasoned rice vinegar

½ cup oyster sauce

½ cup ketchup

2 tablespoons Shrimp Paste Soffrito
(page 194) or well-stirred Barrio
Fiesta brand spicy *ginisang
bagoong*

FOR THE DISH

3 (1- to 1¼-pound) steamed lobsters

½ cup cornstarch

¼ cup plus 2 tablespoons
vegetable oil

3 large eggs, beaten

¾ cup loosely packed very roughly
chopped cilantro (thin stems
and leaves)

¾ cup loosely packed Thai basil
leaves

Lime wedges

The best version of this dish I've had was at a restaurant in Penang,
Malaysia, one of those places with more fish tanks than an aquarium.
I'd always wanted to go to an aquarium where everything on display
was yours to eat, and I ate an ocean's worth of sea creatures that night.
My favorite was transformed into so-called Singapore chile crab—
Singapore and Malaysia both lay claim to the dish, but Singapore
seems to be winning the branding war—a whole crustacean coated
in jammy tomato sauce fragrant with garlic, ginger, lemongrass, and
shrimp paste.

The sauce is the main event. The seafood is just the vehicle. But at Talde, I figured out that lobster stands up even better to the sauce and offers diners a better meat-to-effort ratio. At home, you can use crab, shrimp, even clams and mussels (just cook them in the sauce), and you'll be thrilled by the result. The classic side is soft white bread for sopping up the sauce. But believe me, no one will complain if you use shrimp toast (page 50) instead.

MAKE THE CHILE SAUCE

Combine the oil and shallots in a medium pot, set it over medium-high heat, and cook, stirring occasionally, until the shallots are translucent, about 3 minutes. Add the lemongrass, dried shrimp, ginger, garlic, and chiles and cook, stirring occasionally, until the mixture is very aromatic, about 3 minutes. Stir in the vinegar, oyster sauce, ketchup, shrimp paste soffrito, and 1 cup water. Let it come to a steady simmer and cook, stirring occasionally, until it has just slightly thickened and the flavors have had a chance to meld, about 5 minutes. The sauce keeps covered in the fridge for up to 5 days.

FINISH THE DISH

Twist off the claws and the tail from each lobster. Separate the claws from the knuckles (the chubby part at the base of the claw). Cut the tails in half lengthwise. Use the back of a heavy knife to crack the claws slightly. Use kitchen scissors to snip open the knuckles to reveal the flesh. Reserve the heads and bodies for making stock.

Put the cornstarch in a large bowl, add the lobster parts, and toss well. You want only a very thin coating of cornstarch, so gently knock the parts against the bowl to remove any excess.

Heat a large wok (the high walls of the wok help you toss without things getting messy) or wide heavy skillet over very high heat, add the oil, and let it smoke lightly. Add the lobster pieces and stir well, then cook, stirring once or twice, until the lobster is warmed through, about 3 minutes.

Add all of the chile sauce and cook, stirring the lobster occasionally, until the sauce has thickened slightly and coats the lobster pieces, about 3 minutes. Drizzle the beaten egg into the sauce in a spiral motion. Leave it alone just until it begins to set, about 1 minute, then stir and toss well until it's just cooked, about 15 seconds. Turn off the heat. Add the cilantro and basil, toss until it wilts slightly, and serve on a platter with lime wedges. Eat.

Vietnamese Fish Tacos with Tomato Jam and Herbs

Serves
6 to 8

Want to know how to get a Park Slope family to dig into head-on whole fish? Turn it into fish tacos. It's been amazing to see this dish, which, with its banana leaf wrapper and heap of herbs, looks like something you'd see at an old-school riverside restaurant in Vietnam, become a Brooklyn favorite. It's fun to watch faces go from confused ("How do you eat this?") to excited ("Oh, you make tacos!"). At Talde, we use deboned whole fish, but at home, stacked fillets do nicely.

If you don't mind a little smoke (or as I think of it, excitement), cook the fish as instructed until it's almost done, then turn on the broiler and finish the fish nice and close to the heat source. The tomato jam should get a little charred. The banana leaf might light on fire. That's how we get down at the restaurant.

2 large pieces banana leaf (about 14 by 10 inches each)

2 cups Asian Tomato Jam (page 191)

8 (6-ounce) skin-on branzino, sea bass, or red snapper fillets

About 2 teaspoons vegetable oil

About 18 small flour tortillas

⅔ cup loosely packed Thai basil leaves

⅔ cup loosely packed cilantro leaves

⅔ cup loosely packed roughly chopped dill

2 limes, cut into wedges

Flaky sea or kosher salt

Preheat the oven to 425°F.

Lay one of the banana leaves shiny side down, positioning it so that one of the long edges faces you. Spread ⅓ cup of the tomato jam diagonally on the leaf to form a layer about the width of 2 fillets sitting side by side. Stack two pairs of the fillets to approximate a whole fish (two skin side down on the bottom, two skin side up on top) on the layer of jam, slathering ⅓ cup of the tomato jam between the fillets and another ⅓ cup of the jam on top of the stack.

Fold the two empty corners of the banana leaf over the fish so that they meet in the middle, leaving an inch or two of space between the leaf and the top layer of tomato jam. Use a toothpick or two to fasten the corners together. Repeat the process with the remaining banana leaf, jam, and fish. Drizzle the top of the banana leaf packages with the vegetable oil.

Set the banana leaf packages toothpick sides up on a baking sheet. Bake just until the fish is cooked through, 15 to 20 minutes. To make sure it's done, insert a butter knife into the thickest part of a fillet. Carefully press the knife to your lip. If it's just hotter than is comfortable, it's done.

Meanwhile, briefly heat a few tortillas in a hot dry pan on both sides until they just begin to puff up, then transfer them to a large kitchen towel–lined bowl and cover with a plate to keep them warm while you heat the rest.

When the fish is ready, combine the herbs in a bowl, dress them with a generous squeeze of lime and a sprinkle of salt, and toss gently but well. Open the banana leaves, pile the herbs on the fish, and serve with the tortillas and lime wedges.

Miso-Marinated Salmon, Reuben Style

When you like the Reuben as much as I do, the principles of the sandwich can creep into everything you do. Miso-marinated salmon, for instance, has nothing to do with a Reuben. But suddenly you find yourself sneaking in pastrami spices—even Russ & Daughters, the Lower East Side's ancient Jewish appetizing store, gets down with pastrami-fied smoked salmon—and thinking up ways to incorporate rye, sauerkraut, and Russian dressing. Next thing you know you're in the kitchen at 2 a.m. taking down a mutant Reuben, with that salmon and an inevitable fusion of the classic toppings: kimchi Thousand Island dressing.

MARINATE AND BROIL THE SALMON

Combine the pastrami spice, miso, and sugar in a medium mixing bowl along with 2 tablespoons water and stir well. Add the salmon fillets and toss to coat them well, then cover with plastic wrap and marinate for at least 4 hours or up to 2 days.

Turn on the broiler and position the oven rack about 2 inches from the heat source. Put the salmon on a lightly oiled foil-lined baking sheet. Broil until the fish is dark brown in spots and just cooked through, about 6 minutes. Leave the broiler on.

MAKE THE DRESSING

Combine the kimchi, eggs, mayo, and ketchup in a mixing bowl and stir well. You might need to add salt to taste, depending on the saltiness of the kimchi.

MAKE THE SANDWICHES

Spread the butter on both sides of the bread and toast, flipping once, under the broiler until light golden brown, 2 to 3 minutes.

Put a slice of bread on each of 4 plates. Spread about ¼ cup of the kimchi dressing on each and top with a fillet of salmon. Drizzle on the remaining dressing and sprinkle on the dill. Top with the remaining bread. Eat.

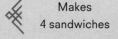 Makes
4 sandwiches

FOR THE SALMON

2 tablespoons Pastrami Spice (page 207)

2 tablespoons *shiro miso* (aka white miso)

1 tablespoon granulated sugar

4 (4-ounce) skinless salmon fillets, preferably center cut

About 1 teaspoon vegetable oil

FOR THE KIMCHI DRESSING

1½ cups drained store-bought cabbage kimchi, thinly sliced

2 hard-boiled eggs, roughly chopped

¼ cup plus 2 tablespoons mayo

2 rounded tablespoons ketchup

Kosher salt to taste

FOR THE SANDWICHES

3 tablespoons room-temperature unsalted butter

8 slices rye or pumpernickel bread

Generous ¼ cup roughly chopped dill

Maple-Glazed Squid with Cabbage, Chinese Sausage, and Pickled Cranberries

At Talde, I make this dish with octopus, cooked low and slow until it's super-tender then griddled to order. But at home, I recommend looking to another springy-chewy sea creature. Squid is often sustainable, typically cheap, and cooks in about the same time it takes to open your computer and Google the plural of "octopus." Glazed to add sweetness and umami, the squid chills out on the plate with charred cabbage, Chinese sausage, and pickled cranberries.

Heat ½ tablespoon of the oil in a large pan over medium heat until it shimmers. Add the sausage in a single layer and cook, flipping once and being especially careful that the sausage doesn't burn, until it's golden brown and crispy, about 5 minutes.

Prepare a grill to cook over high heat.

Combine the soy sauce, maple syrup, and sherry vinegar in a small pan, bring to a boil over high heat, and cook until it thickens slightly, about 3 minutes. Combine in a blender with the butter (or over low heat, whisk in a piece of butter at a time), blend until smooth, and reserve.

Combine the squid and ⅓ cup of the soy sauce mixture in a bowl and toss well. Let the squid marinate at room temperature for about 15 minutes.

Meanwhile, quarter the cabbage lengthwise, keeping the root intact, drizzle the quarters with the remaining 1 tablespoon of the vegetable oil, and lightly season with salt. Grill the cabbage, turning occasionally, until it's charred at the edges and wilted but still slightly crunchy, 6 to 8 minutes. Cut off and discard the tough root end, chop the cabbage into about 1-inch pieces, and spread them on a platter.

Transfer the squid to the grill, reserving the marinade. Season lightly with salt and cook, flipping once, until the squid is charred and just cooked through, 2 to 3 minutes. Brush on some of the marinade twice, stopping a minute or so before the squid is done. Transfer the squid to a cutting board and cut into bite-size pieces.

Drizzle the cranberry pickling liquid evenly over the cabbage and season with salt. Scatter on the squid, sausage, pickled cranberries, and mint leaves. Drizzle on the remaining soy sauce mixture. Eat.

Serves 6 to 8

SPECIAL EQUIPMENT

A grill, preferably charcoal

1½ tablespoons vegetable oil, plus extra for oiling the grill

1 fresh or defrosted frozen cured Chinese sausage (aka *lap chuong*), cut into ⅛-inch-thick slices

¼ cup reduced-sodium soy sauce

¼ cup maple syrup

2 tablespoons sherry vinegar

4 tablespoons cold unsalted butter, cut into several pieces

1½ pounds squid (bodies and legs), cleaned, rinsed, and dried very well inside and out

1 large head Napa cabbage, outermost leaves removed

Kosher salt

About 24 Spicy Pickled Cranberries (page 205), plus ½ cup of the pickling liquid

1 cup loosely packed mint leaves

Vegetables and Salads

Vietnamese Halal Cart–Style Lamb Pitas

My version of the halal cart lamb sandwich delivers the pleasures of the real thing via an Asian detour. Easy pickled cabbage, white and red sauce, and pitas are all pretty much in line with the original. But then I go and rub tender lamb with spices that conjure Vietnamese pho and add an eggplant relish that exists halfway between the Mediterranean and Asia.

PICKLE THE CABBAGE

Combine the vinegar and sugar in a medium mixing bowl and stir to dissolve the sugar. Add the cabbage and press to more or less submerge it in the liquid, then cover and keep in the fridge for at least 4 hours or up to 1 day. Drain before using.

COOK THE LAMB

Preheat the oven to 400°F. Combine the sugar, salt, and all the spices in a small bowl and stir well. Put the lamb on a plate, drizzle on 1½ tablespoons of the fish sauce, and rub to coat the lamb well. Evenly sprinkle the spice mixture on all sides of the lamb, patting it to help the spices adhere.

Heat the oil in a heavy ovenproof skillet over medium-high heat until it shimmers. Sear the lamb on all sides until dark brown, about 5 minutes. Put the skillet in the oven and roast until the lamb is rare to medium rare, 8 to 10 minutes. Let the meat rest on a cutting board for 10 minutes, then thinly slice it against the grain and drizzle on the remaining fish sauce.

MAKE THE PITAS

Wrap the pitas in foil and warm in the oven for 3 to 5 minutes. Let everyone pile the cabbage, eggplant relish, lamb, white sauce, and hot sauce on their pita, fold it like a taco, and eat.

 Makes 4 pitas

FOR THE PICKLED CABBAGE

1 cup unseasoned rice vinegar

2 tablespoons granulated sugar

2 cups thinly sliced red cabbage

FOR THE LAMB

1 teaspoon granulated sugar

½ teaspoon kosher salt

½ teaspoon onion powder

½ teaspoon garlic powder

½ teaspoon ground black pepper

½ teaspoon ginger powder

½ teaspoon fennel seeds, roughly chopped then coarsely crushed with flat of knife

Healthy pinch ground cinnamon

Healthy pinch ground clove

1 (1½-pound) piece of tender, boneless lamb, about 1 inch thick, such as leg steaks, lamb loin, lamb sirloin, or butterflied leg

2 tablespoons Thai or Vietnamese fish sauce

1 tablespoon vegetable oil

FOR THE PITAS

4 (8-inch) pocketless pitas

Eggplant Relish (page 161), at room temperature

Halal Cart–Style White Sauce (page 190)

Dale's "Homemade" Hot Sauce (page 187)

Heirloom Tomato Salad with Tamarind Vinaigrette and Pickled Berries

I don't think I've ever ordered an heirloom tomato salad at a restaurant, even though as soon as summer hits, every last farm-to-table spot starts charging $15-plus for a plate of tomatoes, a splash of vinegar, and some olive oil. Don't get me wrong, I love the result as much as anyone. I just don't need to splurge on what even my nephew could make at home.

Yet, for all my tough talk, guess who serves a tomato salad as soon as heirlooms come in? In the restaurant business, customers rule and they want their heirlooms. I figure if I'm going to make the dish, I might as well trick it out so you don't get the typical salad, though not so much that I break rule number one of top-notch produce: Let it shine. Tamarind vinaigrette, toasted pistachios, and pickled berries add some unexpected flavors and textures, but all in the service of highlighting those awesome tomatoes.

Combine the vinegar and sugar along with 2 tablespoons water in a small container and stir until the sugar dissolves. Add the berries so they're more or less submerged in the liquid, cover, and pickle in the fridge for at least 2 hours or up to 2 days.

Preheat a toaster oven to 350°F. Spread out the pistachios on a toaster oven tray and cook, shaking occasionally, until they're very aromatic, about 3 minutes. Roughly chop them.

Arrange the tomatoes on a plate and sprinkle on the pistachios and the herbs. Add the berries (reserving the pickling liquid for another purpose), sprinkle on the salt, and drizzle on the dressing. Eat.

Serves 4

¼ cup plus 2 tablespoons unseasoned rice vinegar

2 teaspoons granulated sugar

½ cup mixed blueberries, quartered strawberries, and gooseberries

2 tablespoons unsalted roasted pistachios

1½ pounds mixed heirloom tomatoes, cored and cut into bite-size wedges or slices

1 pint cherry tomatoes

¼ cup loosely packed basil leaves, torn at the last minute

¼ cup loosely packed mint leaves, torn at the last minute

Flaky sea salt to taste

¼ cup Tamarind Vinaigrette (page 201), or more to taste

Lola

We called her *Lola*, or "Grandmother" in Ilonggo, the language of my parents' home region. Saying *Lola* was way easier than saying her full name, Cresenciana Tibajares. Lola was my grandma and she was married to my grandpa, Felicisimo Villianosa. When it comes to names, Filipinos of their generation didn't mess around.

After my grandfather passed, Lola moved from the Philippines to Chicago to live with my aunt, and she took care of us when my parents weren't around. She scared me a little. I don't know if I ever saw her smile. She spoke no English, but for some reason developed a profound affection for the Cubs. Mainly, she'd sit around in her Coke-bottle glasses, watching them play on TV, rolling cigars out of tobacco leaves that she smuggled from the Philippines and cured herself, and eating weird shit like Pepsi poured over rice (yep, for real). When she passed away about 20 years back, my parents found 5Gs in cash on her person—some inside her wallet, some inside a shoe and her bra. No idea why.

No one else in my family got down with Pepsi rice, but my parents and I, if not my brother and sister, were all over her other favorite snack: slices of green mango dipped into *ginisang bagoong*, a spicy, salty, rank-ass mixture of vinegar, chile, and fermented shrimp paste. She'd sit there and burn through a pile of the tart, crisp fruit and half a cup of shrimp paste. Half a cup might not sound like a lot, but I never went through more than a few tablespoons. This combination of unripe fruit and seafood, of sourness and saltiness and funk, is as Filipino as anything else I can think of. I liked it, because Lola liked it and because I thought it tasted good, though I'm pretty sure the first reason came before the second.

It's funny to me that I could get down with something like this and at the same time pine after Big Macs and burritos. It shows that old preferences can co-exist with new ones—after all, Lola liked both her green mango snack and her soda-on-rice atrocity. I reflect on this sometimes when I think about the mutt cuisine I cook.

FILIPINO
ADVISORY
EXPLICIT FLAVORS

This dish is too funky for most white people.

Spicy Green Mango Salad

This salad is my ode to my *lola*. Even though I go relatively light on the shrimp paste, add lime juice to cut that funk, and hit the salad with coconut flakes and fried shallots to add a little sweetness, the dish brings that punch-to-the-dome flavor and heat. I love this salad. You know who doesn't, though? Customers at Talde. No dish in the history of the restaurant gets sent back to the kitchen more often. Normally, that's a sign that I need to check myself. In this case, I take it as a sign I did things right.

Preheat the oven to 350°F. Spread the coconut in one layer on a small baking sheet or toaster oven tray and bake, shaking and tossing frequently, until the coconut is crunchy and golden, about 3 minutes. Set aside to cool.

Mix the shrimp paste, lime, chile, and salt in a large bowl. Add the mango and toss (ideally with gloved hands) until it's well coated in the mixture. Season to taste with additional salt and lime juice, then sprinkle on the coconut and fried shallots. Eat.

Serves
4 to 6

3 tablespoons unsweetened coconut flakes

3 tablespoons Shrimp Paste Soffrito (page 194) or well-stirred Barrio Fiesta brand spicy *ginisang bagoong*

2 tablespoons fresh lime juice, or more to taste

1 teaspoon thinly sliced fresh red Thai chile (including seeds)

¼ teaspoon kosher salt

4 cups batons (approximately 3 by ¼ inch) of peeled green mango or tart green apple (see Green Mango, below)

3 tablespoons store-bought Thai or Vietnamese fried shallots or French's French Fried Onions

Green Mango

Green mango isn't just any old unripe mango, but a variety meant to be eaten when it's still crunchy and tart. You'll find it at many Asian markets, especially those with a Southeast or South Asian focus. If you can't find it, go ahead and sub green apple, which has a different texture and some sweetness, but still hits the spot.

#369 Brussels Sprouts with Green Sambal

This blows the standard sprouts with garlic and bacon out of the water. I'm not hating, just saying. Roasting the sprouts at a high heat brings out their sweetness and crunch, and green sambal acts like Southeast Asian pesto, coating each one with its smack-you-in-the-face herbaceousness. I call it #369 to honor Talde's address at 369 7th Avenue as well as the brilliant tradition of ordering from Chinese menus by number.

Preheat the oven to 450°F. Put the Brussels sprouts on a baking sheet that fits them in a single layer. Drizzle on the oil, sprinkle on the salt, and toss well. Spread them out and roast, stirring once, until they're tender and deep brown and crispy in spots, about 25 minutes.

Transfer the sprouts to a bowl or platter, add the sambal, and stir to coat them well. Add the lime juice and more salt and sambal to taste, stir again, and eat.

Serves
4 to 6

1½ pounds Brussels sprouts, trimmed and halved lengthwise (about 8 cups)

¼ cup plus 2 tablespoons vegetable oil

1½ teaspoons kosher salt

¼ cup plus 2 tablespoons Green Sambal (page 195), or more to taste

About 1 tablespoon fresh lime juice

Caesar [see-zer]; VERB
To coat in creamy dressing; to make less healthy: *Tonight we'll toss the Brussels sprouts with green sambal, but tomorrow let's Caesar them.*

Butternut Squash Samosas

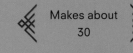

Makes about
30

SPECIAL EQUIPMENT

Deep-fry thermometer

Parchment paper

FOR THE KAFFIR LIME YOGURT

1 cup 2% Greek yogurt

2 fresh or frozen (not dried) kaffir
lime leaves, thick stems removed,
very finely minced

1 teaspoon kosher salt

FOR THE FILLING

1 pound peeled, seeded butternut
squash, cut into approximately
1-inch pieces

½ cup vegetable oil

2½ teaspoons kosher salt

1 tablespoon garam masala

2 large shallots, finely chopped

1 generous tablespoon finely
chopped fresh ginger

1 medium garlic clove, finely chopped

1 fresh red Thai chile, thinly sliced
(including seeds)

¼ pound fresh shiitake mushroom
caps, cut into ¼-inch pieces

½ cup chopped (½ inch) tomato

1 generous tablespoon roughly
chopped cilantro (thin stems and
leaves)

1 teaspoon finely grated orange zest

Continued, opposite

Nobody does vegetarian food like Indian cooks do. And nobody does filled dough like them either. The two categories collide in the samosa, a golden pyramid of pie crust filled with all kinds of good stuff, most commonly potato. I make a crunchy version with wonton wrappers and fill them with butternut squash amped up with spices and aromatics. As with any samosa, half the fun is dipping it into sauces. In this case that's tangy tamarind-apple chutney and yogurt infused with the wild flavor of kaffir lime leaf. If you want, you can skip the wrapping and frying and still have dope curried butternut squash to eat over basmati rice, though if you do, scale back a little on the salt.

MAKE THE KAFFIR LIME YOGURT

Combine the yogurt, kaffir lime leaves, and salt, stir really well, and season to taste with additional salt. Keep covered in the fridge overnight to let the kaffir lime leaf flavor infuse the yogurt. The yogurt keeps in the fridge for up to 1 week. Serve it cold.

MAKE THE FILLING

Preheat the oven to 400°F. Combine the squash, 3 tablespoons of the oil, and 1 teaspoon of the salt in a baking dish large enough to hold the squash in more or less one layer. Roast, stirring once, until the squash is brown at the edges and very soft, 30 to 40 minutes. Drain off any excess oil.

Meanwhile, heat the remaining oil in a medium pan over medium-high heat. Add the garam masala and cook, stirring occasionally, until very fragrant, about 1 minute. Add the shallots, ginger, garlic, and chile and cook, stirring occasionally, until the shallots are translucent, about 2 minutes. Add the shiitakes and tomatoes and cook, stirring occasionally, just until the tomato liquid evaporates, then stir in the remaining 1½ teaspoons salt. Keep cooking, scraping the pan frequently, until the shiitakes are fully cooked, the tomato is very soft, and the spices are dark brown but not burned, about 5 minutes. Remove the pan from the heat, add the squash, and stir and smash until you have a fairly chunky mush. Stir in the cilantro and orange zest.

FORM, FRY, AND SERVE THE SAMOSAS

Form the samosas one at a time, keeping the yet-to-be-used wonton wrappers under a damp towel. Line a baking sheet with parchment paper. Fill a small bowl with water. Put one wrapper on your work surface, wet the edges with your fingers, then put another wrapper on top so they're aligned. Wet the edges of the top wrapper and add a tablespoon of filling to the center. Fold one corner onto another to form a triangle and press the edges very firmly to seal the samosa. Transfer to the prepared baking sheet and continue making samosas with the remaining wrappers and filling. You can keep them covered in the fridge for up to 2 days.

Pour enough oil into a large pot to reach a depth of about 3 inches. Set the pot over high heat and bring the oil to 350°F (use a deep-fry thermometer). Fry the samosas in two or three batches, turning them over once, until they're golden brown and crispy, 2 to 3 minutes. Transfer them to paper towels and tent loosely with foil as they're done, and let the oil return to 350°F before adding the next batch.

Serve with bowls of the chutney and yogurt, and eat.

FOR THE SAMOSAS

60 wonton wrappers (square), preferably "Hong Kong style"

Vegetable oil for deep frying

Apple-Tamarind Chutney (page 191)

Eggplant Relish with Olives, Pistachios, and Fish Sauce

When you taste the olives and pistachios, you're like, "Aha, it's Mediterranean." Then you get a hit of the ginger and fish sauce and you're like, "Oh, it's Asian." This relish disorients you. That's why I like it. Spoon it onto my Vietnamese Halal Cart–Style Lamb Pitas (page 121), use it as a light, nearly vegetarian filling for lettuce wraps, or serve it alongside simply grilled lamb or beef.

Heat 3 tablespoons of the oil in a large skillet over high heat until it begins to smoke. Add half the eggplant and cook, stirring occasionally, until it's deep brown in spots and fully tender, about 5 minutes. Transfer the eggplant to a bowl. Add another 3 tablespoons of oil to the pan and cook the remaining eggplant in the same way, transferring it to the bowl.

Reduce the heat to medium low and add the remaining 2 tablespoons oil. When it shimmers, add the onion and cook, stirring occasionally, until it's very soft but not colored, about 10 minutes. Stir in the tomato, scallions, ginger, garlic, and chile and cook, shaking the skillet occasionally, until the tomato is cooked but not falling apart, about 5 minutes.

Return the eggplant to the skillet and add the fish sauce, vinegar, and sugar, then stir gently so you don't smash the tomato or the eggplant. Increase the heat to high, bring the liquid to a boil, and cook just until the liquid is absorbed but the relish still looks moist, 3 to 5 minutes.

Take the skillet off the heat and gently stir in the pistachios, olives, dried cherries, and orange zest. Transfer the relish to a wide bowl and let it cool to warm or room temperature before you eat it. The relish keeps in the fridge for a few days and tastes even better the day after you make it.

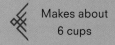

Makes about
6 cups

½ cup vegetable oil

1½ pounds Asian long eggplant, cut into ½-inch pieces (about 8 cups)

1 medium Spanish onion (about ½ pound), cut into ¼-inch pieces

1 medium tomato (about ½ pound), cut into ½-inch pieces

½ cup thinly sliced scallion whites

1 generous tablespoon finely chopped fresh ginger

3 medium garlic cloves, finely chopped

2 teaspoons thinly sliced fresh red Thai chile (including seeds)

½ cup Thai or Vietnamese fish sauce

½ cup unseasoned rice vinegar

2 tablespoons granulated sugar

½ cup roughly chopped unsalted roasted pistachios

½ cup sliced (about ¼ inch) pitted green olives

½ cup dried cherries

1 teaspoon finely grated orange zest

Long Beans Almondine

If Jacques Pépin ever rolls by the crib, I'm feeding him beans almondine. I'll upgrade him from regular green beans to the Asian variety that are as long as LeBron's shoes. Instead of the lemony butter, he'll get a butter–soy sauce emulsion livened up with rice vinegar and garlic. Just don't tell him I throw in a cheat for home cooks: Adding cream makes the otherwise fragile sauce bulletproof. You could go to war with this stuff and it wouldn't break on you. If you're slick with a whisk, do your thing. For the rest of you, a hand blender will be your best bet to make sure the sauce fully emulsifies. Once you've made the emulsion, you might ask yourself, "Should I really use *all* of it for these green beans?" The answer is *oui*, so serve plenty of white rice or bread alongside for sopping up.

MAKE THE SOY SAUCE BUTTER

Heat a medium pan over medium-high heat and add the oil. When it begins to smoke, add the garlic and cook, flipping the cloves once, until deep golden brown on both sides, about 3 minutes. Pour in the soy sauce and vinegar, bring the mixture to a simmer, and turn off the heat. Let the mixture sit for at least 4 hours or, even better, overnight. Discard the garlic.

Pour the cream into a small saucepan, set it over high heat, and boil until it has reduced by about half (it'll have the texture of a cream sauce), about 3 minutes. Stir in the soy sauce mixture, let it come to a simmer, then reduce the heat to very low. Add a third of the butter at a time and whisk vigorously (or even better, use a handheld blender) until it has fully melted before adding the next third. Turn off the heat and cover the pot. The sauce will stay warm and emulsified for up to 30 minutes.

FINISH THE DISH

Preheat the oven to 500°F. Toss the long beans with the oil in a mixing bowl, season lightly with salt, and spread on a baking sheet in one layer. Roast, shaking the sheet occasionally, until the beans are blistered and cooked through (long beans will be slightly chewy—in a good way), 10 to 15 minutes. Transfer the beans to a platter, pour on the soy sauce butter, top with the almonds, and eat.

Serves
4 to 6

FOR THE SOY SAUCE BUTTER

1½ teaspoons vegetable oil

2 medium garlic cloves, peeled

¼ cup reduced-sodium soy sauce

1 tablespoon unseasoned rice vinegar

¼ cup heavy cream

2 sticks (½ pound) room-temperature unsalted butter, cut into ½-inch pieces

FOR THE DISH

1½ pounds long beans, trimmed and cut into 3-inch lengths, or regular green beans, trimmed and halved (about 8 cups)

2 tablespoons vegetable oil

Kosher salt

½ cup slivered, blanched almonds, lightly toasted

Roasted Cauliflower with Masala Tomato Sauce

One of my best friends growing up was a legally blind Indian dude named Raj who listened to death metal and wore ripped-up Slayer and Motörhead concert Ts. I was all about De La Soul and fitted caps. How we stayed friends for so long isn't clear. I'd be at his house when it got dark and his mom would ask if I'd like to stay for dinner. I'd look at what she had cooking on the stove—typically a brown mush or green gruel—and was like, "Nah, I'm good." Funny enough, I was doing exactly what I used to resent white boys for doing to me when I showed up at school with *sinigang* or *kare-kare* for lunch. I was rejecting something just because it was unfamiliar.

Now I love the fact that Indian food sports incredibly complex flavors while also looking like it could give a damn about appearance. And I kick myself for missing out on Raj's mom's food. This might not be the Halle Berry of dishes, but it provides killer flavor with a spiced tomato sauce and a down-low dose of rich, fatty cashews.

MAKE THE SAUCE
Heat the oil in a medium skillet over medium heat until it shimmers. Add the garam masala, fennel, turmeric, caraway, cloves, and cardamom and cook, stirring frequently, until very aromatic, about 2 minutes. Stir in the onion, ginger, garlic, chile, and salt and cook, stirring occasionally, until the onion is translucent and the garlic is lightly browned, 5 to 8 minutes.

Combine the tomatoes and cashews in a blender and blend to a coarse puree with some of the cashews in small chunks. Dump the mixture into the pan and stir well. Reduce the heat and cook at a gentle simmer for 15 minutes to let the flavors come together. The sauce keeps in an airtight container in the fridge for several days or in the freezer for up to 3 months.

FINISH THE DISH
Preheat the oven to 450°F. Put the cauliflower in a small baking dish or medium ovenproof pan and drizzle the oil and sprinkle the salt on the top and bottom of the cauliflower. Roast the cauliflower stem down until it's fully tender with a slight bite, about 35 minutes. Trim the florets from the stem into about 2-inch pieces and cut the stem into thin slices.

Stir the peas into the sauce, wait a few minutes, then add the cauliflower and simmer until they're both heated through. Stir in the mint and add salt to taste. If you're using the panko, sprinkle on top of the dish, turn on the oven broiler, and broil until it's golden brown and crunchy, about 2 minutes. Eat.

**Serves
4 to 6**

FOR THE SAUCE

¼ cup vegetable oil

2 teaspoons garam masala

1 teaspoon ground fennel

1 teaspoon turmeric powder

¼ teaspoon caraway seeds

⅛ teaspoon ground cloves

⅛ teaspoon ground cardamom

1 medium Spanish onion (about ½ pound), cut into ¼-inch dice

3 tablespoons finely chopped fresh ginger

2 medium garlic cloves, finely chopped

1 tablespoon thinly sliced fresh red Thai chile (including seeds)

2 teaspoons kosher salt

1 (14-ounce) can whole tomatoes

½ cup unsalted roasted cashews

FOR THE DISH

1 large head cauliflower, leaves and stalks discarded, stem trimmed to about 1½ inches

2 tablespoons vegetable oil

1 teaspoon kosher salt

½ cup frozen peas

About 10 mint leaves, torn at the last minute

2 tablespoons panko bread crumbs, optional

Mezze Plate, Talde-Style

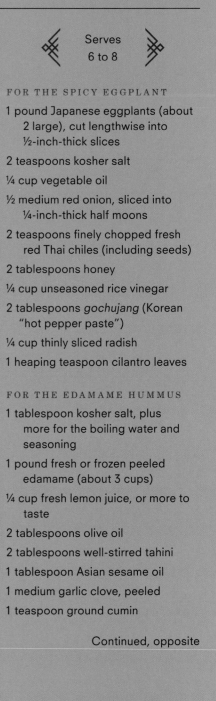

Serves
6 to 8

FOR THE SPICY EGGPLANT

1 pound Japanese eggplants (about 2 large), cut lengthwise into ½-inch-thick slices

2 teaspoons kosher salt

¼ cup vegetable oil

½ medium red onion, sliced into ¼-inch-thick half moons

2 teaspoons finely chopped fresh red Thai chiles (including seeds)

2 tablespoons honey

¼ cup unseasoned rice vinegar

2 tablespoons *gochujang* (Korean "hot pepper paste")

¼ cup thinly sliced radish

1 heaping teaspoon cilantro leaves

FOR THE EDAMAME HUMMUS

1 tablespoon kosher salt, plus more for the boiling water and seasoning

1 pound fresh or frozen peeled edamame (about 3 cups)

¼ cup fresh lemon juice, or more to taste

2 tablespoons olive oil

2 tablespoons well-stirred tahini

1 tablespoon Asian sesame oil

1 medium garlic clove, peeled

1 teaspoon ground cumin

Continued, opposite

When you hit a Greek, Turkish, or Lebanese spot, it doesn't matter what else you order—if you know what's what, you're also going to get the mezze plate. Mine is a little different. The hummus is made with edamame—not chickpeas—which bring their own earthy sweetness. The obligatory eggplant component packs the heat and umami of Korean *gochujang*. And the yogurt isn't labne or tzatziki but raita, the mouth-cooling Indian yogurt condiment, seen through the eyes of a Ranch junkie. If I see a creamy sauce, I have to add a bump of that white powder. Like certain other white powders, adding Ranch to the party doesn't always turn out so good. In this case, though, you get something that looks like raita and tastes like raita, but with a surprise Doritos twist. And speaking of Doritos, I serve them alongside just as often as I do the more predictable pita.

MAKE THE EGGPLANT

Preheat a grill, griddle, or large cast-iron skillet over medium-high heat. Toss the eggplant with 1 teaspoon of the salt, then 2 tablespoons of the oil to coat the slices. Cook, flipping the slices once, until both sides are charred in spots and the eggplant is just cooked through, about 8 minutes. Cut into approximately 2- by ½-inch pieces.

Meanwhile, heat the remaining 2 tablespoons oil in a medium pan over high heat until it shimmers. Add the onion and remaining 1 teaspoon salt and cook, stirring, until it's wilted and golden brown at the edges, about 2 minutes. Add the chiles, stir, and cook until very aromatic, about 1 minute more.

Reduce the heat to medium, add the honey, and let it bubble for about 30 seconds. Stir well and cook for another minute. Stir in the eggplant, rice vinegar, and *gochujang*. Toss well and cook at a moderate simmer until the eggplant is fully soft and has absorbed most of the liquid, about 3 minutes. Let cool to warm or room temperature. (It keeps for up to 5 days in an airtight container in the fridge.) When you're ready to serve, scatter on the radish and cilantro leaves.

MAKE THE HUMMUS

Bring a large pot of water to a boil over high heat. Fill a large bowl with icy water. Add enough salt to the boiling water to make it taste slightly salty, then add the edamame and cook until the edamame are fully tender but not mushy, about 5 minutes. Transfer the edamame to the icy water, reserving 1½ cups of the cooking liquid.

Drain the edamame well and add them to a blender along with the lemon juice, olive oil, tahini, sesame oil, garlic, cumin, and 1 cup of the reserved cooking liquid. Add 1 tablespoon salt and blend until very smooth. Be patient if it doesn't all blend right away. Stir occasionally and as a last resort very gradually add more of the reserved liquid to help it blend. Season with more salt and lemon juice to taste. It keeps in an airtight container in the fridge for up to 5 days.

MAKE THE RAITA AND SERVE THE DISH

Combine the yogurt, Ranch seasoning, cumin, and salt in a bowl and stir until the salt dissolves. Stir in the cucumber and mint.

Serve the hummus, eggplant, and raita, doing your best to make them look dope. Eat.

FOR THE COOL RANCH RAITA

1 cup low-fat plain yogurt (not Greek)

1½ teaspoons Ranch seasoning powder, such as the Hidden Valley brand

½ teaspoon ground cumin

½ teaspoon kosher salt

1 cup seeded, diced (about ¼ inch) cucumber

2 tablespoons roughly chopped mint leaves

Carrot Rendang

I used to hate cooking for vegetarians and vegans. I was on that "I cook what I want and you eat it" trip. Then I opened my own place. Not only did I learn to put my ego aside and appreciate the people who kept me in business, but I also started to have fun cooking within limits. Limits keep you creative. It led to this dish, a remix of Indonesian beef rendang where carrots stand in for the protein. Because it's a dry curry, the carrots don't hide in soupy liquid; they strut in a chinchilla coat of spice and aromatics. Beef better watch its back.

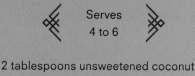

Serves
4 to 6

2 tablespoons unsweetened coconut flakes

2 pounds carrots, peeled and cut into irregular ¾-inch chunks

¼ cup vegetable oil

1½ teaspoons kosher salt

1 cup well-shaken coconut milk

1 cup Rendang Paste (page 196)

1 teaspoon Thai or Vietnamese fish sauce, optional

2 heaping tablespoons roughly chopped cilantro (thin stems and leaves)

2 lime wedges

Preheat the oven to 350°F. Spread the coconut flakes in one layer on a small baking sheet or toaster oven tray and bake, shaking and tossing frequently, until the coconut is crunchy and golden, about 3 minutes. Set aside to cool.

Preheat the broiler. Toss the carrots with the oil and salt, spread them out on a medium baking sheet, and broil just until the carrots are brown at the edges and fully tender but not mushy, 10 to 15 minutes. Drain off any excess oil.

Bring the coconut milk to a boil in a medium skillet over high heat. Let it boil until it "cracks" (it'll look curdled, with the fat and water separated), about 3 minutes. Add the carrots, rendang paste, and fish sauce, stir well, and cook, stirring frequently, until the rendang mixture coats the carrots, about 5 minutes. Use a slotted spoon to transfer the carrots to a plate, leaving the excess oil behind.

Add more salt to taste, then top with the cilantro and coconut flakes and serve with the lime wedges. Eat.

Butternut Squash Hot Pot with Shrimp, Apple, and Shrimp Paste

I must've made butternut squash soup every damn day for an entire year when I was working at Spring (R.I.P.) in Chicago. I got tired of cooking it, but I never got tired of eating it. I loved the way a little apple balanced the squash's sweetness and a drizzle of blue cheese–infused cream added some of that sweat-sock funk. Now when I make the soup I look to shrimp paste for a source of stink that's a bit closer to home. With that and coconut milk, the soup tastes a hell of a lot more complex than it is to cook.

MAKE THE SOUP

Heat the oil in a medium pot over medium-high heat until it shimmers. Stir in the squash, apples, onion, ginger, chile, sugar, and salt, reduce the heat to medium low, and cover the pot. Cook, stirring occasionally, until the onions are translucent but not colored, about 8 minutes. Add the shrimp paste, stir for 30 seconds or so, then pour in the coconut milk along with 2 cups water.

Cover the pot again, adjust the heat to maintain a steady simmer, and cook until the squash is fully soft, 15 to 20 minutes. Stir in the fish sauce, then let the mixture cool to warm. Blend in several batches until very smooth. The soup tastes even better the day after it's made. Covered and kept in the fridge, it keeps for up to 3 days.

SERVE THE SOUP

Bring the soup to a simmer over medium heat, add the shrimp, and cook, stirring occasionally, until they're barely cooked through, about 2 minutes. Add the tofu and long beans, stir gently, and cook until they're warmed through and the shrimp are fully cooked, about 1 minute more. Divide the soup among bowls and spoon on the diced apple. Eat.

 Serves 6 to 8

FOR THE SOUP

3 tablespoons vegetable oil

1 pound peeled, seeded butternut squash, cut into about 2-inch chunks

2 sweet-tart apples, like Granny Smith, peeled, cored, and quartered

1 medium Spanish onion (about ½ pound), sliced into about ½-inch-thick half moons

2 tablespoons finely chopped fresh ginger

1 fresh red Thai chile, thinly sliced (including seeds)

1 tablespoon granulated sugar

2 teaspoons kosher salt

¼ cup Shrimp Paste Soffrito (page 194) or well-stirred Barrio Fiesta brand spicy *ginisang bagoong*

2 (14-ounce) cans well-shaken coconut milk

2 tablespoons Thai or Vietnamese fish sauce

FOR THE EXTRAS

1 pound shrimp, peeled and deveined

1 pound silken tofu, drained and cut into 1-inch cubes

2 cups long beans, chopped (about 2½-inch lengths), briefly boiled, and cooled under cold running water

1 sweet-tart apple, peeled, cored, and diced (about ¼ inch)

Grilled Sweet Potatoes with Soy Sauce, Maple, and Bacon

My mom only ate sweet potatoes for dessert. She'd throw one in the microwave and dig in. No butter, no sweetened condensed milk, nothing. I kept telling her, "Mom, that's not dessert, that's a potato." For a while I thought this reflected our cultural divide. She grew up in the Philippines, where inherently sweet ingredients like corn went into desserts. I grew up in Chicago, where corn was buttered and salted and beans went into burritos. But when I started working in restaurants during Thanksgiving, I saw what the white boys and black guys I worked with made, and I was confused all over again. As I watched them pile the brown sugar and marshmallows on sweet potatoes, I was thinking, "That's just pie without the crust."

Maybe, then, it's just me who likes a more savory preparation. Here, there's as much soy sauce as there is maple syrup. A last-minute shower of crumbled bacon drives the point home.

Put the potatoes in a medium pot, add enough water to cover by about ½ inch, and add enough salt so the water tastes slightly salty. Bring the water to a boil over high heat, reduce the heat, and simmer gently until the potatoes are nearly cooked but still firm, about 5 minutes. Drain and let them cool. You can do this a few days in advance.

Preheat the oven to 400°F. Add the bacon to a foil-lined baking sheet in one layer and bake until brown and crispy, about 15 minutes. Transfer to paper towels to drain, reserving the fat for another purpose.

Combine the soy sauce, maple syrup, and sherry vinegar in a small pan, bring to a boil over high heat, and cook until the mixture thickens slightly, about 3 minutes. Combine in a blender with the butter (or over low heat, whisk in a piece of butter at a time), blend until smooth, and reserve.

Preheat a well-oiled grill to cook over medium-high heat. Skewer the potatoes, leaving a little space between slices and leaving a couple of inches at the bottom of the skewer empty. Brush or drizzle some of the soy sauce mixture all over the potatoes. Grill the potatoes, flipping and brushing or drizzling on sauce occasionally, until the potatoes are lightly charred, shiny, and cooked through, 5 to 8 minutes.

Transfer the skewers to plates, crumble on the bacon, sprinkle on the scallions, and drizzle on a little extra sauce. Eat.

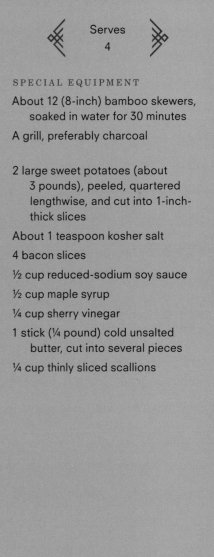

Serves
4

SPECIAL EQUIPMENT

About 12 (8-inch) bamboo skewers, soaked in water for 30 minutes

A grill, preferably charcoal

2 large sweet potatoes (about 3 pounds), peeled, quartered lengthwise, and cut into 1-inch-thick slices

About 1 teaspoon kosher salt

4 bacon slices

½ cup reduced-sodium soy sauce

½ cup maple syrup

¼ cup sherry vinegar

1 stick (¼ pound) cold unsalted butter, cut into several pieces

¼ cup thinly sliced scallions

Buffalo-ed Cauliflower with Blue Cheese

Anything can be Buffalo-ed. And anything that could benefit from a little spice, acidity, and butter deserves to be. Like cauliflower, which I roast whole like chicken, cut into crunchy wing-size pieces, and toss with butter and hot sauce. Crumbling blue cheese on top is a no-brainer.

Preheat the oven to 450°F. Put the cauliflower in a small baking dish or medium ovenproof pan and drizzle the oil and sprinkle the salt all over. Roast the cauliflower stem down until it's fully tender with a slight bite, about 35 minutes. Trim the florets from the stem into 3-inch-long pieces (or about the size of chicken wingettes), then cut the stem into thin slices. You can do this a few days in advance.

Combine the Sriracha and Frank's in a large pan, stir, then add the cauliflower and toss to coat. Set the pan over medium-high heat. When the sauce sizzles, add the butter and cook, tossing and stirring, until the butter has melted, the cauliflower is heated through, and the sauce looks slightly creamy, 3 to 5 minutes. Sprinkle on the cheese and add salt to taste. Eat.

 Serves 4 to 6

1 large head cauliflower (about 2 pounds), leaves and stalks discarded, stem trimmed to about 1½ inches

2 tablespoons vegetable oil

1 teaspoon kosher salt

¼ cup plus 1 tablespoon Sriracha

¼ cup plus 1 tablespoon Frank's RedHot sauce

6 tablespoons room-temperature unsalted butter, cut into chunks

½ cup crumbled blue cheese

Buffalo [**buhf**-*uh*-loh]; VERB
To coat in a mixture of hot sauce and butter; to make more delicious; to improve: *Uh-oh, Leroy cooked these shrimp? We should buffalo them, stat.*

Desserts

Halo-Halo

My aunt Catalina lived in Chicago and ran a grocery store in Great Lakes, Illinois, about 45 minutes north and strategically located next to a naval base packed with Filipinos. So of course, she had an industrial ice shaver—how else could she make enough *halo-halo*? Tagalog for "mix mix," *halo-halo* is the dessert to beat in the Philippines. It's basically a snow cone topped with all sorts of stuff—sweetened condensed milk (dope), candied chickpeas (nasty), bootleg Rice Krispies (solid), cubes of coconut gel (a must), and *macapuno* strings (the sweet, gelatinous flesh of a mutant coconut, preserved in syrup). She'd just plug in the machine, lay out the fixings salad-bar style, and make that money.

The only two traditions I keep intact are the coconut gel and *macapuno* strings. Otherwise, I came up with my own toppings for Talde's version: Rice Krispies step aside for my childhood favorite, Cap'n Crunch. Instead of straight-up condensed milk, I make a lemongrass bubble tea base that I swear smells like Froot Loops—in a good way. Dried mango simmered in coconut milk turns fleshy and tart, and everyone who tries it asks, "What is that?" as if you had invented bacon.

Halo-halo really does require an ice shaver, which costs about $25, to achieve the proper texture. But since you got to do what you got to do, I won't tell you *not* to grind up ice in a food processor.

SIMMER THE MANGO
Combine the coconut milk, mango, and salt in a small saucepan along with ¼ cup water and bring to a simmer over high heat. Reduce the heat and gently simmer until the mango is rehydrated but not falling apart, about 20 minutes. Let cool, cover, and keep in the fridge until it's well chilled, but no more than 2 hours.

MAKE THE MILKY LEMONGRASS TEA
Combine the coconut water, lemongrass, lime leaves, and chile in a small saucepan and bring to a boil over high heat. Turn off the heat, cover the pan, and let the mixture steep for about 20 minutes. Strain, pressing then discarding the solids. Stir in the condensed milk until smooth. Cover and keep it in the fridge until it's well chilled, but no more than 2 hours.

MAKE THE HALO-HALO
Right before you're ready to eat, layer the ice, the mango mixture, and the solid ingredients in 4 tall, wide glasses or bowls. Pour the lemongrass tea over each bowl. Eat one.

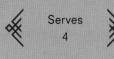

Serves
4

FOR THE MANGO

1 (14-ounce) can well-shaken coconut milk

1 cup unsweetened dried mango slices

¼ teaspoon kosher salt

FOR THE MILKY LEMONGRASS TEA

2 cups coconut water, such as the Vita Coco or Zico brand

2 large lemongrass stalks (bottom 1 inch, top 8 inches, and outer layer removed), lightly smashed and cut into 1-inch pieces

2 fresh or frozen (not dried) kaffir lime leaves

½ fresh red Thai chile, halved lengthwise (including seeds)

¼ cup sweetened condensed milk

FOR THE HALO-HALO

8 cups shaved ice (ideally from an ice shaver)

1 cup cooked large pearl tapioca

1 cup *macapuno* strings (aka coconut sport)

1 cup drained *nata de coco* (aka coconut gel)

1 cup mixed fresh fruit, such as bananas, mango, pineapple, blueberries, or lychee, sliced if necessary into bite-size pieces

1 cup Cap'n Crunch or your favorite sugar cereal

Potato Chip and Pretzel Squares with Caramel-Chocolate Ganache

The best desserts remind you of being a kid. So it's fitting that this recipe was inspired by one. I was playing ball on the Lower East Side when I saw him leave a bodega juggling a bag of pretzels, a bag of chips, a chocolate milk, and a Snickers bar. I bet you that kid had never been to restaurants with pastry chefs, but he definitely understood the way they think: Sweetness plus a little saltiness equals incredible. I'm no pastry chef myself, but I set out to turn those four snacks into one insanely good sweet. So I crush the pretzels and chips to make a crust (no stand mixer necessary) and top them with a chocolate caramel ganache, for which you barely have to do more than stir. I like this dessert best served cold—like a candy bar straight out of the fridge.

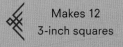
Makes 12
3-inch squares

SPECIAL EQUIPMENT

13- by 9-inch rimmed baking sheet

Parchment paper

FOR THE CRUST

5 ounces plain salted potato chips (preferably Ruffles), coarsely crushed (about 3¼ cups)

5 ounces salted pretzels, coarsely crushed (about 2¾ cups)

¼ cup granulated sugar

1 tablespoon all-purpose flour

1½ sticks (⅜ pound) unsalted butter, melted

FOR THE GANACHE

7 ounces bittersweet dark chocolate, roughly chopped (about 1¼ cups)

1 teaspoon kosher salt

1 cup granulated sugar

2 tablespoons corn syrup

1 cup room-temperature heavy cream

4 tablespoons room-temperature unsalted butter

1 teaspoon pretzel salt

MAKE THE CRUST

Preheat the oven to 350°F. Line the baking sheet with parchment paper.

Combine the chips, pretzels, sugar, and flour in a food processor and pulse until the mixture has the texture of very coarse bread crumbs, stopping occasionally to stir to make sure the texture is even. Pour in the butter and pulse just until the mixture is evenly moistened. Add the mixture to the baking sheet and press to form an even layer. Bake the crust until it's evenly peanut-butter brown, 10 to 15 minutes. Let the crust cool completely.

MAKE THE GANACHE

Put the chocolate and kosher salt in a heatproof mixing bowl and set aside.

Combine the sugar, corn syrup, and 3 tablespoons water in a medium saucepan. Set the pan over medium-high heat and let the mixture get liquidy, about 2 minutes. Cook, without stirring but rotating the pan on the stove if some spots turn brown much faster than others, until it turns a mahogany color, 3 to 5 minutes. Pour in the cream, bring it to a boil over high heat, and cook, stirring occasionally, until any caramel that hardened has melted back into the mixture, 1 to 2 minutes.

Stir in the butter until it melts, then pour the hot mixture into the bowl with the chocolate and stir until the chocolate has completely melted. Immediately pour the chocolate mixture onto the pretzel crust, tilting the baking sheet so the ganache spreads out in an even layer on top of the crust. Sprinkle on the pretzel salt.

Let the ganache cool, then cover and chill in the fridge until the ganache is firm and cold. Cut into approximately 3-inch squares and serve right out of the fridge. The squares keep tightly wrapped in the fridge for up to a week and in the freezer for up to 3 months.

Mickey D's–Style Fried Apple Pies

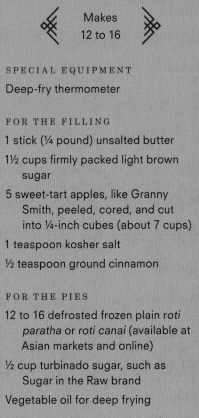

Makes
12 to 16

SPECIAL EQUIPMENT
Deep-fry thermometer

FOR THE FILLING

1 stick (¼ pound) unsalted butter

1½ cups firmly packed light brown
    sugar

5 sweet-tart apples, like Granny
    Smith, peeled, cored, and cut
    into ¼-inch cubes (about 7 cups)

1 teaspoon kosher salt

½ teaspoon ground cinnamon

FOR THE PIES

12 to 16 defrosted frozen plain *roti
    paratha* or *roti canai* (available at
    Asian markets and online)

½ cup turbinado sugar, such as
    Sugar in the Raw brand

Vegetable oil for deep frying

Everyone who's about my age remembers the Tragedy of 1992. That
was when McDonald's betrayed us all by retiring their deep-fried apple
pie and replacing it with a second-rate baked version. I was depressed
about this for a good two decades until I discovered that with some
store-bought *roti paratha* and a pot of hot oil, I could relive the chain's
glory days on the regular. Since then I've messed around with all kinds
of fillings: Strawberry and rhubarb to embrace the season. Peanut butter and jelly to embrace my inner fat kid. But I always return to the
classic: sweet-tart apple inside a flaky golden-brown, sugar-studded

crust. Just take that first bite carefully, because like the original, when you get these straight out of the fryer, the filling is the second-hottest substance on earth after lava.

MAKE THE FILLING

Melt the butter in a wide skillet over medium heat. Add the brown sugar and stir well, breaking up clumps. Let the mixture simmer until the sugar has mostly dissolved, about 5 minutes. Raise the heat to medium high, stir in the apples, salt, and cinnamon, and cook, stirring occasionally, until the apples are tender but not mushy, about 8 minutes. The sugar will seize up but will melt into the liquid that the apples release as they cook. Transfer the mixture to a bowl and let it cool completely. You can keep it in the fridge for up to 3 days.

FORM THE PIES

Work with one roti at a time, keeping it between the plastic squares it comes in (the roti is very sticky) and keeping the others in the fridge as you form each pie. Put a roti on a work surface. Use your palm to stretch the roti slightly, starting in the center and applying gentle pressure as you move toward the edges.

Peel off the top layer of plastic. Stir the filling, then add 3 tablespoons to ¼ cup (depending on the diameter of the roti) of the filling to the center of the roti. Holding two corners of the remaining plastic square, fold the roti over the filling to form a semi circle, gently forcing the air out but keeping the filling in. Firmly press the rounded edge of the roti to create a seal, then crimp with a fork. Use a sharp knife to make three slashes on the top (so it doesn't burst), cutting through the roti layer and leaving ½ inch or so between slashes. Sprinkle some sugar (about 1 teaspoon) on the top, then fold the plastic over and use your hands to gently press so the sugar adheres. Do the same on the other side of the pie.

Repeat with the remaining roti and filling. Chill the pies in the fridge for at least 30 minutes before frying. You can keep them covered in the fridge for up to 12 hours, or freeze them—first uncovered on a plate, then in bags with parchment paper in between the pies—for up to 3 months.

FRY THE PIES

Preheat the oven to 200°F and set a rack over a baking sheet. Pour enough oil into a large pot to reach a depth of about 3 inches. Set the pot over medium-high heat and bring the oil to 350°F (use a deep-fry thermometer). Fry the pies 4 or so at a time, carefully turning them over halfway through if they float to the surface, until golden brown and crispy, 3 to 4 minutes per batch. (If you're frying frozen pies, they'll take about 6 minutes.)

Transfer them to the rack and keep them warm in the oven. Let the oil come back to 350°F between batches. Let them cool slightly before you eat.

The King

René Redzepi has his Nordic Food Lab, where he and his peeps explore vinegar, blood, and crickets. David Chang has his fermentation chamber, where he and his squad mess with microbes. I, too, have a venue for experimentation, where new food is born. It's called the deep fryer. My methods are complex: I throw stuff in—meat, kelp, miso, lettuce—and see what happens. The greatest discovery I've made is that hot oil turns canned biscuit dough into donuts. I named this creation for Elvis, the famous glutton who'd've loved the caramel topping decked out with peanuts, bananas, and bacon.

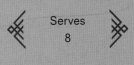

Serves
8

SPECIAL EQUIPMENT

Deep-fry thermometer

FOR THE CARAMEL TOPPING

¼ cup plus 2 tablespoons granulated sugar

½ cup heavy cream

6 tablespoons unsalted butter, cut into several pieces

¼ cup bourbon

2 firm-ripe bananas, peeled and cut into ¼-inch-thick slices

½ cup coarsely crushed unsalted roasted peanuts

2 thick-cut slices bacon, cooked and chopped into ½-inch pieces

FOR THE DISH

Vegetable oil for deep frying

½ cup turbinado sugar, such as Sugar in the Raw

1 (16-ounce) tube original flavor Pillsbury Grands! Flaky Layers refrigerated biscuits

1 tablespoon flaky sea salt

MAKE THE TOPPING

Put the granulated sugar in a medium pan, set it over medium heat, and let the sugar melt. Cook, without stirring but rotating the pan on the stove if some spots turn brown much faster than others, until it turns a mahogany color, 3 to 5 minutes. Pour in the cream, bring it to a boil over high heat, and cook, stirring occasionally, until any caramel that hardened has melted back into the mixture, 1 to 2 minutes.

Stir in the butter until it melts, then pour in the bourbon, stand back, and cook at a boil for a minute or so (don't freak out if you see flames; they'll go out by themselves). Stir in the bananas, peanuts, and bacon, let the mixture come back to a boil, then turn off the heat. Keep it in a warm place while you finish the dish.

FRY THE BISCUITS AND FINISH THE DISH

Preheat the oven to 200°F and set a rack over a baking sheet. Pour enough oil into a large pot to reach a depth of about 3 inches. Set the pot over medium-high heat and bring the oil to 350°F (use a deep-fry thermometer).

Dump the turbinado sugar on a plate, and open the biscuit tube. One by one, separate each biscuit and add it to the sugar, turning and gently pressing to coat it with a layer of sugar on the top, bottom, and sides.

Fry in two batches—they'll float, so either use a fryer basket to weigh them down or use tongs to flip them over once—until they're peanut-butter brown, about 5 minutes per batch. Transfer them to the rack and keep them warm in the oven. Let the oil come back to 350°F between batches.

Divide the fried biscuits among 8 plates, spoon about ¼ cup of the topping on each, and top with a generous pinch of the salt. Eat.

Avocado Milk Shakes

Many of the cooks at my restaurants are Latino, and this shake blows their minds. For them, avocado exists in an exclusively savory context. They grew up mashing creamy chunks with salt, lime, and chiles. They eat slices with salty beans and charred beef and warm tortillas. But in Asia, the avocado is a relatively new import that we treat like a fruit. You're more likely to see it in desserts and other sweet preparations like this one. As much as I like guacamole, the Filipino in me sees the fatty flesh of avocado as nature's custard and wants to blend it with sweetened condensed milk into this shake so thick it's almost like ice cream.

Serves 4

2 medium-size ripe Hass avocados, peeled and pitted
¾ cup sweetened condensed milk
3 cups ice cubes

Scoop the avocado flesh into a blender, pour in the condensed milk, then add the ice cubes. Blend on high, stirring if necessary, just until the mixture is completely smooth. Divide among 4 small glasses and serve with bubble tea straws or spoons. Drink.

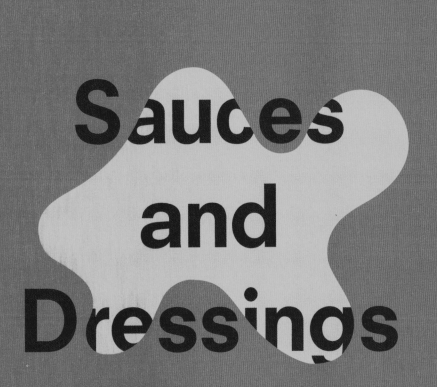

Sauces and Dressings

Garlic-Chile Vinegar

Makes about 2 cups

At my parents' house in Chicago, no eating goes down without this stuff nearby. My mom, the Queen of Recycling, would keep it in all sorts of weird-ass containers, like pancake syrup bottles. A superior Southeast Asian version of black pepper in a shaker, this mixture lets everyone at the table add acid and heat to whatever he or she is eating, whether that's fried rice or spaghetti and meatballs.

2 cups distilled white vinegar
6 or so garlic cloves, peeled
1½ teaspoons black peppercorns
4 or so fresh red Thai chiles, stemmed

Combine the ingredients in a glass jar, cover tightly, and let sit at room temperature for at least 4 days. It keeps for several months at room temperature.

Jalapeño Aioli

Makes about ½ cup

Fresh chiles like jalapeños have a rep for heat, but for me they're more about flavor. This aioli celebrates their sharp, grassy quality as well as their burn. And, OK, fine: It's technically just mayo, but "aioli" sounds like something you can't buy at the bodega.

   A large food processor might not be able to fully blend the chile, but a slightly chunky aioli is still damn good. Make it for Crab Fried Rice (page 71), but use it anywhere and everywhere you would Hellman's.

2 large egg yolks
1 medium fresh jalapeño chile, roughly chopped (including seeds)
1½ teaspoons fresh lime juice
1 teaspoon Thai or Vietnamese fish sauce
¼ teaspoon kosher salt
½ cup vegetable oil

Combine the egg yolks, jalapeño, lime juice, fish sauce, and salt in a small food processor and process until fairly smooth. With the food processor running, slowly and steadily drizzle in the oil in a very thin stream. You'll have a smooth, creamy sauce that looks like a loose, pale green mayo. Use within a couple of hours.

Kimchi Yogurt

Makes a generous 4 cups

There is no kimchi in my kimchi yogurt. Back when I came up with this sauce, we were getting this awesome jarred kimchi. But we couldn't figure out a way to source it consistently, so my cooks and I thought, "Fuck it," and set out to make it ourselves. We started as I always do when I try to make a better version of a commercial product: We looked at the ingredients list. This time, I had to bribe a Korean friend to translate. Then we tinkered until we had an incredible spice mixture that conjured kimchi without the pain of fermenting. And this irresistible sauce was born. It's meant for my Korean Fried Chicken (page 104), but there are few things it doesn't improve, from grilled eggplant to roasted cauliflower to grilled fish.

1 teaspoon coriander seeds
½ teaspoon fennel seeds
½ teaspoon black peppercorns
2 cups Frank's RedHot sauce
2 cups low-fat plain yogurt (not Greek)
¼ cup Thai or Vietnamese fish sauce
1½ tablespoons Asian sesame oil
½ teaspoon chile powder
½ teaspoon paprika
½ teaspoon chicken bouillon
½ teaspoon turmeric powder
½ teaspoon garlic powder
¼ teaspoon ground cardamom

Combine the coriander seeds, fennel seeds, and black peppercorns in a small cold pan, and set it over medium-high heat. Toast, shaking the pan often, until they're very fragrant, about 3 minutes. Let them cool, and grind in a spice grinder or crush to a powder in a mortar.

Combine the ground spices and the remaining ingredients in a large bowl and stir very well. Let the mixture sit for at least an hour before using. The kimchi yogurt keeps in an airtight container in the fridge for up to 3 weeks.

Kung Pao Sauce

Makes about 2¼ cups

Kung pao chicken went from an underground dish to one that's served at every takeout joint in America. The version that gets prime billing on menus alongside General Tso's barely resembles the regional specialty born in Sichuan Province. Mine straddles the two. It's meant for Kung Pao Chicken Wings (page 30), but will give anything, deep-fried or not, that fly sweet-salty flavor plus a punch of umami and the strange but awesome burn of Szechuan peppercorns. Just bring the sauce to a simmer and toss in simply cooked cauliflower, shrimp, eggplant, even fried potatoes.

¼ cup plus 2 tablespoons vegetable oil

1½ teaspoons annatto seeds (aka achiote seeds; available at Latin markets)

1½ teaspoons Szechuan peppercorns

½ star anise

1 tablespoon Asian chile oil

½ cup Chinese chile-bean paste (*toban djan*), such as the Lee Kum Kee brand

½ cup Thai sweet chile sauce, such as the Mae Ploy brand

¼ cup plus 2 tablespoons oyster sauce

¼ cup Shaoxing wine, dry sherry, or bourbon

¼ cup unseasoned rice vinegar

1 tablespoon Asian sesame oil

Combine the vegetable oil, annatto seeds, Szechuan peppercorns, and star anise in a small pan, set it over medium heat, and let the oil sizzle. Cook, shaking the pan occasionally, until you smell the Szechuan peppercorns (they have a sort of minty-nutty aroma), about 1 minute. Take the pan off the heat and stir in the chile oil.

Combine the remaining ingredients in a large mixing bowl. Strain the oil into the mixing bowl, discarding the spices. Whisk until the mixture is emulsified like a dressing. You'll no longer see a layer of oil on the surface.

It keeps in an airtight container in the fridge for up to 3 weeks or in the freezer for up to 3 months.

Dale's "Homemade" Hot Sauce

Makes 2 cups

A squeeze bottle of this stuff sits on every table at Talde and Pork Slope. Every week, I get some hot-sauce head begging me to share how I make it. I always start the same way: "It's really hard..." I can see him pulling out his mental notebook, preparing to scribble down the name of an obscure chile that I source from New Mexico or Manila and the blend of aromatics that I probably sauté and simmer for hours. That's why I have so much fun with the punch line: Take two fine American products and mix them together. Sriracha (engineered and produced in California) has so much going on, but it lacks the acidity I love in hot sauce. Frank's RedHot sauce (shouts to Springfield, Missouri) has the acidity and some bonus cayenne flavor. Together, they're unstoppable.

1 cup Sriracha

1 cup Frank's RedHot sauce

Combine and stir well. The sauce keeps for up to 1 month in the fridge.

Chicken Nug Sauce Trio

The not-new but definitely improved Mickey D's holy trinity is right here. My BBQ sauce kills Ronald's. Making the honey mustard yourself is almost as easy as pulling the lid off the little container but turns out a hundred times tastier. And for the sweet chile sauce, I get real lazy and just open a bottle of the superior Asian stuff.

BBQ Sauce

Makes about 3 cups

1 tablespoon vegetable oil

½ cup diced (¼ inch) Spanish onion

2 medium garlic cloves, thinly sliced

1 teaspoon kosher salt

1 cup of your favorite BBQ sauce

1 cup distilled white vinegar

¾ cup ketchup

½ cup firmly packed dark brown sugar

1 tablespoon Worcestershire sauce

1 tablespoon Thai or Vietnamese fish sauce

2 canned chipotle chiles in adobo

Heat the oil in a small saucepan over medium heat until it shimmers. Add the onion, garlic, and salt and cook, stirring occasionally, until the garlic smells toasty and the onion is soft, about 5 minutes. Add the remaining ingredients, increase the heat, and bring the mixture to a boil. Reduce the heat to maintain a gentle simmer for 15 minutes to let the flavors meld. Let it cool to warm, then transfer to a blender and blend until smooth. Let it cool to room temperature before serving.

The sauce keeps in an airtight container in the fridge for up to 2 weeks.

Honey Mustard Sauce

Makes ¾ cup

½ cup honey

¼ cup Dijon mustard

Combine and stir well.

Sweet Chile Sauce

Any Asian sweet chile sauce, such as the Mae Ploy brand.

Halal Cart–Style White Sauce

Makes about 1 cup

Halal carts serve two sauces: red and white. Red is just decent hot sauce. If you get home and realize they forgot the red, it's not the end of the world, because you probably have something in the pantry that'll hit the spot. But white is another matter. It happens to be the most mysterious substance on earth. I still don't know what's in the real version, but this tastes pretty damn close.

½ cup 2% Greek yogurt
½ cup mayo
1 tablespoon well-stirred tahini
1 tablespoon fresh lemon juice
2 teaspoons kosher salt

Combine the ingredients and stir well. The sauce keeps in an airtight container in the fridge for up to 2 days.

Tahini Mustard Sauce

Makes about 1 cup

You can't eat a soft pretzel without mustard. But straight-up mustard would overwhelm Pretzel Pork-and-Chive Dumplings (page 77). You need something to tone down the mustard's sting. Because dumplings are Asian and New York's pretzel vendors are almost always Middle Eastern, I looked to a common culinary thread: sesame. Creamy tahini and fragrant sesame oil get it done, giving this dip a richness with just enough mustardy bite.

½ cup hot Chinese mustard (or Dijon, if you have to)
2 tablespoons well-stirred tahini
2 tablespoons unseasoned rice vinegar
2 tablespoons vegetable oil
2 tablespoons Asian sesame oil
1 teaspoon granulated sugar
1 teaspoon kosher salt

Combine the ingredients in a bowl and stir really well.

Bacon-Tamarind Caramel

Makes about 2 cups

The recipe for this spreadable caramel—revved up with fish sauce and bacon, balanced by tangy tamarind, and enriched with coconut milk—gives you way more than you need for Perilla Leaf Bites (page 25). I figure if you're down to make caramel, you deserve a stash of this long-lasting, life-changing condiment. You'll find yourself slathering it on crackers, spreading it on sandwiches, and dipping in any vegetables that go good with pork.

10 ounces bacon, ground either by you or your butcher, or frozen then very finely chopped
1 cup tamarind concentrate (not pulp or paste)
½ cup well-shaken coconut milk
¼ cup Thai or Vietnamese fish sauce
1 cup granulated sugar

Put the bacon in a medium saucepan and set it over medium heat. Let the bacon cook, stirring occasionally once it starts sizzling and cooking in its own fat, until it's brown and crispy, about 15 minutes. Use a slotted spoon to transfer the bacon to a small bowl to cool. Pour the bacon fat into a heatproof container and reserve it for another purpose. Don't clean the pan.

Combine the tamarind concentrate, coconut milk, and fish sauce in a separate bowl and stir well.

Add the sugar to the pan along with just enough water (about ¼ cup) to give the sugar the texture of wet sand and stir well, scraping the pan as you do. Set the pan over medium heat and let the mixture get liquidy, about 3 minutes. Keep cooking at a gentle simmer, stirring only if it's browning too fast in spots and watching closely as the mixture goes from white to blond to light brown, 5 to 7 minutes more. Lower the heat slightly and let it turn a light caramel color, 1 minute or so more.

Immediately pour in the tamarind mixture and stir. The caramel will clump and harden. That's OK—it'll melt soon. Let the mixture come to a steady simmer and cook, occasionally stirring and scraping the pan, until the mixture has reduced by about half (it'll have the texture of tamarind concentrate) and turned an even darker shade of brown, 10 to 15 minutes.

Take the pan off the heat, stir in the bacon, and care-fully transfer to a heatproof container. It'll thicken to a spreadable texture once it's cool.

The caramel keeps in an airtight container in the fridge for up to 1 month.

Asian Tomato Jam
Makes about 2 cups

There's some India and a little Vietnam in this condiment of tomatoes cooked to a jam-like consistency. While it's meant for Vietnamese Fish Tacos (page 141), you'll find yourself using it for simpler dishes, too, like straight-up fish fillets or to flavor a pot of steamed mussels.

1½ pounds tomatoes (about 3 large), cored and halved
½ cup vegetable oil
1 tablespoon ground coriander
2 teaspoons turmeric powder
½ teaspoon ground cardamom
½ teaspoon mustard seeds (yellow or black)
6 Asian dried red chiles
3 large shallots, cut into ¼-inch slices
1 tablespoon finely chopped garlic
1 tablespoon finely chopped fresh ginger
½ cup Thai or Vietnamese fish sauce
3 tablespoons granulated sugar
½ cup fresh lime juice
¼ cup thinly sliced scallion greens

Preheat the oven to 450°F. Put the tomatoes on a baking sheet, drizzle with a couple tablespoons of the oil, and toss gently. Roast them cut sides down until they're very soft and well charred, about 30 minutes.

Heat the remaining oil in a large skillet over medium-high heat. When the oil shimmers, add the coriander, turmeric, cardamom, mustard seeds, and chiles and cook, stirring occasionally, just until the mustard seeds start to pop, 1 to 2 minutes. Add the shallots, garlic, and ginger and cook, stirring, until the shallots are soft, about 8 minutes.

Stir in the roasted tomatoes, fish sauce, and sugar, and cook at a vigorous simmer, stirring and breaking up the tomatoes occasionally but leaving the mixture very chunky,

until it has thickened to a texture just slightly looser than jarred tomato salsa, about 10 minutes.

Let it cool to warm. Fish out the dried chiles and discard them, then stir in the lime juice and scallions. If you add the lime juice and scallions just before you use it, the jam keeps in an airtight container in the fridge for up to 1 week.

Apple-Tamarind Chutney
Makes about 1½ cups

Few countries can mess with India's condiment game. It's got pickles on power forward, raita as point guard, and chutneys as center. Tamarind chutney, the tangy purplish one, is like Shaq, towering over all others. Its only weak-ness, like free throws for the Big Daddy, is that it's often too sweet. Mine fixes that, leading with tartness then end-ing on a sweet, spicy note for the alley-oop.

2 tablespoons vegetable oil
1 teaspoon garam masala
1 teaspoon yellow mustard seeds
½ cup diced (¼ inch) red onion
1 tablespoon finely chopped fresh ginger
1 fresh red Thai chile, thinly sliced (including seeds)
2 sweet apples, like Fuji, peeled, cored, and each cut into about 8 wedges
½ cup unseasoned rice vinegar
3 tablespoons fresh orange juice
2 tablespoons dark brown sugar
1 tablespoon tamarind concentrate (not pulp or paste)
1 teaspoon reduced-sodium soy sauce

Combine the oil, garam masala, and mustard seeds in a medium pan, set it over medium-high heat, and cook, stir-ring occasionally, just until the mustard seeds begin to pop, 1 to 2 minutes. Add the onion, ginger, and chile and cook, stirring occasionally, until the onion is translucent, about 2 minutes.

Add the apples, vinegar, orange juice, brown sugar, tamarind concentrate, soy sauce, and 2 tablespoons water. Stir well, cover the pan, and bring the liquid to a simmer. Remove the cover and simmer, stirring occasion-ally, until the apples are fully soft, 10 to 15 minutes. Let cool to room temperature then blend until completely smooth.

It keeps in an airtight container in the fridge for up to 5 days and in the freezer for up to 3 months.

Wasabi Salsa Verde

Makes about ½ cup

All the elements of Italian salsa verde are here. I've just flipped the script. The herb blast comes from cilantro rather than parsley. Fish sauce provides the umami of anchovies. Because I spoon it over rib eye steak (page 125) and I love the combo of beef and horseradish, I add the Asian equivalent with the sinus-tickling bite of wasabi.

2 tablespoons sherry vinegar
1½ tablespoons finely chopped shallots
½ teaspoon Thai or Vietnamese fish sauce
½ teaspoon reduced-sodium soy sauce
¼ teaspoon wasabi oil (available at Japanese markets and online), plus more to taste
¼ cup olive oil
2 tablespoons very finely chopped cilantro (thin stems and leaves)

Combine the vinegar, shallots, fish sauce, soy sauce, and wasabi oil in a bowl and stir well. Drizzle in the olive oil, whisking as you do. Right before you're ready to eat it, whisk well again and stir in the cilantro. Taste and *gradually* add up to another ¼ teaspoon of wasabi oil, depending on the brand and your taste.

XO Romesco

Makes 2 cups

Most culinary cultures have curries. Or at least I can't help but think of them as curries. I mean, what is mole but a Mexican curry? You cook a bunch of ingredients, then puree them, chop them, or mash them in a mortar. I think of romesco as Spain's curry—tomatoes, peppers, onions, and garlic cooked to bring out their sweetness, perked up with vinegar, and enriched with nuts and bread. A dose of umami-packed XO sauce, Hong Kong's romesco, makes perfect sense, at least to me.

The result is delicious served with charred asparagus, grilled fish, or skirt steak.

1 cup olive oil
1 medium red bell pepper, stemmed, seeded, and cut into 1½-inch pieces
1 medium tomato, cored and cut into eighths
1 medium Spanish onion, cut into 2-inch pieces
3 medium garlic cloves, roughly chopped
2 Asian dried red chiles
1 slice soft white bread, cut into 1-inch pieces
¼ cup sliced blanched almonds
3 tablespoons XO sauce
¼ cup sherry vinegar
1 teaspoon kosher salt

Heat the oil in a medium skillet over high heat until it shimmers, add the pepper and tomato and cook, without stirring, until they're both blistered and dark brown on the undersides, about 5 minutes. Flip the pepper and tomato pieces, then add the onion pieces and cook, stirring occasionally, until they're dark brown in spots, about 3 minutes.

Add the garlic and chiles and cook, stirring occasionally, until the onion pieces are very soft, about 5 minutes. Stir in the bread and almonds, reduce the heat to medium, and cook, stirring and scraping the pan occasionally, until the almonds are golden brown and the peppers are very soft, 10 to 15 minutes. Stir in the XO sauce, cook for a minute, then take the pan off the heat.

Transfer the mixture to a food processor, add the sherry vinegar and salt, then pulse until the mixture is thick, well blended, but still slightly chunky. You can use it right away, but it tastes even better after a few days.

The sauce keeps in an airtight container covered in a layer of oil for up to 2 weeks.

XO Tartar Sauce

Makes about 1 cup

Tartar sauce has always needed some swag. And nothing's got swag like XO sauce, a Hong Kong invention named for "extra old" cognac—that good stuff. Never mind that the sauce doesn't even have cognac in it. It does have dried scallops, though, which are just as baller.

½ cup mayo
3 tablespoons XO sauce
1 tablespoon Sriracha
¼ cup diced (¼ inch) celery
1 tablespoon fresh lime juice

Combine the ingredients and stir. Let it sit for a few hours or, even better, overnight, before serving.

Garlic-Vinegar Mayo

Makes about 1 cup

I'm a mayo slut: I'm always up for some. Especially on sandwiches. I'm not sure there's a sandwich in existence that isn't improved by a generous layer. Jarred mayo makes a great jumping-off point. Here it becomes a looser, brighter version of itself, one with the sophistication of a homemade emulsion but the ease of an everyday sandwich spread.

1 cup mayo
2 tablespoons distilled white vinegar
1 teaspoon garlic powder
½ teaspoon finely ground black pepper (preferably from freshly toasted and ground peppercorns)

Combine the ingredients and stir well. It keeps in an airtight container in the fridge for up to a week.

Beef and Bean Chili

Makes about 6 cups

There's a reason that chili is in the sauce section of this book. Because while I'll definitely rock a bowl of chili for dinner, to me, chili is more verb than noun. Instead of serving chili with some rice or corn bread, I prefer to chili foods like nachos (page 45), hot dogs, cheeseburgers, and (why not?) salad. Keep this in your fridge or freezer until something worthy comes out of the oven or off the grill.

1 tablespoon vegetable oil
1 pound ground beef, preferably 80 percent lean
1 medium Spanish onion, chopped into ¼-inch pieces
2 medium garlic cloves, thinly sliced
1 tablespoon all-purpose flour
2 tablespoons tomato paste
1 tablespoon kosher salt
1 teaspoon ground black pepper
1 teaspoon chili powder
½ teaspoon ground cayenne
½ teaspoon ground cumin
½ teaspoon ground coriander
1½ cups dark, inexpensive beer, such as Negra Modelo
¼ generous cup finely chopped canned chipotles in adobo
1 (28-ounce) can whole tomatoes, drained and roughly chopped
1 (15-ounce) can navy or other beans, drained
1 tablespoon Worcestershire sauce

Heat the oil in a large, wide pot over high heat until it smokes. Add the beef and cook, occasionally stirring and breaking up the clumps, until it's well browned and just cooked through, 5 to 8 minutes. Reduce the heat to medium, then add the onions and garlic. Cook, frequently stirring and scraping the pot, until the onions are translucent, about 5 minutes. Stir in the flour and cook, stirring frequently, for about 2 minutes.

Add the tomato paste, salt, pepper, chili powder, cayenne, cumin, and coriander and cook, stirring, until the spices are very aromatic, about 2 minutes. Add the beer and chipotles, bring the mixture to a simmer, and cook until the liquid has lost the bite from the alcohol, about 5 minutes. Add the tomatoes, beans, and Worcestershire along with ½ cup water, bring the mixture to a simmer, then reduce the heat and simmer gently until the chili thickens slightly and its flavor both intensifies and melds, about 45 minutes. Season to taste with salt.

Eat right away, or keep in airtight containers in the fridge for up to 5 days or in the freezer for up to 3 months.

Pepperoni Marinara

Makes about 4 cups

Growing up, most of my homeboys were from church, our friendships cemented during Bible study. We were all Asian, in need of the company of others like us but also excited to be away from our eye-rollingly foreign families. Our youth pastor must have sensed this, because after class he took us to Pizza Hut, God bless him. Remember how back in the day you could actually sit down at a Pizza Hut? I'll never forget the smell when we stepped in, the tomato-and-pepperoni sharpness that was so different from the smell of vinegar and soy sauce we all knew well.

As pathetic as this sounds, this—not some checkered tablecloth joint called Gino's or Sal's—is where my love for red-sauce Italian food comes from. And this sauce, which I ripped off from my man Mike Isabella, a fellow *Top Chef* contestant, is just as comforting to me as my mom's chicken adobo. The salty tang of pepperoni and the brightness of chopped pickled cherry peppers get any pasta poppin'. But my favorite way to eat it is as a dip for English muffins. Just add ½ pound of cubed unfancy mozzarella and heat until the cheese has fully melted.

1 tablespoon olive oil

½ pound thinly sliced pepperoni, finely chopped or pulsed in the food processor

1 teaspoon red chile flakes

1 cup diced (¼ inch) Spanish onion

2 medium garlic cloves, thinly sliced

1 tablespoon all-purpose flour

1 (28-ounce) can crushed tomatoes

½ cup finely chopped drained B&G pickled cherry peppers (including seeds)

Heat the oil in a medium pot over medium heat until it shimmers. Add the pepperoni and chile flakes and cook, stirring, until the pepperoni releases plenty of fat, about 5 minutes. Stir in the onion and garlic and cook, stirring, until the oil releases again, about 5 minutes more.

Push the onion, garlic, and pepperoni to one side of the pot and let the oil pool in the other. Stir the flour into the oil, then stir everything together. Cook, stirring occasionally, for about 2 minutes. Add the tomatoes and pickled peppers and simmer gently, stirring occasionally, for 15 to 20 minutes, until the flavors come together.

The sauce keeps in an airtight container in the fridge for up to 5 days or in the freezer for up to 3 months.

Shrimp Paste Soffrito

Makes about 1½ cups

Let's get one thing straight: You can absolutely ignore this recipe and substitute the spicy variety of Barrio Fiesta brand *ginisang bagoong*—often labeled as "sautéed shrimp paste"—when you make Spicy Green Mango Salad (page 155), Singapore Chile Lobster (page 138), and Short Rib Kare-Kare (page 129).

I say that not just because I'm a lazy cook who likes to save himself work if he can, but also because what you can order online is actually a little better than what you'll get from my recipe. Mine is just an attempt to re-create this jarred product before I could get it regularly and at a low enough price to make it work within the weird world of restaurant economics.

Now that you know it's optional, I'll tell you that making this stuff at home involves toasting *belacan* (Malaysian fermented shrimp paste sold in blocks on the shelves of many Asian markets), and toasting *belacan* stinks your kitchen up like nothing else. Wait, forget "kitchen"; it stinks up your whole crib. You're meant to toast the *belacan* not "until fragrant" or any of that bullshit; you want to toast it until you think there's a problem, until it smells like something has gone horribly wrong.

If you're up for it, you damn well better make a big batch, because you don't want to stink up your apartment more times than you have to and because it keeps well in the fridge and freezer (mainly because the main component is already rotten). Even better, do the toasting outside on a medium-hot grill if you can. Then your girl won't hate you. Your neighbors probably will, though.

2¼ ounces *belacan* (a quarter of an 8.8-ounce brick), coarsely crumbled with gloved hands

½ cup vegetable oil

3 tablespoons annatto seeds (aka achiote seeds; available at Latin markets)

1 pound tomatoes, cored and roughly chopped

1 medium Spanish onion (about ¾ pound), roughly chopped

10 medium garlic cloves, roughly chopped

1 (1-ounce) knob peeled ginger (about 2 by 1½ inches), roughly chopped

10 fresh red Thai chiles, stemmed and roughly chopped (including seeds)

2½ teaspoons turmeric powder

½ cup distilled white vinegar

3 tablespoons granulated sugar

Preheat the oven to 400°F. Put the *belacan* on two layers of aluminum foil and fold to make a package. Put it on the oven rack and bake, turning it over once, just until it smells really, really nasty but before your neighbors call the police, about 5 minutes. Set the package aside.

Combine the oil and annatto seeds in a large skillet, set it over medium heat, and wait for the seeds to sizzle slightly, about 5 minutes. Strain the bright-red oil, discarding the seeds.

Return the oil to the pan, set it over medium heat, and add the tomatoes, onion, garlic, ginger, chiles, and turmeric. Cook, stirring occasionally, until the onions are very soft, 15 to 20 minutes. Stir in the toasted *belacan* and cook for 5 minutes more to infuse the mixture with its flavor. Let the mixture cool to warm. Puree the mixture in a blender with the vinegar and sugar until very smooth.

Store the soffrito in an airtight container in the fridge for up to 1 month or in the freezer for up to 6 months.

Green Sambal

Makes 1½ cups

Straight up, this is a little annoying to make at home. But I wouldn't put it in the book if it wasn't worth the effort. Think pesto if the Italians had access to lemongrass, galangal, and kaffir lime leaf—the Jordan, Pippen, and Rodman of Southeast Asian cooking. I left out the more ethnically appropriate candlenuts, though. They're both hard to find and, to be honest, kind of wack compared to pistachios.

At Talde, I get lazy molecular gastronomy–style, flash-freezing the ingredients with liquid nitrogen then buzzing them into a powder in a Vitamix. At home, your best tools are a blender and patience. Better to blend, stir, blend, and stir than to painstakingly pound everything in a mortar.

I use green sambal to coat roasted Brussels sprouts (page 157), but that's just a start: Put it out as a table sauce, spoon it onto fish or grilled shrimp, dissolve it into coconut milk to make a curry, or use it as a sauce for noodles, even pasta, just to see your friends' faces when they discover there ain't no basil and pine nuts up in here.

¼ cup unsalted roasted pistachios

1½ teaspoons coriander seeds

8 tiny fish (sold at Asian markets from bins near the dried shrimp and bean sprouts) or medium dried shrimp

2 tablespoons Thai or Vietnamese fish sauce

1 (½-ounce) peeled fresh or frozen galangal (about 1½ by 1 inch), roughly sliced against the grain

1 (½-ounce) knob peeled ginger (about 1½ by 1 inch) roughly sliced against the grain

2 garlic cloves, roughly chopped

5 large lemongrass stalks (bottom 1 inch, top 8 inches, and outer 2 layers removed), roughly sliced

¼ cup plus 2 tablespoons roughly chopped cilantro stems

2 medium fresh or frozen (not dried) kaffir lime leaves, thick stems removed

2 medium shallots, roughly chopped

3 medium-size jalapeño chiles, stemmed and roughly sliced (including seeds)

1 fresh green Thai chile, or more to taste, stemmed

1 ounce palm sugar (½ disk), roughly chopped, or 2 tablespoons firmly packed dark brown sugar

¾ cup vegetable oil

Combine the pistachios, coriander seeds, and dried tiny fish in the food processor and process until you have a very coarse powder (if you use dried shrimp, they'll stay chunky). Add the fish sauce and galangal and blend until fairly smooth, prodding the mixture to help it blend. Add the ginger, garlic, lemongrass, cilantro stems, kaffir lime leaves, shallots, chiles, sugar, and ¼ cup of the oil. Process until you have a slightly coarse paste, stopping and stirring often to help it blend.

Pour the remaining ½ cup oil into a small pot and add the sambal mixture. Set it over medium heat, stirring constantly, until the oil bubbles around the edges. Increase the heat to medium high and cook, frequently stirring and scraping the pot, until it begins to split and vivid-green oil pools on top of the sambal, 5 to 8 minutes.

Use it right away or let it cool. The oil will rise to the surface. Store the sambal with the oil on the surface in an airtight container in the fridge for up to 1 week. If you're not using it within a day and want to keep the bright-green color from fading, cool the sambal quickly after frying: Fill a big bowl with some ice and some water. Set a smaller bowl in the ice water, pour in the sambal, and stir until it's fully cool.

Rendang Paste

Makes about 2⅔ cups

Peak summer in Penang, Malaysia. It's hot. Really, really hot. I'm there on a junket with a bunch of chefs. On the first night, we hit a Chinese-run club—the only place you can drink in the predominantly Muslim country—and start wildin' out. Dangerously cheap bottle service leads to dancing to techno, power slides like Swayze in *Dirty Dancing*, and a rough morning after. We're all struggling the next day when we drag ourselves to an a.m. cooking class.

A Chinese-Malay woman welcomes us into her home, which has been in her family for 150 years and where it feels like it's 150°F. And there we are desecrating it with all the booze spilling from our pores. She assigns us each a dish to cook. I get a dead-simple sticky rice dessert, but my man Chris Rendell does not. He gets rendang, a curry popular in Malaysia (though probably Indonesian in origin) that's so thick that it's more coating than sauce. I finish cooking in about 10 minutes. I'm straight lounging while Chris peels candlenuts, preps 18 other ingredients, then pounds them in a mortar so big that it requires a bear hug to lift. An hour later, he's on the floor sweating, head in his hands, when our teacher informs him he's only half done, that it's now time to stand over a hot wok and fry the paste. The secret to rendang, she tells him, is always being there to stir. I totally would've helped, if I hadn't been busy napping.

The secret to my rendang is a blender. The paste is still a pain in the butt to make, but it keeps in the fridge for weeks and in the freezer for months, and will turn even humble carrots (page 166) into a memorable dish.

2 cups vegetable oil

3 large shallots, roughly chopped

5 Asian dried red chiles, soaked in 1 cup water until soft

1 tablespoon kosher salt

1 (2-ounce) knob peeled ginger (about 4 inches), roughly sliced

1 (2-ounce) knob peeled fresh or frozen galangal (about 4 by 1½ inches), roughly sliced

6 large lemongrass stalks (bottom 1 inch, top 8 inches, and outer 2 layers removed), roughly chopped

½ cup roughly chopped unsalted roasted almonds

1 medium garlic clove, peeled

1 tablespoon turmeric powder
1 teaspoon ground black pepper

Combine 1 cup of the oil, the shallots, the soaked chiles and 2 tablespoons of their soaking liquid, and the salt in a food processor and process to a coarse puree. Add the remaining paste ingredients one at a time, processing until smooth before adding the next one and gradually adding a little water if necessary to help it blend.

Heat the remaining 1 cup oil in a medium pot over medium heat until it shimmers. Add the paste and cook, using a wooden spoon to stir almost constantly and scrape the pot to prevent sticking as best you can, 20 to 25 minutes. After 10 minutes or so, you'll notice that the paste has released some of its oil. After 15, the oil will look frothy and the paste will look slightly broken. When it's ready, there will be almost as much oil as there is paste and the paste will have the texture of ricotta cheese.

Together in an airtight container, the paste and oil keep in the fridge for up to 2 weeks or in the freezer for up to 3 months.

Beef or Chicken Rendang

To use the paste to make the more typical protein-based rendang, cook some of the paste in vegetable oil until it smells really good. Next, add some beef chuck or chicken thighs cut into 2-inch pieces, stir well, and then add enough coconut milk to cover. Bring the coconut milk to a boil, then reduce the heat to maintain a gentle simmer. Cook until the meat is tender and the coconut milk is almost all evaporated, about 2 hours. Then cook, stirring constantly, until the sauce turns a mahogany color, about 15 minutes more.

Chinese-Sausage Gravy
Makes about 6 cups

Southern milk gravy is basically just a trashier version of the velouté I made in French kitchens. Trashier in a good way. Both are essentially sauces thickened with a simple roux, but only one contains sausage and cures hangovers. You tell me which sounds better.

My riff one-ups the original with a quick, two-ingredient shrimp stock and *lap chuong*—the narrow, sweet-salty cured Chinese sausage sold in most Asian markets. Try to find it, but even if you use breakfast sausage instead, this gravy will be just as at home on biscuits as it is on Shrimp Toast (page 50).

FOR THE QUICK STOCK
3 cups fresh or frozen shrimp shells (from about
    1½ pounds shrimp)
½ medium Spanish onion, roughly chopped

FOR THE GRAVY
1 stick (¼ pound) unsalted butter, cut into several pieces
3 ounces fresh or defrosted frozen cured Chinese sausage
    (aka *lap chuong*), cut into ¼-inch pieces (½ cup)
¼ cup finely chopped Spanish onion
2 tablespoons thinly sliced scallion (white parts only)
1 tablespoon finely chopped fresh ginger
1 medium garlic clove, finely chopped
1 teaspoon thinly sliced fresh red Thai chile (including seeds)
½ cup all-purpose flour
½ cup Shaoxing wine, dry sherry, or bourbon
1 tablespoon ground black pepper
1½ teaspoons kosher salt
1 teaspoon chicken bouillon

MAKE THE QUICK STOCK
Preheat the oven to 375°F. Spread the shrimp shells on a baking sheet and roast until they turn pink with golden brown edges and are very aromatic, 5 to 7 minutes. Combine the shells, onion, and 5 cups water in a small pot, bring it to a simmer, and simmer gently until the water has taken on the shrimp flavor, 20 to 25 minutes. Strain the stock into a heatproof measuring cup, discarding the onion and the shells. Ideally, you will have about 4 cups. If your stock reduced too much, add enough water

to measure 4 cups. It won't be as shrimpy, but it will still be good. You can store the stock in the fridge for up to 3 days or in the freezer for up to 3 months. Warm it over low heat before continuing with the recipe.

MAKE THE GRAVY

Melt the butter in a medium pot over medium heat. Add the sausage, onion, scallion, ginger, garlic, and chile and cook, stirring occasionally, until the onion is translucent but not colored, about 3 minutes. Stir in the flour and cook, stirring frequently, until the flour no longer smells raw (it should not turn any shade of brown), 3 to 5 minutes.

Add the Shaoxing wine (the mixture will clump), increase the heat to medium high, and cook for 1 minute, stirring constantly. Gradually add the shrimp stock (about a cup at a time), whisking constantly. Let the mixture come to a simmer, and cook, whisking, until it has thickened enough to just coat the back of a spoon, about 2 minutes. Stir in the pepper, salt, and chicken bouillon. Use it right away, or let it cool to room temperature and store in an airtight container in the fridge or for up to 5 days or in the freezer (preferably in 2-cup portions) for up to 6 weeks.

Chinese Black-Bean Brown Butter

Makes about 1¾ cups

You'll have plenty of this salty, aromatic brown butter left over after making Fish with Black-Bean Brown Butter (page 135). Which is all good, because the butter keeps well in the fridge or freezer and tastes great on just about anything. The first step—browning the butter—is painless, but newbies to the process should use a stainless steel or another light-colored saucepan to make it especially easy to see the butter change color.

3 sticks (¾ pound) unsalted butter
1 tablespoon finely chopped shallot
1 tablespoon finely chopped fresh ginger
1 tablespoon finely chopped garlic
½ cup black bean in chile oil sauce, such as the Lao Gan Ma brand

1 tablespoon finely grated orange zest
2 tablespoons oyster sauce
1 tablespoon reduced-sodium soy sauce
1 teaspoon granulated sugar
1 teaspoon Worcestershire sauce

BROWN THE BUTTER

Set a fine-mesh strainer over a heatproof bowl. Melt the butter in a large saucepan over medium-high heat. Let it bubble and crackle, stirring occasionally. After about 4 minutes, it will stop bubbling aggressively and you'll be left with a light-golden froth on the surface.

Reduce the heat to medium low and cook, occasionally using a spoon to push the froth aside to check on the butter, until the solids in the butter turn a caramel color, about 2 minutes more. Cook it a little more, until the color gets a shade or two darker. Immediately pour it through the strainer into the bowl and discard the solids.

FINISH THE BUTTER

Wipe the pan clean, add 2 tablespoons of the brown butter, and set it over medium-high heat. Add the shallot, ginger, and garlic and cook, stirring, until lightly browned, about 2 minutes. Stir in the black bean sauce and orange zest. Turn off the heat and smash the beans for 30 seconds or so. Stir in the oyster sauce, soy sauce, sugar, and Worcestershire, then the remaining butter.

Let the mixture cool, then chill in the fridge, covered, stirring occasionally until it solidifies. Or, to cool it quickly, pour into a bowl set in another bowl of ice. Stir and scrape the bottom often until the butter is the texture of fudge.

The butter keeps in the fridge for up to 2 weeks and in the freezer (preferably in small portions) for up to 6 months.

Miso-Ponzu Dressing

Makes about 1½ cups

You know how just about anything you order at Japanese restaurants comes with a salad with throwaway greens and a few carrot shreds? You're like, fine, I guess I'll eat it because salad is good for me. Then you remember the creamy-looking orange-ish dressing it comes with and you're suddenly excited to dig into that romaine. Well, this dressing is even better than that one. And you're not stuck putting it on some wack-ass salad.

2 ounces drained firm tofu
¼ cup unseasoned rice vinegar
¼ cup reduced-sodium soy sauce
¼ cup apple cider or juice
2 tablespoons fresh orange juice
1 tablespoon fresh lemon juice
1 tablespoon fresh lime juice
1½ teaspoons *shiro miso* (aka white miso)
¼ cup plus 2 tablespoons vegetable oil

Combine all the ingredients except for the oil in a blender and blend until smooth. With the blender running, add the oil in a slow, steady stream. The dressing keeps for up to 2 weeks in the fridge. Stir well before using.

Buttermilk Ranch

Makes about 1½ cups

In the early 1800s, the legendary French chef Antonin Carême classified four mother sauces. Almost a century later, Auguste Escoffier added a fifth. Let me propose a sixth: Ranch dressing. Ranch is my jam. I'd been putting Ranch and Sriracha on my pizza years before my boy Rich-y Blais brilliantly coined the term *Srirancha*. I like it so much that things get weird, and food starts getting dipped into Ranch—shrimp toast, dumplings—that really shouldn't. You might start crossing lines, too, because my version is way better than Wish-Bone's.

¾ cup mayo
½ cup sour cream
¼ cup well-shaken buttermilk
3 tablespoons Ranch seasoning powder, such as the Hidden Valley brand

Combine the ingredients and stir. Let it sit for at least an hour or, even better, a day. It keeps in an airtight container in the fridge for up to 1 week.

Tamarind Vinaigrette

Makes about 1½ cups

Bright and creamy enough to improve any salad—of heirloom tomatoes (page 151), cucumbers, or sturdy greens—this dressing is also bold enough to serve as a banging dip for steak, pork, shrimp, spring rolls, whatever. The complex acidity of tamarind and the meaty, nutty flavor of toasted garlic turn a lazy man's dressing into one with serious depth.

½ cup vegetable oil
2 medium garlic cloves, finely chopped
½ cup tamarind concentrate (not pulp or paste)
½ cup firmly packed light brown sugar
3 tablespoons Thai or Vietnamese fish sauce

Combine the oil and garlic in a small pan, set it over medium-high heat, and cook, stirring often, just until the garlic begins to turn golden brown at the edges, 1 to 2 minutes. Take the pan off the heat and let the garlic sizzle, stirring, until it turns mahogany brown, about 1 minute more.

Combine the tamarind, sugar, and fish sauce in a blender and blend until smooth. With the blender running, gradually pour in the oil and garlic and blend until smooth.

The dressing keeps in an airtight container in the fridge for up to 1 week.

Coconut–Brown Butter Syrup

Makes about 2 cups

Shouts to Vera Tong Obias, aka the Dragon Lady, aka the Tony Stark of the baking game. Vera is the skilled pastry chef turned owner of Du Jour Bakery in Park Slope who generously taught me to make this syrup. It destroys Aunt Jemima. It embarrasses maple syrup. And it's on every table at Talde come pancake hour.

2 sticks (½ pound) unsalted butter cut into pieces
1¼ cups firmly packed light brown sugar
2 teaspoons kosher salt
1 teaspoon vanilla extract
½ cup well-shaken coconut milk

Set a fine-mesh strainer over a heatproof bowl. Melt the butter in a small pan over medium-high heat. Let it bubble and crackle, stirring occasionally. After about 4 minutes, it will stop bubbling and you'll be left with a light-golden froth on the surface. Reduce the heat to medium low and cook, occasionally using a spoon to push the froth aside to check on the butter, until the solids in the butter turn a shade or two darker than caramel, about 2 minutes more. Pour it through a strainer into the bowl and discard the solids.

Combine the brown sugar with ½ cup water in a small pan, set over high heat, and bring to a furious bubble. Cook, without stirring, until the mixture is the consistency of thick syrup, about 3 minutes.

Pour the brown butter into the brown sugar mixture. Stir in the salt and vanilla extract, then gradually whisk in the coconut milk.

The syrup keeps in an airtight container in the fridge for up to a month. It solidifies and separates slightly when cool, so stir well and gently reheat before serving.

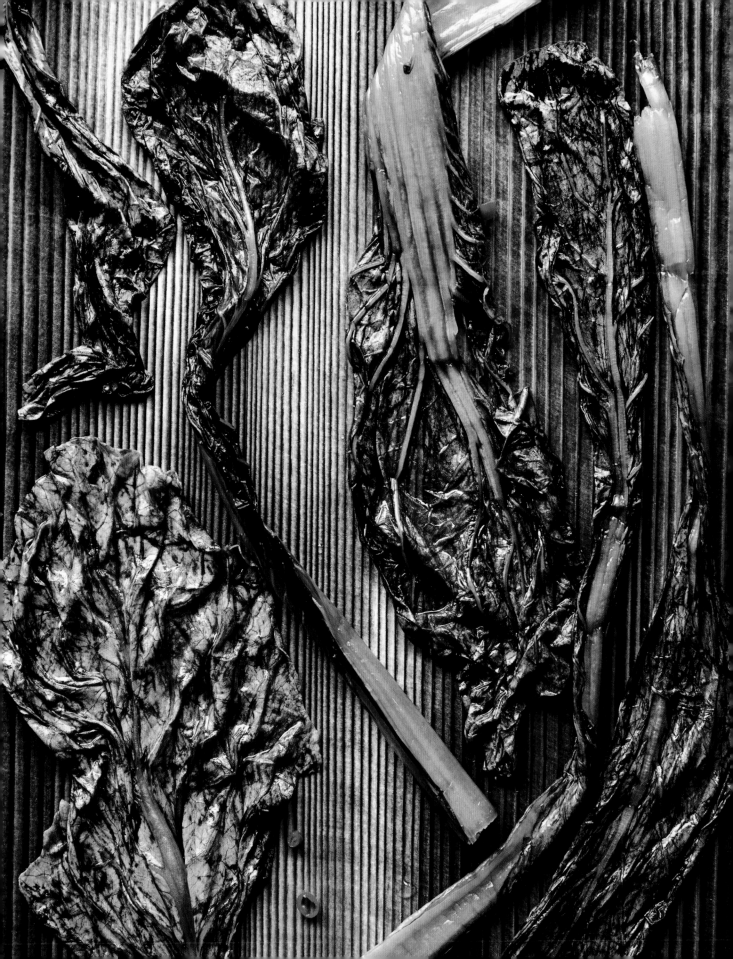

Pickles and Other Stuff

Banh Mi Pickles

Makes about 3 cups

Without these crunchy, sweet, tart pickles, a banh mi is just another sandwich.

1½ cups unseasoned rice vinegar

¾ cup granulated sugar

¼ pound carrot, peeled and cut into long, thin matchsticks (1 generous cup)

¼ pound daikon radish (preferably from one that's less than 2 inches in diameter), peeled and cut into long, thin matchsticks (1 generous cup)

Combine the vinegar and sugar in a 1-quart container, put on the lid securely, and shake until the sugar dissolves. Add the carrot and daikon so they're submerged in the liquid. Cover and pickle for at least 1 hour at room temperature or in the fridge for up to 2 weeks.

Pickled Shallots

Makes about 1 quart

At Talde, I put these bright-pink pickles on my sausage sliders (page 34) and shiitake sliders (page 35). But when I'm snacking between shifts I find myself putting them on virtually anything that could do with some crunch and acidity.

2 cups unseasoned rice vinegar

¼ cup Asian chile oil

2 tablespoons granulated sugar

1 tablespoon kosher salt

1 tablespoon coriander seeds, toasted in a pan until aromatic and finely ground

10 ounces large shallots, sliced into ¼-inch-thick rounds (about 3 cups)

1 (1-ounce) knob peeled ginger (about 2 by 1½ inches), cut into 2- by ⅛-inch matchsticks (about ¼ cup)

Combine the vinegar, chile oil, sugar, salt, and coriander in a bowl and stir to dissolve the sugar and salt. Combine the shallots and ginger in a tall container (or divide evenly between two) and pour in the vinegar mixture. It should just about cover the shallots.

Let the mixture sit for a few hours at room temperature, stirring once. Eat while they're crunchy or, even better, keep them covered in the fridge for at least 24 hours or up to 1 month.

Spicy Pickled Cranberries

Makes 2 cups

These little grenades of sweet-tart flavor will become a key weapon in your arsenal, whether you're making Maple-Glazed Squid with Cabbage (page 145) or trying to spice up a traditional Thanksgiving dinner.

2 cups unseasoned rice vinegar

1 tablespoon *gochujang* (Korean "hot pepper paste")

1 tablespoon Thai sweet chile sauce

1 teaspoon granulated sugar

¼ teaspoon kosher salt

½ pound fresh or defrosted frozen cranberries (about 2¼ cups)

¼ cup thinly sliced long, red, moderately spicy chiles (including seeds), such as Fresno

Combine all of the ingredients except the cranberries and chiles in a tall container and stir or shake until the *gochujang* and sugar dissolve. Add the cranberries and chiles, cover, and let pickle in the fridge for a few hours or, even better, overnight. They keep in an airtight container in the fridge for up to 3 months.

Cauliflower Kimchi

Makes about 2 quarts

Before the short ribs and squid even hit the tabletop grill, Korean restaurants bring on the fun, presenting every table with a dozen little dishes to amuse your *bouche*. They're called *banchan* and always include several types of the fermented pickle called kimchi—made from cabbage, daikon radish, and cucumber, among other things. And every time, there will be one dish in the array that's just weird. Too many times, that's cauliflower, steamed and tossed with a strangely sweet mayo. I always wish that the cauliflower would be more like the kimchi. And here (minus the fermentation), it is.

1 cup *gochujang* (Korean "hot pepper paste")

¼ cup unseasoned rice vinegar

2 tablespoons Thai or Vietnamese fish sauce

1 tablespoon Asian sesame oil

1 teaspoon red chile flakes

1 large head cauliflower, cored and cut into bite-size florets (about 8 cups)

1 cup loosely packed roughly chopped (about 1-inch lengths) scallion greens

Combine the *gochujang*, vinegar, fish sauce, sesame oil, and chile flakes in a large mixing bowl and stir until smooth. Add the cauliflower and scallions, toss to coat very well, and transfer to one large or several smaller clean airtight containers.

Let it pickle in the fridge until the cauliflower is tender but still slightly crunchy, at least 2 days or up to 3 weeks (the longer, the better).

Pickled Mustard Greens

Makes about 2 cups

Sure, you can buy already pickled mustard greens from Asian markets, but the store-bought kind are usually mad salty and often a creepily neon-green color. Either soak them in water before you use them or make your own. Mine are especially bright from rice vinegar and full of umami thanks to fish sauce. Sprinkle them on Red-Cooking Pork Shank with Crisp Rice Noodles (page 90) or eat them like you'd eat a dill pickle—with everything.

2 cups unseasoned rice vinegar

¾ cup Thai or Vietnamese fish sauce

½ cup granulated sugar

1 teaspoon turmeric powder

4 fresh red Thai chiles, stemmed

1 medium garlic clove, peeled

1¼ pounds *yu choy* (aka Chinese mustard greens), bottom 1 inch trimmed, halved crosswise (about 8 tightly packed cups)

Blend the vinegar, fish sauce, sugar, turmeric, chiles, and garlic until smooth. Distribute the *yu choy* among two 1-quart containers, then pour in the vinegar mixture.

Cover and keep in the fridge, shaking occasionally, for at least 3 days. The pickled greens keep in the fridge in an airtight container for up to 3 months. Roughly chop and let come to room temperature before you use them.

Char Siu Marinade

Makes about 1 cup

This marinade might contain a bunch of ingredients, but once you have them, all you do is dump, stir, and slather the mixture on any quick-cooking cut of pork. High heat caramelizes the sugars and creates complex sweetness reminiscent of *char siu*, the glistening reddish slabs of pork that hang in what seems like every window in Chinatown.

¼ cup plus 2 tablespoons oyster sauce

¼ cup plus 2 tablespoons hoisin sauce

¼ cup granulated sugar

2 tablespoons ketchup

2 tablespoons honey

1 tablespoon brandy or whiskey

1 tablespoon vegetable oil

1½ teaspoons Asian sesame oil

¾ teaspoon Asian chile oil

2 medium garlic cloves, finely chopped

¼ teaspoon five-spice powder

¼ teaspoon ginger powder

¼ teaspoon garlic powder

⅛ teaspoon ground white pepper

Combine the ingredients in a big bowl, and stir until the sugar has dissolved and there are no lumps remaining. Covered, it keeps in the fridge for up to 1 week or in the freezer for up to 3 months.

Pastrami Spice

Makes about 6 tablespoons

This spice mixture brings the essence of pastrami to whatever it touches, whether meat or beet.

2 tablespoons kosher salt

1 tablespoon coriander seeds

1 tablespoon fennel seeds

1 tablespoon black peppercorns

1 tablespoon hon dashi powder or chicken bouillon

1 tablespoon red chile flakes

1 tablespoon onion powder

1 tablespoon garlic powder

3 cloves

Combine everything in a blender or spice grinder and process to a fairly fine powder. The spice mix keeps in an airtight container in a cool dark place for up to 2 weeks.

Pastrami [puh-**strah**-mee]; VERB
To coat or sprinkle with a mixture of ground coriander, black pepper, garlic powder, and other seasonings; to evoke a sense of pastrami: *Yesterday I pastrami-ed deviled eggs, then today I pastrami-ed skirt steak.*

Ramen Broth

Makes about 12 cups

This broth has Beyoncé body—I mean, it's thick. Three different types of bones team up, contributing their flavor and gelatin to make a rich but balanced broth. Not only that, but because you cook it for a long time at a simmer (rather than the bare bubble of French stocks), you also extract fatty marrow that gets all up in the broth to make a cloudy, dairy-looking emulsion. To this stock I add what I call "ramen booster"—a mixture that includes hon dashi powder, soy sauce, and oyster sauce. In other words, some top-quality MSG. The ramen masters of the world might scoff at my shortcut, but I bet you won't.

¾ pound pork neck bones, cut crosswise into approximately 3-inch pieces if necessary by your butcher

½ pound chicken bones, such as backs, necks, and wings

¼ pound beef shin bones, cut crosswise into approximately 3-inch pieces if necessary by your butcher

¼ cup plus 2 tablespoons reduced-sodium soy sauce

1½ tablespoons hon dashi powder

1½ tablespoons kosher salt

2¼ teaspoons granulated sugar

2¼ teaspoons oyster sauce

Combine the bones in a large pot and add enough water to cover. Cover the pot and bring the water to a boil over high heat. Drain the bones, rinse them briefly under running water, and put them back in the pot.

Pour in 6 quarts water, cover, and bring the water to a boil over high heat. Partially cover the pot and reduce the heat to maintain a steady simmer. Cook, skimming off any scum, until the broth is milky white and the bones have had plenty of time to release their flavor and marrow, about 6 hours. Strain the broth through a fine-mesh strainer. If necessary, add water so the stock measures 12 cups.

Pour the stock into a clean pot and bring it to a simmer. Add the soy sauce, dashi powder, salt, sugar, and oyster sauce, then stir until the dashi powder, salt, and sugar have completely dissolved.

Let the broth cool and store in airtight containers in the fridge for up to 5 days or in the freezer for up to 6 months.

Everything Roti Bread

Makes 8

Only one thing could threaten to dethrone the everything bagel. This right here.

2 tablespoons poppy seeds

2 tablespoons sesame seeds

2 tablespoons pretzel salt

2 tablespoons store-bought Thai or Vietnamese fried shallots or French's French Fried Onions, crumbled

About 3 tablespoons vegetable oil

8 defrosted frozen plain *roti paratha* or *roti canai* (available at Asian markets and online)

Preheat the oven to 350°F.

Combine the poppy seeds, sesame seeds, salt, and fried shallots or onions in a bowl and stir well. Rub a large baking sheet (or two if the roti won't all fit on one) with oil. Brush or rub both sides of the roti with oil (about 1 teaspoon per roti), then arrange them in one layer on the baking sheet, leaving a little space separating them. Sprinkle about 1 tablespoon of the poppy seed mixture evenly onto each one and press lightly with your hands to help the spices stick. Bake the roti until they turn golden brown and begin to puff up, 12 to 15 minutes.

Stack them on a plate, which will help keep them warm, and serve right away.

Everything [ev-ree-thing]; VERB
To coat (a bagel or other carb) with a mixture of salt, poppy seeds, sesame seeds, et al.; to make festive: *Come on, it's my birthday, let's everything those dumplings!*

Ingredient Glossary

Annatto Seeds

Typically used for the color they impart and not for their very mild flavor, annatto (or achiote) seeds look like little red pebbles. They're sold in Latin markets and many supermarkets. Better to leave them out and sacrifice color than to sub with achiote paste, which contains other spices.

Asian Dried Red Chiles

Some cooks get picky about the provenance of their chiles, but any bag of small (2 to 3 inches long and ½ inch wide), evenly red dried chiles you spot at an Asian market will work for the purposes of this book.

Banana Leaves

The leaf of the banana tree can act like parchment paper with flavor. The leaves are occasionally available fresh but most often frozen in Asian and Latin markets (where they might go by *hoja de plátano*).

Bean Sprouts

Some supermarkets and health food stores offer little containers of crisp fresh bean sprouts. Asian markets tend to sell them from bins or big bags. Either way, if given the choice, choose mung bean sprouts, which have slim yellow tips, instead of soybean sprouts, which have fat ones.

Chinese Sausage

There are many kinds of Chinese sausage, known as *lap chuong*, so for the recipes in this book, zero in on the firm cured links that look like skinny salami. They're sold at Chinese markets in plastic packages or loose—often near the butcher case, occasionally in the refrigerated case, and sometimes hanging. Kam Yen Jan is a common packaged brand that I like.

Coconut Milk

Coconut milk contains no dairy, just the rich, fatty flavor of the fruit. I'm pretty much down with any Asian brand of coconut milk, the most common of which are Aroy-D, Savoy, and Chaokoh. I tend to avoid brands whose labels seem a little too amped about convincing you that they're Thai.

Dried Shrimp

Salty, slightly sweet, and full of umami, dried shrimp are like the ocean's version of bacon. Most Asian grocery stores stock dried shrimp loose or in bags in the refrigerated section. Unless a recipe says otherwise, buy the medium size (sometimes you'll just see the letter "M" on the bag).

Dumpling and Wonton Wrappers

Do yourself a favor and buy wrappers, aka skins, instead of trying to make them. You'll find superior ones in the refrigerated cases at Asian markets but you might also see acceptable versions in supermarkets. Each recipe in this book specifies the appropriate shape (round or square) and variety (yellow Hong Kong style or eggless white Shanghai style).

Fish Sauce

The Jay Z of ingredients, fish sauce is untouchable. A few dashes of the golden, translucent liquid will improve just about anything, upping umami without adding fishiness. You'll find bottles at major supermarkets nowadays, but Asian markets typically have the best brands.

Fried Shallots

Less-lazy cooks can look up how to fry thinly sliced shallots to a golden crisp. Me? I just buy them in little plastic jars in Thai, Vietnamese, and other Asian markets. Occasionally, you'll see freshly fried shallots in bags, which are even better. Worse comes to worst, get French's French Fried Onions.

Galangal

This Thai rhizome looks like paler ginger and tastes less sharp and awesomely citrusy. Thai and some Chinese markets sell it fresh in the produce section, but more often you'll see it in the freezer. Don't defrost before you use it.

Ginisang Bagoong

Often labeled "sautéed shrimp paste," this Filipino product is a spicy, funky paste of chiles, vinegar, and fermented shrimp. I make a version myself (see page 194), but only if I don't have access to the Barrio Fiesta brand's jarred version. Look for the spicy variety in Asian markets, especially Southeast Asian ones, and online.

Gochujang

Sold in plastic tubs (usually not in bottles) and often translated as "red pepper paste" or "hot pepper paste," this is Korea's ketchup, a smooth, sweet-salty burgundy-colored condiment that has umami from fermented soybeans and heat from dried chiles. You'll find it at any Korean market, at some Asian ones, and online, often under the Haechandle or Chung Jung One brand.

Hawaiian Buns

These soft, fluffy, slightly sweet rolls make the best slider bun in the business, though potato or challah rolls kill it, too. King's Hawaiian is a dope brand. Its website, kingshawaiian.com, tells you where to find the buns and even lets you order them online.

Hon Dashi Powder

The chicken bouillon cube of Japan, this instant version of the country's fundamental stock made from kombu (a type of kelp) and *katsuobushi* (smoked, dried bonito fish) delivers tons of flavor and umami. Look for it—the most common brand is Ajinomoto—in boxes, envelopes, and jars at Japanese markets or online. You might see it labeled as "bonito fish soup stock."

Kaffir Lime Leaves

The leaves of the kaffir lime tree have the most amazing aroma, as if someone packed all the fragrances of Thai food into one glossy leaf. Seek them out in the refrigerated or freezer case at good Thai markets and some Asian and Indian grocery stores. They freeze really well and don't need defrosting. Ignore dried leaves.

Kimchi

During the past decade spicy, funky kimchi went from the sauerkraut of Korea (loved deeply but only by some people) to one of America's favorite pickles. It's made from many vegetables but, most iconically, cabbage. Look for jars in the refrigerated section of many urban supermarkets and, of course, Korean and other Asian markets. Most Korean-owned bodegas have it, too.

Lemongrass

You'll find this aromatic, lemony stalk in Asian markets and even some supermarkets, especially in big cities. For the recipes in this book, you'll typically have to trim an inch from the bottom and 8 inches from the top, and peel off the outer layers until you get to the parts that aren't really woody. The older the stalk, the more you might have to trim.

Miso

Japanese cooks use many varieties of the fermented soybean paste called miso. My recipes call for one of them: *shiro miso*, aka white miso, aka sweet miso. Nowadays you can find it not only at Japanese markets but also at health food stores and many supermarkets.

Oyster Sauce

Yet another thick, brown umami-packed sauce in the Asian repertoire, oyster sauce is indeed made from oysters and tastes salty-sweet. Lee Kum Kee is a common brand.

Palm Sugar

Feel free to substitute the same weight of dark brown sugar for this sugar that is popular in Southeast Asia. Made from the sap of the sugar palm, it is often sold in hard disks and should be roughly chopped before using in my recipes.

Pretzel Salt

With slightly larger, more opaque grains than kosher salt, this is the stuff you see on soft pretzels and everything bagels. Spice shops, baking supply stores, and some supermarkets sell it. It's also easy to buy online.

Ramen Noodles

Not all ramen noodles come in dried bricks and with seasoning packets. Japanese grocery stores often stock fresh ramen, pale yellow strands that have a slight, pleasant bitterness and cook up to an especially springy texture. If you can only find frozen noodles, that's cool, too. No need to defrost them before boiling.

Ranch Seasoning Powder

Sold in spice shakers and envelopes in most non-bougie supermarkets, Ranch seasoning is a magical mix of dried garlic, dried onions, dried buttermilk, salt, secrets, and typically some form of delicious, nutritious MSG (see page 95). Look for the "Original" flavor.

Rice Flour

I specify Asian rice flour in my recipes, because the white-boy brands have a coarser grind and batters made with them won't have the right texture. So get yourself to an Asian market, buy some rice flour (not sticky rice flour, which is a different product), and keep it in your fridge for up to 6 months.

Rice Noodles

I call for three types of rice noodles in this book, which are available in most Asian markets. Fully dried thin, flat rice noodles you'll find in packages on shelves; semi-dried (not fully soft but not brittle either) thin rice noodles you'll find in vacuum-packed bags in the refrigerated case. In the case of these two noodles, the shape (thin and round versus thin and flat) matters much less than the level of dryness. The third type is fresh rice noodles (see page 91 for details).

Rice Vinegar

Sometimes called rice wine vinegar, this stuff is easy to find nowadays—at major supermarkets, health food stores, and Asian markets. I prefer Japanese brands, such as Marukan and Nakano. Avoid "seasoned" rice vinegar, which contains sugar and salt (check the ingredients listed on the label to be sure).

Roti Paratha

Also known as *roti prata* and *roti canai*, this buttery flatbread was adapted by Malaysian and Singaporean cooks from the Indian original. If you've ever watched someone make real roti, you know that you should be thrilled that you can buy it already made in the freezer section of Southeast Asian and some Indian markets as well as online. Different brands vary slightly in diameter, so use your judgment when you use roti for Pepperoni-Pizza "Very Warm" Pockets (page 28), Mickey D's–Style Fried Apple Pies (page 178), and Everything Roti Bread (page 208). The Kawan brand is what I use at Talde and is widely available.

Sesame Oil

Asian brands, such as the Japanese Kadoya, are your best bet for this dark brown oil made from roasted sesame seeds.

Soy Sauce

Soy sauce comes in many varieties and from many countries. For the recipes in this book, use Japanese soy sauce that says "reduced-sodium" or "less sodium" on the label, not for health reasons but because this kind has a higher flavor-to-saltiness ratio.

Szechuan (or Sichuan) Peppercorns

Available at Chinese markets and good spice stores (including Penzeys.com, which will mail you the spice), Szechuan peppercorns are not true peppercorns but the dried berries of an Asian bush. They have an unusual flavor, like Kool cigarettes mixed with orange peel and walnuts, and make your mouth tingle in a cold way rather than in a hot one.

Tahini

Middle Eastern markets and many supermarkets sell tahini, a loose paste of ground sesame seeds, like peanut butter that's not made with peanuts. Liquid often separates and rises to the surface, so make sure to stir well before using.

Tamarind Concentrate

The tamarind fruit is a pod with tart, sticky flesh and big seeds. You can buy the whole pods and you can buy blocks of the flesh, but for the recipes in this book, I call for concentrate, essentially the flesh that's been mixed with water, strained of seeds and fibers, and reduced to a thick liquid. Look for plastic and glass jars in Indian and Asian markets. I use the Por Kwan brand, which is labeled "Nuoc Me Chua" and "Sour Soup Base Mix" and available online as well as in stores.

Thai Basil

Sometimes called sweet basil, the herb sports purple stems and a licorice-like aroma. Thai markets, and some Indian and Chinese markets, sell it in the produce section or in the refrigerated case. Some farmers' markets sell it, too.

Thai Chiles

Though any very spicy fresh chiles can stand in for these, look for small green or red chiles, sometimes called bird or finger chiles, that are about 2 inches long. If searching the produce section of Asian markets

fails, try the freezer case. These chiles freeze well and there's no need to defrost them before using.

Toban Djan

Spelled many ways but typically translated as "chile bean sauce," this slightly spicy, super-salty paste made from fermented soybeans is earthy and almost meaty. The popular Lee Kum Kee brand is available in many supermarkets as well as Asian markets.

XO Sauce

This Hong Kong invention is an oily, chunky product made from pricey dried scallops, Chinese ham, chiles, shallots, and garlic, among other stuff. It isn't cheap, but a little goes a long way. Lee Kum Kee is a solid brand.

Yuzu Juice

Yuzu is an especially aromatic Japanese citrus that's hard to find fresh in the U.S. The bottled versions sold at Japanese markets and online hit the spot. You can also make a good approximation by combining equal parts lemon, lime, and orange juices.

Acknowledgments

Shout-outs to Grand Central Publishing, especially Sara Weiss, Brittany Hamblin, Karen Murgolo, Deb Futter, Jamie Raab, Tareth Mitch, and Tom Whatley. And to designer Berkeley Poole.

Shout-outs to Lauren Smythe, Kim Witherspoon, and the rest of the Inkwell Management team.

And to my main man JJ Goode, for making me wake up at the god-awful hour of 9 a.m. for months and for making me do all this work. You're a gifted writer, my friend. Thank you for making me sound *somewhat* literate.

Shout-outs to photographer William Hereford and to Rebekah Peppler for making me and my food look particularly fly.

Shout-outs to Kristin Donnelly and Lauren Salkeld for messing up their home stoves testing my recipes.

Shout-outs to every chef out there that kicked my ass up and down the kitchen, starting with Carrie and Michael Nahabedian. Without you guys, I wouldn't be where I am today.

Thanks to Geoff Felsenthal, for teaching me how to cook and for taking a chance on a little punk motherfucker who could never get his station set up and who never made those fucking potato pancakes with kimchi.

Thank you to Stephen Starr, for the inspiration and for not firing me when you should've fired me five times.

Shout-outs to Brian Ray and Daniel Skurnik. Thank you for the 6 a.m. inspiration over a bottle of Maker's.

Shout-outs to the EPIS crew—Dennis, Derrick, and Ben.

Big up to Khuong—we doin', homie.

Shout-out to the Mass-holes over at Homarus for hooking us up with fatty crustaceans.

And to Korin Japanese Trading for always being there.

Shout-outs to my business partners, David Massoni and John Bush. We doin' it.

Thank you to all my chefs and staff at my restaurants—Talde, Thistle Hill Tavern, and Pork Slope—especially Andrew aka Big Boy, Janine, Daniel, Drew, Bun, and Fabian.

And thank you to our investors.

Special shout-outs to the guys who helped me open Talde: Margarita, Julian, Andrew, Kyle, Janine, and Bill. Without your dedication, we wouldn't be here.

R.I.P. MAHAL.

Thank you to my baby, Agnes.

Shout-outs to the entire Villanosa and Talde family. Thanks for making me crazy, feeding me, and supplying me with endless material for poking fun at our Filipino ethnicity. And to all my aunties—all 6,000 of them out there—shout-outs for the great food.

Thank you to my brother, Ian, and his son, Kai, especially for taking care of the stupid dog.

Thank you to my mom and dad, for believing in me and giving me the opportunity to follow my dreams.

Thank you to Jesus Christ, my lord and savior.

Index

About the Authors

My name is Dale Talde. I've been cooking since '98,
been playin' ball since I was ten. I eat, live, and die for this.

My name is JJ Goode. I have the best job.
I write cookbooks with chefs. I suck at basketball.